the glorious
VEGETABLES OF ITALY

the glorious

VEGETABLES OF ITALY

DOMENICA MARCHETTI

photographs by

SANG AN

CHRONICLE BOOKS

SAN FRANCISCO

Library of Congress Cataloging-in-Publication
Data available.

ISBN 978-1-4521-0886-5

Manufactured in China

Designed by Sara Schneider
Prop styling by Glenn Jenkins
Food styling by George Dolese
Assistant food styling by Elizabet Nederlanden
Typesetting by DC Type

Cynar is a registered trademark of Campari. Rogue Creamery
Smokey Blue is a registered trademark of Rogue Creamery.

10 9 8 7 6 5 4 3 2

Chronicle Books LLC
680 Second Street
San Francisco, California 94107
www.chroniclebooks.com

ACKNOWLEDGMENTS

I have always been an enthusiastic consumer of vegetables, so writing (and cooking) this book has been a dream come true. I'd like to thank those who helped in its creation:

To my editors at Chronicle Books, Bill LeBlond and Amy Treadwell, a heartfelt thanks for your enthusiastic support of my work, and for your patience and understanding while I dealt with a most untimely hand injury!

Thanks to my friend and agent, Lisa Ekus, and her excellent staff at the Lisa Ekus Group, for your expert advice and guidance through this project.

I would like to express my gratitude to designer Sara Schneider, who once again took several hundred pages of my words and transformed them into a beautiful book; and to photographer Sang An, whose stunning images present Italian vegetables in all the glory they deserve. Thank you also to George Dolese, Glenn Jenkins, and Elizabet Nederlanden.

At Chronicle Books, I would also like to thank Peter Perez and David Hawk, who always work so hard on my behalf. It is a pleasure to work with you. Shouts out also to production coordinator Tera Killip, and to Doug Ogan, Claire Fletcher, and Marie Oishi. And a big thanks to Ellen Wheat for your eagle-eye copyediting.

Seeds from Italy founder Bill McKay and current owner Dan Nagengast generously shared their knowledge of, and love for, Italian heirloom vegetables. Thank you for your dedication to spreading the word about these glorious Italian varieties and for making them accessible this side of the Atlantic. Of course, seeds need to be nurtured to grow into beautiful, edible vegetables. For this I thank farmers, from those who set up stalls every week in the parking lot of my local library in Virginia to those across the ocean who work the terraced hills of Italy and beyond. A special tip of the hat to Aubrey King of Twin Springs Fruit Farm, in Orrtanna, PA, whose candy-sweet buttercup squash inspired several recipes in this book, including the Winter Squash Panna Cotta (page 248) and the Buttercup Squash and Ricotta Crostata (page 242).

I'm grateful to the friends who generously shared their recipes, tips, expertise, and thoughtful advice, especially Amy Albert, Nancy Baggett, Cathy Barrow, Amy Brandwein, John Coletta, Marcello De Antoniis, Joe Gray, Diane Morgan, and Titti Pacchione. A special thanks to Olga Berman for her lovely author's photo.

Thanks also to the many friends who are always supportive and who continue to inspire me and keep me motivated, especially my American Food Roots team Bonny Wolf, Michele Kayal, and Carol Guensburg.

And finally, I am grateful to my family for always supporting me cento per cento: my parents, Gabriella and Frank; my sister, Maria; my niece, Gina; and my brother-in-law Tony; and my brothers-in-law Darren and John; and my nephew Xander; and to my cousins Coco and Cheryl. And most especially to Nick, Adriana, and Scott, who are sort of like the leafy green vegetables of my life. They nourish me every day.

contents

INTRODUCTION

In 2008, my family and I took a trip to Venice. Five years later, my most vivid memory of that trip is not of the Piazza San Marco, or the cathedral, or the gondolas wending their way through the canals. It is of the incredible display of vegetables at the Rialto farmers' market. The selection of radicchio alone was enough to make me dizzy—fat, scarlet bouquets of Chioggia and Verona; furled red and white fingers of Treviso; pale green and pink-speckled heads of Castelfranco. Behind them spilled blood-red tomatoes and peppers, and atop those sat a big, squat winter squash, sliced in half, its orange flesh practically glowing. What a show!

In many ways, Italian cooking is really a celebration of vegetables. Think about all the vegetables that are featured prominently in Italian dishes: artichokes, asparagus, beans—green and dried—broccoli, cauliflower, cabbage, carrots, chard, chicory, eggplant, kale, mushrooms, onions, peppers, potatoes, spinach, tomatoes, and more. The variety is breathtaking, and the ways in which these vegetables arrive at the table is even more so.

There is a practical reason for this, of course: Until fairly recently, meat was too costly to be served in large portions every day, but vegetables have always been plentiful. The Italian peninsula is blessed with a long growing season—year-round in some parts—and the climate is reflected in the wealth of the vegetable harvest, from the many varieties of ruffled radicchio found in the Veneto region to the famed meaty San Marzano tomatoes of Campania.

Italian home cooks prepare these vegetables thoughtfully—with love, really—integrating them into seasonal soups and pastas, mixing them into nourishing frittatas and savory tarts, showcasing them on top of pizza, and giving them equal time with meat and seafood at he center of the meal. I promise you that a serving of Grilled Summer Vegetables alla Parmigiana (page 194), layered with eggplant, peppers, zucchini, and smoked scamorza cheese, is every bit as satisfying as a Sunday pork roast.

Of course, vegetables are also served in their purest form, fresh and at the height of their season, lightly cooked and dressed only with good olive oil. If you have ever sat down to eat at an Italian trattoria, you might recall the platters of vegetables set out on the communal table to entice diners—silky grilled eggplant slices, glossy strips of roasted peppers, and whole baby artichokes anointed with olive oil.

It has always mystified me to see the contortions that so many American parents go through trying to get their kids to "like" vegetables—dousing them in ranch dressing, "hiding" them in baked goods or falling back on fries. I honestly can't remember vegetables being an issue at our house when I was growing up. They were just always there; in fact, not always but very often, they were my favorite part of the meal.

Thanksgiving is a good example. Yes, we all looked forward to the turkey. But it was really the vegetable dishes that my mom prepared to go with the turkey—saucy, braised sweet-and-sour cabbage, garlicky rapini, sautéed cauliflower punched up with anchovies and oil-cured olives—that made the meal. (Incidentally, you will find these recipes within the pages of this book.)

In Italy, where I spent my summers, nearly every day began with a trip to a farmers' market. My mother and her three sisters sniffed, prodded, poked, and haggled over the price of every vegetable that went into their sack. It is no surprise that my adult self adores most vegetables, and I would be hard-pressed to come up with one that don't enjoy.

The good news is that those of us who love vegetables are no longer the exception in the United States. Farmers' markets have sprung up everywhere over the last few decades, seducing cooks and consumers with their gorgeous vegetable offerings. What's especially wonderful about this growing trend is that so many of the vegetables featured in these markets are the same vegetables that are at the heart of Italian cooking. Elegant long-stemmed fennel with creamy white bulbs; dark bumpy leaves of Tuscan kale, scarlet radicchio, and delicate baby zucchini with yellow blossoms still attached—all of these were once hard to find but are now common at many farmers' markets and some supermarkets. Even at the tiny farmers' market that sets up in the parking lot of my local library every Wednesday, I am able to choose between a dozen types of summer squash, from conventional long zucchini to the fat, baseball-size heirloom globe variety Tondo di Piacenza.

This book is my tribute to Italy's many glorious vegetables, from the tender green fava beans of early spring to the bright, sweet orange-fleshed pumpkins of autumn. To be honest, I had never thought about just how much vegetables figured into my daily cooking repertoire until I started working on this project—a process that took me back to the three previous books I have published with Chronicle. From the poached zucchini blossom soup in *The Glorious Soups and Stews of Italy* to the elegant savory carrot crostata in *Big Night In* to the cannelloni with braised radicchio in *The Glorious Pasta of Italy*, I realized that I had been paying tribute to vegetables for years!

But that is the real glory of vegetables—they keep on inspiring.

The recipes in this book offer a mix of tradition and innovation. Some are treasured recipes handed down to me by my mom and my aunts— all great home cooks; others are recipes that I have collected during my travels around Abruzzo, the beautiful region where my family originated, and around the Italian peninsula. And others I created in my own kitchen, guided by the seasons and by whatever comes home with me from the market.

Before you start cooking, I encourage you to read the Gallery of Italian Vegetables (page 15) in chapter 1, which includes descriptions of and tips for preparing the vegetables featured in this book. Think of it as a "speed dating" session with these vegetables, some of which you may already know—or *think* you know. (Did you realize that carrots make an excellent filling for ravioli?) The first chapter also contains essential information on equipment and ingredients, including the Italian cheeses that appear in many of the recipes. There are also a number of basic "building block" recipes—broths, sauces, and simple vegetable preparations that are used in a variety of ways throughout the book

For example, Roasted Mushrooms (page 69) do double duty as a filling for calzoni (page 174) and as one of the layers in Vegetable Lasagne (page 148), and they also make an excellent side dish on their own.

Chapters 2 through 7 make up the heart of the book and are organized by course, from antipasti to side dishes. It is important to note that while this book is about vegetables, it is not a vegetarian cookbook. That is why you will see recipes that call for pancetta as a garnish or flavoring agent. In Main Courses, I have included three dishes that feature meat or seafood with vegetables, recipes in which both elements are integral and one complements the other. With the exception of those three main dishes, almost every other recipe can be made vegetarian.

At the end of the book are two bonus chapters. One is a selection of desserts, including a classic Winter Squash Panna Cotta (page 248), and one of my all-time favorite creations, a light citrus-scented Carrot Polenta Cake with Marsala (page 246). The final chapter includes preserves and condiments. Italian cooks are resourceful and have been practicing the art of preserving foods for centuries. Vegetables preserved in vinegar (*sott'aceto*) or oil (*sott'olio*) are an essential part of *la dispensa*, the Italian pantry. This chapter is short, but it holds some treasures—my mother's recipe for Giardiniera (pickled vegetables, see page 256); simple Small-Batch Tomato Sauce (page 263); and my jewel-toned Tomato Marmalade (page 264), so savory and full of ripe tomato flavor that you may find yourself eating it out of the jar with a spoon.

Whether served on a classic oval white platter or preserved in a jar, vegetables are at the heart of the Italian table. I hope the recipes in this book will inspire you to make them the heart of yours, too.

Buon appetito!

chapter 1
VEGETABLE ESSENTIALS

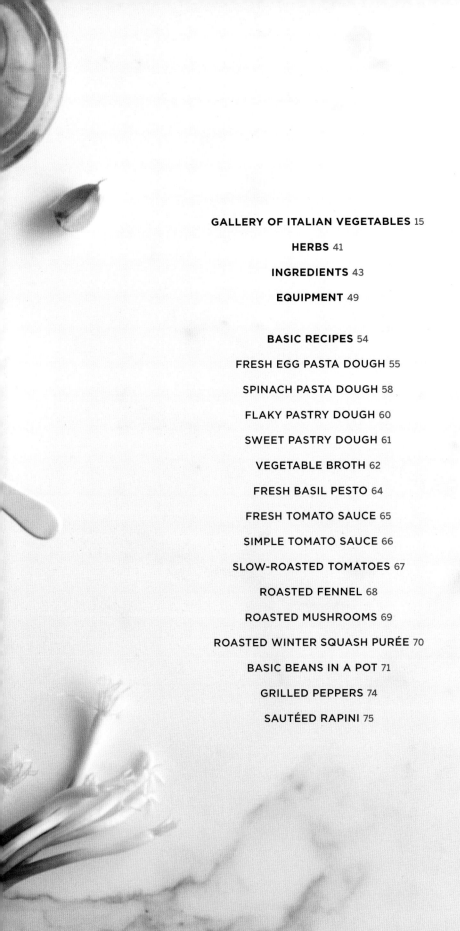

VEGETABLE ESSENTIALS

Andiamo in giardino—let's go into the garden—is a phrase you hear often in Italy. As a child it confused me. There seemed to be no word for yard. But now it makes perfect sense. Wherever there is a plot of land in Italy, there is something growing, whether it's row upon row of staked tomatoes or a hardy mound of rosemary. Even the most modest city balcony holds pots of geraniums and basil. Italians love to be outside, and who can blame them? The entire peninsula is, essentially, a beautiful garden, filled with a profusion of glorious vegetables, from artichokes to zucchini.

These vegetables are at once familiar and surprising. Did you know, for example, that radicchio, that scarlet-streaked salad favorite, completely changes character, turning sweet and mellow, when it's cooked? That cauliflower and kale belong to the same family? Or that fennel seed and anise seed, both popular in Italian recipes, come from entirely different plants?

This chapter opens with an entry for each vegetable, with useful information on how to choose, clean, and prepare it. Following that section you'll find information on equipment, Italian pantry ingredients, and cheeses, and a section of basic recipes—fundamental recipes for broths, sauces, pasta, and simply cooked vegetables that are used in many of the recipes throughout the book. (For a list of the book's recipes in which each vegetable is used, don't forget to use the index.) Take some time to read through the descriptions and be sure to refer back to this section for helpful information.

GALLERY OF ITALIAN VEGETABLES

In the Gallery of Italian Vegetables, I introduce you to the vegetables that are the heart and soul of Italian cooking and are featured in the recipes in this book.

ARTICHOKES/*CARCIOFI*
SEASON: SPRING AND FALL

It's fitting, isn't it, that this gallery should begin with the artichoke, one of spring's first vegetables, and also one of the first that come to mind when you think of Italian cooking. Artichokes, a member of the thistle family that also includes sunflowers, have been cultivated in Italy since Roman times, and who knows how long they were around before that? There is a defiance about the artichoke plant, an invasive, survivalist look to its thorny leaves and leathery flower heads that makes you think that not only might it have been around since prehistoric times but also that it might still be here after the apocalypse.

It's those flower heads—buds, actually—that are the edible part of the plant. (If left to blossom, they would eventually become large purple flowers.) Italian cooks do everything with artichokes, from deep-frying them to using them to make Cynar, a sweet and bitter liqueur.

Artichokes produce both a spring and a fall crop. There are numerous varieties, and they range in color from gray-green to purple-tinged to deep violet. They can be fat and round in shape or elongated. The artichokes grown commercially in the United States come from California. They are best eaten soon after being harvested, so look for good, fresh ones. They can be expensive, so be sure you are getting what you pay for. Look for tightly packed leaves with few spots or blemishes. The artichoke itself should feel heavy. Baby artichokes are just that—buds that have not yet reached maturity. They, too, should look bright, with tightly packed leaves.

TO CLEAN: Large artichokes must be carefully trimmed before cooking. Trim the stem off the artichoke, leaving about 2 in/5 cm, and peel off the tough outer skin of the stem. Immerse the stem in a bowl of cold water mixed with the juice of 1 or 2 lemons to prevent discoloration. Snap off the tough leaves on the bottom of the artichoke. Continue to snap off outer leaves until you reach the pale tender center leaves of the artichoke. Cut off the top third of the artichoke. Use your fingers to pry open the center, and with a round-tipped knife or a small spoon, scrape out the fuzzy choke. Trim around the bottom of the artichoke to remove any tough parts and plunge it into the lemon water. Drain before cooking.

For baby artichokes, trim off the end of the stem, remove tough outer leaves, and cut off the top of the artichoke. Immerse in lemon water to prevent discoloration.

TO PREPARE: Mature, whole, trimmed artichokes can be stuffed with seasoned bread crumbs and braised in broth and wine. Or quarter or slice them and fry in batter, or sauté in olive oil with garlic and parsley. Serve as a side dish or use in frittatas, risotto, or to dress pasta.

Baby artichokes can be battered and fried whole, braised, sautéed, or baked. The tenderest babies can be thinly sliced and served raw, seasoned with olive oil, lemon, and shavings of Parmigiano-Reggiano.

ARUGULA OR ROCKET/*RUCOLA, RUCHETTA*
SEASON: SUMMER

I did not like arugula as a child. I thought it tasted like dirt and always picked it out of my salad. At some point when I was a teenager, my taste buds did a complete turnabout. Since then I have loved that "dirt" flavor, and arugula leaves dressed with olive oil and a drop of lemon juice is my favorite salad. (If there are some Parmigiano shavings on top, so much the better.)

Arugula belongs to the mustard family, which makes sense considering its spiciness. Baby arugula is fairly mild and the peppery bite becomes more pronounced as the leaves mature. If you are buying arugula at the store or a farmers' market, look for deep green leaves that are crisp and free of holes. Yellowing around the edges is a sign that the arugula is no longer fresh.

Arugula flowers are a recent discovery for me. They are the delicate cream-and-purple-striped cross-shaped flowers that appear on the stems of bolting arugula plants. They are edible and surprisingly tasty given how delicate they look—mildly spicy and even a little sweet. I see them from time to time at farmers' markets, though they are still something of a rare find; you may have to grow your own arugula to experience the flowers. Scatter them atop a green salad or a potato salad; use them as a garnish for a spring soup; or fold them into a frittata. They are highly perishable, turning yellow and wilting within a day or two of picking, so don't pick them until you plan to use them.

TO CLEAN: Remove any roots and woody stems, especially from more mature leaves, and immerse in cold water. Drain and spin dry or pat dry with paper towels or a clean kitchen towel.

TO PREPARE: Italians put arugula in salads, along with a mix of lettuces, radicchio, and barely ripe tomatoes. But it has plenty of other uses. Scatter a handful on top of a hot pizza (see page 170) so that it *just* wilts but stays fresh, bright green, and slightly crunchy. You can do the same with hot pasta. Arugula pesto is a bright alternative to the classic version made with basil.

ASPARAGUS/*ASPARAGI*

SEASON: SPRING

I believe that the less you mess with asparagus, the better. It already has every-thing going for it: looks—*elegant* seems to be the word most associated with it—and a distinct flavor that seems to be a distillation of spring itself. Nine times out of ten I do nothing more with asparagus than blanch it until it is just tender, and then season it lightly with good olive oil, a sprinkle of salt, and a squeeze of fresh lemon juice.

Slim green asparagus is what you'll mostly find in supermarkets and farmers' markets in the United States, though fat-speared hybrids are becoming more widely available. An Italian variety of purple asparagus, known as Violetto d'Albenga, is less common here but worth looking for; it's sweeter and less fibrous than green. White asparagus is nothing more than green asparagus that has been deprived of light. It is milder in flavor and more tender than green asparagus and is especially popular in parts of Europe including Belgium, France, Germany, and the Netherlands. Whatever your color preference, be sure to choose firm stalks with tight buds at the tip. Open buds quickly turn slimy and are a sure sign that the asparagus is past its prime. If you are not cooking the asparagus soon after harvesting or buying, set the stalks upright in 1 inch/2.5 cm of water, or wrap the bottoms in a damp paper towel and refrigerate.

TO CLEAN: Rinse the spears under cold water. The easiest way to trim them is to snap off the tough ends. Or you can peel the tough portion of the spears with a small paring knife, starting from the bottom and working your way up. This takes a little more work, but you end up with more of each spear to enjoy.

TO PREPARE: Steam or blanch asparagus for 3 to 4 minutes, until just tender. Dress with olive oil and lemon juice or white wine vinegar. Asparagus is also good grilled or sautéed with a little red spring onion. Toss cooked sliced asparagus spears with pasta, or stir into risotto or into eggs for a frittata.

BEANS/*FAGIOLI E FAGIOLINI*

SEASON: SUMMER FOR FRESH; FALL FOR SHELL; YEAR-ROUND FOR DRIED

Beans are a big, broad family. They encompass everything from tender green snap beans to the coin-size dried borlotti beans used to make classic *pasta e fagioli*. The difference, essentially, is in the stage at which they are harvested. Fresh snap beans, or green beans, are immature pods that are picked before the beans inside have developed. Shell beans mature in the pod but are picked, shelled, and cooked while still fresh. Dried beans are left to dry in the pod and then harvested; they must be reconstituted in water before using in recipes. If left on the vine, all beans will pass through the three stages, though different varieties are cultivated for harvesting at different times. Fresh shell beans, such as cranberry or borlotti beans, are a treat, but they aren't available year-round. Dried beans are always available, so they are a convenient alternative.

SNAP BEANS: These include green beans, yellow wax beans, and purple beans such as Trionfo Violetto (which turn green when cooked).

TO CLEAN: Choose beans that are no thicker than a pencil and that are firm and crisp. Snap off the stem ends and rinse under cold water.

TO PREPARE: Steam or blanch the beans until just tender. Dress with olive oil and lemon juice. Or serve with slices of tomato and a little crumbled ricotta salata cheese on top. For a dish that is a little more substantial, try Smashed Green Beans and Potatoes with Pancetta (page 230).

FLAT BEANS: Known as Roma or Romano beans, these are a type of snap bean and are meant to be eaten while the bean seed is still immature inside the pod. The green variety is a shade lighter than standard green beans. There are several variations, including a yellow Roma bean, known as Meraviglia di Venezia (Marvel of Venice), and beautiful Dragon Tongue beans, which are pale, creamy yellow streaked with purple.

TO CLEAN: Clean them as you would snap beans (preceding).

TO PREPARE: Flat beans have an appealing meaty texture and full, earthy bean flavor, which makes them suitable for braising and longer sautéing, as in the recipe for Sautéed Dragon Tongue Beans with Lemon Zest and Peperoncino (page 221). For a classic preparation, *fagiolini all'uccelletto*, simmer the beans gently in fresh tomato sauce until tender.

SHELL BEANS: You will typically find shell beans at the market in late summer through fall. Their pods are tougher than those of snap beans, and you use the mature yet still tender beans nestled inside. Creamy white cannellini and mottled borlotti—also known as cranberry beans—are among the most common Italian shell beans. But if you look around, you might come across less common varieties, such as violet-streaked bird egg beans (see page 119). When choosing shell beans, look for full pods, with no mold or mildew or browning at the tips.

TO CLEAN: I don't usually rinse shell beans, as the edible bean inside is protected by the pod. Shell beans should pop open fairly easily if you snap the tip and pull down on the "string" or seam along the length of the pod.

TO PREPARE: Cook shell beans in simmering broth or water, with herbs added for additional flavor. Drain them and use them in any number of ways: dress with olive oil, garlic, and chopped fresh flat-leaf parsley; add to hearty pasta or grain soups; or dress with a vinaigrette and serve with hard-boiled eggs and good-quality canned tuna.

DRIED BEANS: These have a longer shelf life than fresh or shell beans. Beans that have been dried recently cook more quickly than older dried beans. If the beans are too old, they may not cook evenly, and in fact they may never become completely tender.

TO CLEAN: Rinse in a colander under cold running water before cooking.

TO PREPARE: Dried beans should be soaked and then simmered in liquid before using in recipes. Once cooked, dried beans can be used in the same types of recipes as shell beans. For detailed instructions on cooking dried beans, see Basic Beans in a Pot (page 71).

BEETS/*BARBABIETOLE*

SEASON: LATE SPRING THROUGH WINTER; AVAILABLE YEAR-ROUND

Remember when beets only came in a can? I'm kidding, of course, but it is nice to see this onetime salad bar staple finally getting the attention it deserves. Fresh beets—and their purple-veined green tops—are popular in northern Italian cooking. The roots are used in salads and the greens are sautéed in olive oil or tossed into soups. Farmers' markets and well-stocked supermarkets now carry a variety of beets in addition to the familiar deep red–fleshed type. Golden beets are mild in taste and have tender tops that are veined orange. They give off a gorgeous marigold-hued liquid when you cook them. Chioggia beets look like a scarlet and white bull's-eye target when you slice them crosswise. Look for beets with tops that are fresh looking and not wilted.

TO CLEAN: Slice off the beet tops for cooking. Scrub the roots gently but thoroughly under cold water. Immerse the greens in cold water and swirl them around to remove dirt and grit. Rinse thoroughly.

TO PREPARE: I like to cook whole beets in the oven at a fairly high tempera-ture (400°F/200°C/gas 6). This concentrates their rich, sweet flavor. Place them upright in a baking dish and drizzle a little olive oil over them. Cover with foil and bake until tender, 30 to 45 minutes depending on their size. Let cool, then peel off their skins with a paring knife and cut the beets into slices or wedges. Make a simple dressing by whisking together olive oil, red wine vinegar, a pinch of salt, and any beet juice that has accumulated in the baking dish. Pour over the warm beets and toss. Beet greens can be shredded and added to soups, sautéed with garlic for a side dish, or cooked and stirred into frittatas or used as a filling for ravioli.

melanzana

broccoli

funghi

aglio

fave

fiori di zucca

carciofi

cavolo

finocchio

peperoni

rucola

fagioli

barbabietole

cavolfiore

fagioli

pomodori

cicoria

zucchine

BROCCOLI/*BROCCOLI*

SEASON: EARLY SPRING AND FALL; AVAILABLE YEAR-ROUND

Broccoli was one of my mom's fallback vegetables. She made it often because it was so easy to prepare—she simply cut the head into florets with a good length of stem attached, blanched them, and served them dressed with oil, with lemon wedges on the side. I do the same thing, and this simple preparation is my favorite way to eat broccoli.

Broccoli is a member of the cabbage family that also includes Brussels sprouts, cauliflower, and kale. *Broccoli di rape*, also known as rapini, broccoli rabe, and cima di rapa, is a pungent leafy green with small florets that Italians love. It belongs to the same family of vegetables that includes turnips and radishes. Broccolini, which seems to have earned a permanent place in the produce section of the grocery store, is not Italian at all, but rather a cross between standard broccoli and gai lan (Chinese broccoli). It's sweeter and milder than broccoli, with long, tender stems. It takes well to Italian flavors, however, and I cook it often at home the way I do regular broccoli, so I've included it here.

In all cases, look for vibrant, deep green heads or bunches with firm, succulent-looking stems, florets with closed buds, and leaves that show no sign of yellowing.

TO CLEAN: Rinse broccoli and broccolini under cold running water. For rapini, cut or snap off the tough stem ends and separate the leaves. Immerse the leaves and florets in cold water to remove dirt and grit.

TO PREPARE: Broccoli is great simply dressed, but it also goes well with assertive flavors, including garlic, capers, anchovies, briny olives, and hot peppers. Blanched broccoli (and broccolini) can be sautéed in olive oil with any (or all) of those ingredients. Sautéed Rapini (page 75) is a classic Neapolitan side dish, and in Puglia, cooked rapini are tossed with orecchiette pasta.

CABBAGE/*CAVOLO*

SEASON: LATE SUMMER THROUGH WINTER; AVAILABLE YEAR-ROUND

Just saying the word *cabbage* makes some people wrinkle their noses. I know what they're thinking. Boiled cabbage. Cabbage and potatoes. Cabbage soup. I like all of those, by the way, but cabbage has much more to offer. Fresh cabbage, raw or quickly cooked, is crunchy, nutty, and sweet, and needs no more adornment than oil and vinegar or lemon juice and a good shower of coarse black pepper. It only becomes strong when it's boiled to death. On the other hand, long-simmered cabbage—especially hearty red varieties—can be delicious when prepared properly. Braised cabbage has a rich flavor and an appealing pulpy texture, which is why it is great in soups and stews. Savoy cabbage (*cavolo verza*) has beautiful crinkled, emerald outer leaves and creamy pale green interior leaves. It is sweeter and more tender than the smooth green head cabbage, and is a key ingredient in Ribollita (page 113), Tuscany's celebrated rustic bread soup. Choose heavy heads of cabbage, with firm, unblemished leaves.

TO CLEAN: Slice the heads into quarters lengthwise and cut out the cores with a paring knife. With a large, sharp knife, cut the quarters crosswise into shreds, however thin or thick you like.

TO PREPARE: Shred raw cabbage thinly and marinate in a dressing of oil, vinegar, and crushed fennel seeds; or braise in wine, broth, or cream and serve as a side with fish, pork, chicken, or sausages.

CARDOONS/*CARDONI*
SEASON: LATE SPRING THROUGH FALL

Cardoons look something like giant stalks of celery but taste something like artichokes, to which they are related. Like artichokes, they come from large, spiny-leafed thistle plants that produce purple spiky flowers. Cardoons are popular in Italy and France, but not widely available elsewhere, though that appears to be changing as more restaurants feature cardoons on their menus. In Abruzzo, where my family is from, diced cardoons are added to turkey or capon broth and served as a first course on Christmas Day. Cardoons can seem intimidating because their stalks can grow waist-high; but trimmed properly, they have myriad uses and are a nice change from more familiar fall and winter vegetables.

TO CLEAN: Discard tough outer stalks and use only the tender stalks and heart. Remove any leaves and cut the stalks into 3- or 4-in/7.5- to 10-cm pieces. Remove all the strings and immerse the trimmed stalks in a bowl of cold water mixed with the juice of 1 or 2 lemons to prevent discoloration. Cook the trimmed cardoons in boiling salted water for 30 to 45 minutes or until tender before using in recipes.

TO PREPARE: Add cooked cardoons to hearty bean soups or frittatas, or fry them in batter as you would zucchini blossoms. Cooked cardoons can be baked in a gratin dish, topped with seasoned bread crumbs and grated Parmigiano.

CARROTS/*CAROTE*
SEASON: SPRING THROUGH EARLY SUMMER FOR BABY CARROTS; LATE SUMMER AND EARLY FALL FOR MATURE CARROTS; AVAILABLE YEAR-ROUND

The carrot is the workhorse of the vegetable world. This underappreciated root finds its way into more recipes than any other vegetable I can think of—salads, soups, stews, braises, roasts, sides, even desserts and drinks! I am always happy to sing the praises of carrots, for their glorious color, their appealing crunch, their nutritional benefits, and their versatility. Carrots are essential to Italian home cooking; minced finely with celery, onion, and parsley, they help create a mixture known as a *battuto*. When sautéed in olive oil, this mixture becomes a *soffritto* and is the foundation of countless soup, sauce, and stew recipes.

In recent years, red, golden, purple, and white carrots have made an appearance on the market, but in my opinion it's hard to improve on the beauty and sweet flavor of a freshly dug orange carrot. Nantes di Chioggia and Berlicum are two popular Italian varieties of orange carrot. Look for carrots that are crisp and smooth, with no soft spots or browning.

TO CLEAN: Young carrots need only to be washed; older carrots should be washed and scraped or peeled.

TO PREPARE: Carrots are essential in flavoring Italian broths, whether vegetable, chicken, or meat. Italians often serve sautéed or roasted carrots as a side dish; roasting brings out the vegetable's natural sweetness. Puréed cooked carrots can be used in soups, as ravioli filling, and in *sformati* (molded vegetable dishes).

CAULIFLOWER/*CAVOLFIORE*
SEASON: SPRING FOR BABY CAULIFLOWER; FALL FOR MATURE CAULIFLOWER; AVAILABLE YEAR-ROUND

I mostly think of cauliflower as a winter vegetable, but some varieties are harvested in summer, and it is more or less available year-round in the supermarket. Many farmers' markets now also carry baby cauliflower in the spring. I find these little heads, about the size of my palm, impossible to resist. I bake them whole, seasoned with herbs and cheese or anchovy dressing. Cauliflower belongs to the same family as broccoli, Brussels sprouts, cabbage, and kale, and Italian cooks appreciate its sweet, slightly sulfuric taste. I like all parts of cauliflower, including the leaves and stems, so I look for heads from which the leaves haven't been stripped. The freshness of the leaves will tell you how fresh the cauliflower is. The creamy white curds (florets) should be tightly packed and free of brown specks—sometimes these spots are shaved off, so be sure to look closely. Cauliflower that has been hanging around too long smells—and tastes—like it.

In addition to white cauliflower, there are varieties with light green heads, such as cavolfiore di Macerata, and purple-headed varieties such as cavolfiore di Sicilia Violetto, which turns green when cooked. In Italy, cauliflower is a key ingredient in *giardiniera*, the classic mix of pickled vegetables. It is served dressed lightly with olive oil, but, like broccoli, it also goes well with assertive flavors.

Romanesco cauliflower, sometimes known as Romanesco broccoli, is neither cauliflower nor broccoli but is part of the same family and tastes a bit like both. It is the M.C. Escher of vegetables. The lime-green conical head is patterned in a logarithmic spiral known as the Fibonacci sequence; each floret that comprises the head repeats the ornate spiral pattern on several smaller scales. You will find the same spiraling pattern in seashells, pinecones, pineapples, and the face of a sunflower, but the Romanesco is perhaps the most exquisite example. Think of it as edible art. It is slightly more tender and sweeter than conventional cauliflower, and is good raw, steamed, or baked.

TO CLEAN: Trim the stem and remove the leaves. Separate the head into florets and rinse briefly in cold water.

TO PREPARE: Cauliflower stems are tender, so don't discard them. Just add them to whatever you're cooking. The florets, stems, and leaves can be briefly steamed and served with oil and lemon juice, or tossed with olive oil and roasted at 375°F/190°C/gas 5 until caramelized and tender.

CELERY/*SEDANO*

SEASON: YEAR-ROUND

I enjoy celery's distinctive aromatic flavor and succulent crunchy texture, and I always have a bunch in the vegetable bin in my refrigerator. Like carrots and onions, celery is an essential flavoring ingredient in Italian cooking, especially in broths, sauces, and soups. It is also, with cauliflower, one of the primary vegetables in Italian *giardiniera* (pickled mixed vegetables). Although you can always find celery in the supermarket, I recommend looking for it at farmers' markets in summer and fall; I find it tastes better and the leafy tops haven't been lopped off. Celery leaves have a lot of flavor and are tasty tossed into salads and added to broths. Look for bunches with fresh, leafy tops that are not wilted. Avoid celery that has split or dry-looking stalks.

TO CLEAN: Separate the stalks from the base and rinse under cold running water. With a paring knife, cut off the bottom of the stalk and gently pull up to remove any tough strings.

TO PREPARE: I use outer stalks for soups and sauces and reserve the tender inner stalks and the heart for salads. The best way to cook celery is to braise it in broth and wine, which yields stalks that are tender but not mushy. Sprinkle braised stalks with grated Parmigiano and put under the broiler to brown.

CHICKPEAS/*CECI*

SEASON: SPRING FOR FRESH; YEAR-ROUND FOR DRIED

I probably use chickpeas (a.k.a. garbanzo beans) more than beans in everyday cooking. I like their earthy flavor and their firm, slightly crumbly texture. I even like canned chickpeas, which seem to keep their integrity better than beans, and I usually keep a can or two in my pantry. Dried chickpeas, which must be soaked in water and then cooked for a lengthy period, are available in most supermarkets. Fresh chickpeas still in their pods are becoming more available at ethnic markets and farmers' markets. They require less cooking time than dried ones. Italian cooks use chickpeas in warm or cold salads and in hearty soups. Chickpea flour is used to make flatbreads and even pasta.

TO CLEAN: Rinse dried chickpeas in a colander under cold running water.

TO PREPARE: For detailed instructions on how to cook dried chickpeas, see the recipe for Basic Beans in a Pot (page 71). Cooked chickpeas can be served warm, with a little of their cooking liquid, seasoned with herbs and garlic or onions, and drizzled with good olive oil. *Pasta e ceci* (pasta with chickpeas) is a classic southern Italian thick soup, which I make often at home with good canned chickpeas and diced tomatoes, adding onions and rosemary to the broth for flavor.

CHICORY/*CICORIA*

SEASON: FALL THROUGH WINTER

There's bitterness in every family. But in the chicory family, it is the reigning trait. And that is a good thing. Ruffled scarlet radicchio and frilly green and white curly endive, both members of the chicory family, add beauty, texture, and character to salads. Other members include escarole, Belgian endive, and puntarelle, a chicory with thin stems and thin leaves. Eating puntarelle is a Roman rite in early spring. The stems are immersed in ice-cold water, which removes a little of their bitterness and makes them curl. Then they are tossed with a dressing of anchovy, garlic, oil, and vinegar.

The variety of radicchio that grows in the Veneto is astonishing. There are so many types that they are named after the towns they hail from. Radicchio di Chioggia and radicchio Rosso di Verona have compact, softball-size red and white heads. These are the types you see most often in supermarkets. Radicchio di Treviso is long and shaped something like a head of Romaine lettuce but with scarlet-and-white striped leaves. Radicchio Variegata di Castelfranco has pale green leaves with red streaks and splatters. The most dramatic looking is radicchio Rosso di Treviso Tardivo, a late-season variety with long, slim, red and white leaves that look like curled fingers at their tips. Seeds from Italy (see Sources, page 266) sells seeds for these types of radicchio and many more chicory varieties.

Many of the chicories, including radicchio, Belgian endive, and escarole, have second identities. When you wilt them in heat or braise them, they lose much of their bitter bite, soften in texture, and take on a nutty flavor. I use sautéed radicchio as an unusual but delicious vegetarian filling for homemade cannelloni.

TO CLEAN: For loose-headed varieties, remove the leaves from the core and rinse in cold water. For tight-headed varieties, either gently pry the leaves from the core or cut the heads lengthwise into quarters and peel off the quarter leaves from the core. Rinse in cold water.

TO PREPARE: Radicchio, endive, and curly endive, also known as frisée, can be mixed with Romaine, butter lettuce, and red leaf lettuce, as well as arugula. I like these chicories dressed assertively, with anchovy dressing or oil and good vinegar and topped with crumbles of Gorgonzola cheese. Escarole is a fairly tough green, and though it can be eaten raw, Italians prefer it boiled and dressed simply with olive oil and lemon juice. It is also used to add body and flavor to soups.

CHIVES (see Onions and Garlic, page 33)

EGGPLANT/*MELANZANA*
SEASON: MIDSUMMER THROUGH EARLY FALL
There is magic in eggplant. For centuries, Italians and other Mediterranean cultures have used this vegetable as a poor man's substitute for meat. Dipped in flour, egg, and bread crumbs and panfried, sliced eggplant does a great job of mimicking veal or chicken cutlets. Layer those slices in a baking dish with mozzarella cheese and tomato sauce and you have one of the world's favorite comfort foods: eggplant Parmesan.

Eggplant is prized all over the world for its versatility and its affinity for so many flavors. In Italian cooking, eggplant pairs beautifully with anchovies, basil, garlic, peppers, olives, tomatoes, and vinegar. It can be sautéed, fried, baked, roasted, or grilled. Pickled eggplant is a staple in the Italian pantry. The classic large, oval, purple-black eggplant is but one of many varieties. There are long, slim Asian hybrids and small, white egg-shaped specimens that look exactly like . . . eggs! Some have purple and white streaks and others are pale pink. There's even a small, bright red-orange variety that looks like a tomato, which isn't surprising, considering that eggplant and tomatoes are both members of the nightshade family. Look for fruits that are smooth and shiny with no scuffs or bruises. They should feel heavy; if the eggplant feels light, chances are it is old and its flesh will be pithy and bitter.

TO CLEAN: Rinse under cold water and slice off the stem and flower ends.

TO PREPARE: If the skin is thick, peeling the eggplant is probably a good idea; otherwise you can peel or not, as you like. To remove bitter juices from mature eggplants, slice them and sprinkle with salt. Layer them in a colander and set a plate with a weight on top. Let the eggplant "sweat" for 30 to 60 minutes. Wipe dry before cooking. Sliced eggplant can be brushed with olive oil and grilled or roasted. You can also sauté or fry eggplant slices with or without a coating of bread crumbs; just be careful to monitor how much oil you use, as the porous eggplant soaks it up like a sponge (eggplant that has been salted and weighted down absorbs less oil). In summer, I love tossing cubes of sautéed eggplant with pasta and fresh tomato sauce. Small eggplants can be hollowed out and filled with rice, bread crumbs, or meat stuffing and baked.

FAVA BEANS/*FAVE*
SEASON: SPRING

Whoever coined the phrase "hill of beans" must have been thinking about favas. You start out with a big pile of fat green pods, and by the time you are done shelling and boiling and peeling, you are left with a tiny mound of lime-green beans, each about the size and width of a tiddlywink. You have to ask yourself if it's worth the trouble.

For me the answer is yes. Fresh fava beans—actually a member of the pea family—are rich and buttery and grassy. Nothing else tastes like them. Their season is short, and so yes, once or twice during those few weeks in April and early May, I set aside the time to clean favas, which I toss with pasta, add to spring stews, or purée as a topping for crostini. It may sound silly, but the work they require and their brief season somehow make me appreciate them more. Look for bright green satiny pods and avoid those with blackened tips.

Dried fava beans are available year-round in most supermarkets. These are older beans that have matured and dried on the vine. The beans are big and yellow, and like other dried beans must be reconstituted in liquid before being used in recipes. They have a heartier flavor and coarser texture than fresh favas, and add substance to winter soups and stews.

TO CLEAN: Shell fresh fava beans by prying open the pods at the seam. This is not difficult, but it takes a little more force than opening pea or shell bean pods. Once you have shelled the beans, boil them for 1 to 2 minutes in salted water, and then plunge into a bowl of ice water to stop the cooking process. Drain the beans and remove their tough outer skins by squeezing each one gently between your thumb and finger. The yield from 1 lb/455 g of beans in the pod is a scant cup of shelled and peeled beans—about 5 oz/140 g.

TO PREPARE: Shelled and peeled favas can be cooked briefly with butter and herbs and served as a side dish, added to salads, or served as an antipasto with Pecorino Romano and other sheep's milk cheeses. Add favas to spring risotto, or toss them with cooked pasta, along with pecorino and finely julienned prosciutto.

FENNEL/*FINOCCHIO*
SEASON: SPRING THROUGH EARLY SUMMER; FALL

A certain amount of confusion surrounds fennel, so let's start by clearing that up. Fennel and anise are not one and the same. The two plants come from the same family, but anise is grown primarily for its seeds, which are used as a spice. Fennel, also known as Florentine fennel, is that oddly beautiful vegetable with the fat white bulb, long straight green stalks, and gentle feathery fronds. The plant produces lacy yellow flowers. Almost all of it is edible, from the bulb to the flowers. Fennel seeds are used to season sausages, salami, and other cured meats. Raw fennel bulb has a satisfying crunch and a bright sweet flavor that does indeed taste of anise. When cooked, fennel becomes sleek and tender, and it caramelizes beautifully because of the natural sugar it contains.

In addition to Florentine fennel, there is also wild fennel, which has similar long stalks, feathery fronds, and yellow flowers but no bulb. It goes well with many vegetables including carrots, tomatoes, onions, and winter squash. The tiny granules of fennel pollen are harvested from wild fennel and used as a spice. Fennel pollen has a rich fragrance that is akin to fennel seed, but with a hint of curry in it. It pairs beautifully with fish.

TO CLEAN: Slice the thick stems off the fennel where they meet the bulb. Peel off any tough outer layers from the bulb. Slice the bulb lengthwise into quarters and cut away the core from the center of each quarter. If you are not using cut fennel immediately, put it in a bowl of water mixed with lemon juice to prevent browning.

TO PREPARE: Fennel has many uses in the kitchen because it pairs well with so many other ingredients. Add sliced raw fennel to salads, especially salads with crunchy endive, apples, raisins or dried cherries, and citrus fruit. Sweet roasted fennel makes a fine accompaniment to roast pork, chicken, or fish, and I love it as a topping for pizza. Don't discard the fennel stalks; the tender ones can be roasted along with the sliced bulb, and the tough parts can be used to flavor broth. Mince the fronds and use them as an herb to flavor soups and roasts.

GARLIC (see Onions and Garlic, page 33)

KALE/*CAVOLO*

SEASON: LATE FALL THROUGH WINTER

There's a reason the Italian word for kale—*cavolo*—is the same as the Italian word for cabbage. They are members of the same large family of mustard plants that also includes broccoli, cabbage, and cauliflower. There are many kinds of kale, but the one most associated with Italian cooking is Tuscan kale, also known known as *cavolo nero* (black kale), lacinato kale, and dinosaur kale. It is quite elegant, in my opinion, with long, slim, crimped leaves that are a deep blue-green. It has a hearty flavor, somewhat pungent but also sweet, and an excellent texture that retains its body even when braised or cooked in soups. Tuscan kale usually comes bundled in small bunches weighing about 8 oz/225 g. Choose bunches with firm, dark leaves and succulent-looking stalks.

TO CLEAN: Trim off ends and rinse leaves in cold water.

TO PREPARE: Raw kale can be finely shredded and tossed with a robust dressing, such as creamy Gorgonzola or an anchovy vinaigrette. Sauté coarsely chopped or shredded kale with olive oil and lots of garlic. Toss in a handful of cooked chickpeas, if you like. Or spread sautéed kale in a baking dish, top with grated cheese, and bake.

LEEKS (see Onions and Garlic, page 33)

LENTILS/*LENTICCHIE*

SEASON: YEAR-ROUND

Le lenticchie portano fortuna, my mom often said when she served us lentil soup. "Lentils bring good luck." In Italy they are served on New Year's Eve or New Year's Day, for the same reason black-eyed peas are served in the American South—in the hope that the coming year will be prosperous. Lentils are grown in several regions in Italy, including Umbria and Abruzzo. They are similar to brown lentils, but they are slightly smaller and they hold their shape during long cooking. Lentils have an affinity for carrots, spinach, and onions, and are especially good when seasoned with bay leaf.

TO CLEAN: Rinse in a colander under cold running water; remove any tiny stones or bits of grit that might be present.

TO PREPARE: I have never found it necessary to soak lentils the way dried beans must be soaked. They should be cooked in plenty of broth or water, because they absorb liquid readily. Season the cooking liquid with half an onion, a handful of parsley sprigs, and a bay leaf. Lentils can be served warm or cold as a salad; in hearty soups; and in stews—sausage and lentil stew is a classic winter dish.

LETTUCE/*LATTUGA*
SEASON: SPRING THROUGH FALL

There are many lettuces beyond the commercially grown Boston, iceberg, and Romaine varieties you see at the supermarket—although the selection is much better than it was a decade or two ago. Lettuce can range from tender to toothsome, buttery to crispy, ruby red to bright green, often with a mix of both colors. The leaves can be crimped or frilly, lobed or spiked. If you don't have a garden or a spot big enough to accommodate lettuces, check out the selection at farmers' markets. Using just-picked fresh mixed lettuces makes a salad more interesting and delicious, not to mention prettier. I like to use a combination of two lettuces and arugula or one of the chicories, usually radicchio. But some-times, a simple salad composed of tender butter lettuce dressed with olive oil and good wine vinegar or lemon juice is all I need.

TO CLEAN: If the leaves are loose, rinse them in several changes of cool water (I use the outer bowl of my salad spinner). If the lettuce is a head, pull off and rinse only the amount you need for the salad and store the rest of the head in an open bag in the vegetable crisper of the refrigerator. Spin the leaves dry or roll them in a clean kitchen towel to dry them thoroughly.

TO PREPARE: Dress tender salads judiciously: it is easy to overwhelm them. For a simple dressing, whisk together 2 or 3 parts very good olive oil with 1 part lemon juice or wine vinegar (or a little of both). Add a sprinkle of salt and toss in a small smashed garlic clove. Let the dressing sit for a while and then remove the garlic before dressing the salad. For the hearty salads I put together, I usu-ally use crunchier lettuces as well as other ingredients, from dried fruit and nuts to shaved or shredded cheese. These salads are more in the style of American or Italian American salads.

MUSHROOMS/*FUNGHI*
SEASON: SPRING, FALL; AVAILABLE YEAR-ROUND

Mushrooms are not technically vegetables—they are fungi—but since they are treated like vegetables I've included them here. Italians cook with a variety of wild and cultivated mushrooms, including the pretty horn-shaped chanterelle and the everyday champignon that is akin to the button mushroom. But it is the porcino, with its fat thumb of a stem and meaty cap, that is the undisputed king of Italian mushrooms. In fall, along mountain roads throughout Italy, you will come across cars parked in whatever narrow spot is available, temporarily aban-doned by their owners who are off in search of the fragrant fungus. Although they do grow wild in North America, porcini are not widely available to those of us who are not skilled mushroom foragers. The few times I have seen them at upscale supermarkets, they have been prohibitively expensive, so I use dried porcini in their place. Dried porcini lack the full meaty texture of fresh ones, and you can't grill them, but they are wonderfully fragrant, with a deep aroma that lies somewhere between rich earth and bitter chocolate.

I always try to mix the selection of mushrooms when I cook them, to provide a variety of flavors and textures. I like portobellos and shiitakes, as well as frilly oyster mushrooms and brown cremini.

I should mention truffles here, as both black and white truffles are found in Italy. The black ones are exorbitantly expensive and the white ones even more so. They can be as small as hazelnuts or as large as misshapen golf balls. Their rich aroma is overpowering and permeates everything around them. The fragrance defies description and would be smothering if it weren't so intoxicating. Truffles elevate the simplest foods, from scrambled eggs to noodles tossed with butter. Are they worth the ridiculous price? I guess everyone has his or her own view on that. If you are like me and can't afford them, I recommend you make some friends among the 1 percent who can.

TO CLEAN: Trim the stems off mushrooms, or cut them off entirely if they are tough. You can brush the dirt off mushrooms with a soft-bristled brush or damp paper towels. I prefer rinsing them in water and gently rubbing off any grit with my fingertips. I then put them to dry in a bowl lined with paper towels.

TO PREPARE: Fresh mushrooms can be sautéed or roasted. Dried porcini must be reconstituted with boiling water. Place the mushrooms in a small bowl and pour boiling water over them. Let them steep for 20 to 30 minutes. Drain the porcini in a fine-mesh sieve lined with damp paper towels, taking care to reserve the strained liquid to use in soups, risotti, sautés, and stews.

OLIVES
SEASON: FALL FOR HARVESTING; YEAR-ROUND FOR EATING
Olives are complicated. There are hundreds of cultivars of the olive tree in Italy alone, many, such as Cerignola and Gaeta, named after the towns in which they flourish. Different olives have different characteristics. Some are mild, others are fruity, and still others bitter. Some, such as Frantoio and Leccino, are grown specifically for the olive oil they produce, while others, such as fat Cerignolas, are picked for their meaty fruit.

Olives can be harvested either unripe, when they are firm and green, or ripe, when they are purple or black. Fresh olives are bitter and must be cured before eating. Methods include oil-curing, brine-curing, and salt- or dry-curing. The variety of olive, plus the degree of ripeness and curing method, and the herbs and spices added to the mix, all determine how the fruit will ultimately taste. I am especially fond of those glossy black oil-cured olives with wrinkly skins. They are first cured in salt and then in oil, a process that turns them soft and removes their bitterness, giving them an intense, rich, salty flavor.

Generally, I prefer to buy olives in bulk. Most supermarkets now have olive bars that offer a good selection and good quality. I find they are almost always better than canned olives. I have found that bottled olives can vary in quality, so choose a brand you trust.

TO PREPARE: Drain olives before using them in recipes, but don't discard all the brine—I often use a spoonful or two to flavor pasta sauces and bruschetta toppings. Whole olives can be pitted easily with an olive pitter or by slicing around the pit with a small, sharp paring knife.

ONIONS AND GARLIC/*CIPOLLE E AGLIO*

SEASON: SPRING FOR YOUNG ONIONS AND GARLIC, SUMMER AND FALL FOR MORE MATURE ONIONS AND GARLIC; AVAILABLE YEAR-ROUND

Onions contribute much to the character of Italian cooking. They provide an essential flavor base for broths, soups, many sautés, and certainly stews and braises. The onion family is large, comprising chives, scallions, spring onions, bulb onions, leeks, shallots, and garlic. It is part of the same family that includes lilies.

Onions are harvested at various stages of development. In spring, farmers' markets carry young onions—both red and white—with small, immature bulbs and green stalks still attached. As the months go by you'll notice that the bulbs get bigger, until eventually you begin to see more mature onions in their familiar papery skins. I am partial to basic yellow or red onions for chopping finely and using as a flavor agent, usually together with carrots and celery. When onions are the star of the show, I look for something more special, like the small, squat cipolline, which are great for pickling, and the ornament-shaped red torpedo onions, such as Rossa Lunga di Firenze or Rossa di Tropea.

I am never without a head of garlic in my pantry. Supermarket garlic is fine, but in spring my farmers' market carries young garlic still attached to its long stem. It is tender and free of brown spots or the bitter green sprouts that you often find in older garlic. At farmers' markets, you will also find curlicue garlic scapes, which are the tender flower stems of the plant. They can be sautéed or turned into garlic scape pesto. More farmers' markets now carry the beautiful long-stemmed globes of purple or white flowers from chive, onion, and garlic plants. You can put them in a flower arrangement, but they have a better use. Snip off the pretty flowers and sprinkle them on top of a tomato or green salad. They're delicious. Be sure to choose fresh onions—chives, scallions, spring onions, and young bulb onions—that have firm green stalks with no sign of wilting. For older onions, choose firm, thin-skinned specimens with no soft spots or specks of mildew. Avoid old onions that are sprouting.

TO CLEAN: Fresh young onions should be rinsed to remove dirt at the bulb end. Take extra care when washing leeks, which grow in sandy soil and retain grit. It is not necessary to wash storage onions or garlic before peeling.

Slice off the root ends before slicing or chopping. Use only the white and pale green parts of leeks, but feel free to use most of the green of scallions and spring onions.

TO PREPARE: Add onion halves or quarters, stuck with a whole clove if you like, to chicken or vegetable broth. Onions are great roasted with other vegetables such as cauliflower and potatoes. Cipolline are especially good in *agrodolce*—a sweet and sour vinegar sauce. Both red and yellow onions are delicious cooked very slowly in butter and olive oil over a low flame until they are creamy and caramelized. Use this as a topping for pizza or crostini or as a base for onion soup.

PEAS/*PISELLI*
SEASON: SPRING FOR FRESH; AVAILABLE FROZEN YEAR-ROUND

I didn't start buying fresh peas in their pods until I began frequenting my weekly farmers' market about fifteen years ago. My kids were toddlers then, with beautiful tiny hands and chubby little fingers that were perfect for shelling. *(Pause for a nostalgic sigh.)* Now they are at school all day and into the evening, so the task falls to me, though they certainly enjoy the fruits of my labor, especially in the form of a dish of *pasta e piselli*. If you are buying peas in the pod, know that 1 lb/455 g yields only 4 oz/115 g of shelled peas, so be sure to buy enough.

Frozen peas are fine—good, even—and certainly less work than the fresh ones, but fresh peas have such a short season that I can't help but take advantage of it when I see them at one of the stalls. Fresh peas should be eaten soon after they are picked because their sugars turn to starch quickly and they lose their delicate sweetness. Look for full, crisp, shiny pods. But stay away from larger dry-looking pods that are bulging with peas; these are likely to be older and unappealingly starchy. Fresh peas should be cooked the same day you harvest or buy them. Otherwise blanch and freeze them: remove them from their pods and immerse them in boiling water for a minute or two. Drain them quickly and then plunge them into a bowl of ice water to stop the cooking and preserve their bright green color. Peas that are frozen without blanching will turn starchy.

TO CLEAN: Fresh peas are easy to shell; simply pry open their pods with your thumbs and coax out the peas.

TO PREPARE: Blanched fresh peas can be mixed into rice or grain salads, or puréed, seasoned, and spread on crostini. Not surprisingly, peas go well in sautés with other spring vegetables such as spring onions, asparagus, young carrots, and herbs such as marjoram. Classic Italian preparations for peas include peas sautéed with onion and a little prosciutto, and peas cooked in a light tomato sauce.

PEPPERS, SWEET AND HOT/*PEPERONI E PEPERONCINI*
SEASON: MIDSUMMER THROUGH EARLY FALL

If it is difficult to imagine Italian cooking without onions, it is impossible to imagine it without peppers. In fact, fried onions and peppers—green or red—are a divine combination, even more so if you plop a fried or poached egg on top. In addition to fried, Italians enjoy peppers raw, roasted, stuffed, and pickled.

Hot peppers are equally adored. In certain parts of Italy, such as Abruzzo, where my family is from, just about every restaurant sets out a bowl of dried or preserved *peperoncini* (hot peppers), the way American restaurants set out salt and pepper shakers. I had a cousin who used to pop whole fiery-hot *peperoncini* into his mouth and chew them as if they were caramels.

Peppers come in a glorious array of shapes, sizes, and colors. Most start out green and mature to red, yellow, or orange, though cream-colored and purple peppers are also gaining in popularity. The rectangular bell peppers are used for stuffing, frying, and roasting, and the tapered, horn-shaped varieties, which generally have a thinner skin, are fried and grilled. Cherry peppers, the little fat round ones, can be sweet or hot, and their size generally ranges from 1 to 2 in/2.5 to 5 cm in diameter. Recently, small red, yellow, and orange peppers known as snacking peppers have come onto the market. Besides being a healthy snack, they are great for pickling.

I am still trying to find a tiny, extremely spicy variety of cherry pepper that I enjoyed at my friend Margherita Pacchione's house. She had preserved them in oil and sent me home with a jar. They had such flavor! I was shamefully parsimonious about using and sharing them. The classic *peperoncino* from Abruzzo is a long, skinny, horn-shaped pepper, which also goes by the name of *diavolino* (little devil). In September when they are in high season, you will find them strung together in bunches hanging from doors and out on balconies to dry.

TO CLEAN: Rinse sweet peppers under cold water. If you are grilling or roasting the peppers whole, leave the stems on so you can turn them with tongs as they char (see page 74). Otherwise, cut around the top of the pepper and remove the stem and attached seeds. Use a paring knife to cut the good flesh around the stem. Discard the stem and seeds. Cut the peppers in half or quarters, depending on their shape and size, and use the paring knife to remove any pith. Slice or dice as you please.

For hot peppers, rinse under cold water. You may want to use rubber or latex gloves when handling hot peppers as a precautionary step. Slice the stem off the peppers and cut them in half. Scrape out the seeds if not using—they are the hottest part of the hot pepper—and chop finely. I like the seeds so I usually leave them in and chop them along with the rest of the pepper.

TO PREPARE: Peppers are a front-and-center vegetable. Unlike zucchini or eggplant, they won't absorb the flavors of other vegetables, but they are happy to impart their own. They go well with almost any other vegetable, and in countless preparations. Raw, they are spicy and crunchy; grilling or roasting turns them silky. Toss cooked peppers with pasta and cheese, put them on pizza, and add them to tarts or frittatas. They work well with other assertive flavors, like anchovies, capers, garlic, olives, and onions. Hot peppers should not be used with abandon, even if you are a lover of spice. Too much can be overwhelming. Start with the smaller amount called for in a recipe and add more if you want to crank up the heat. Hot peppers are great with hearty greens such as rapini, kale, and cabbage.

POTATOES/*PATATE*

SEASON: LATE SPRING FOR BABY POTATOES, SUMMER FOR NEW POTATOES; FALL THROUGH WINTER FOR MATURE AND STORAGE POTATOES

It can be hard to shake a stereotype. That, I fear, is the case with potatoes. So often they end up on the plate as the requisite starch, the plate filler, the after-thought side dish. I like the way Italian cooks treat the potato with the respect it deserves. After all, it is the key ingredient in one of Italy's most famous con-tributions to the culinary world—gnocchi. Italians turn potatoes into croquettes, pizza, patties, gratins, and tortes. They also love to combine potatoes with other vegetables—tomatoes, green beans, peppers, and eggplant.

Baby new potatoes begin popping up at farmers' markets in spring. Some are smaller than walnuts. They are delicious roasted whole—no need to peel. The term *new potatoes* refers to potatoes that have not yet been put into cold storage for long keeping. That's what you'll find at farmers' markets and many supermarkets from spring into fall. The cold storage potatoes are the ones you find at the supermarket in winter. The texture and character of potatoes differ depending on how much starch and moisture they contain. Russets are the classic baking potato, dry and fluffy when baked or mashed. Red potatoes are waxier and make good gratins and potato salads. Yellow potatoes are my favorites. Their flesh is creamy and dense, and their flavor has a sweet note. I actually prefer mashed yellow potatoes to the fluffy russets because of their flavor and buttery texture. In fact, I use a mix of yellow and red potatoes to make gnocchi rather than the standard russets. This is considered heresy among some purists, but I find the combination yields gnocchi that are fluffy and tender, yet substantial.

When buying potatoes, choose ones that feel firm and crisp. Avoid those with skins that have begun to turn green or eyes that are sprouting, since they are old.

TO CLEAN: New potatoes don't really need to be peeled because their skins are usually thin. Just scrub them with a brush under water to remove dirt.

TO PREPARE: Boil potatoes whole in their skins in salted water until just tender. Peel if you like and dress with good olive oil, sea salt, and a shower of parsley. Or cut potatoes into chunks, toss with olive oil, salt, and pepper, and roast at 400°F/200°C/gas 6 until golden brown. Potatoes are excellent roasted together with onions and cauliflower. And *pasta e patate* (pasta with potatoes) is one of my favorite high-carb comfort dinners.

SPINACH AND TENDER GREENS/*SPINACI E VERDURA TENERA*
SEASON: SPRING, FALL

Spinach is the virtuous vegetable. There's something about those deep green leaves and clean mineral flavor that makes me feel like I'm adding years to my life span when I take a bite. Although it's good in a mixed salad, I actually prefer spinach when it's been cooked—not a lot, just quickly wilted in a pan with a little olive oil and garlic. In Italy, spinach comes to the table in many forms—tossed with pasta, worked into pasta dough, as gnocchi, in *sformati* (savory custards), and in tortes and frittatas.

Wild spinach, called *orapi* in Italian, grows in abundance in the hills of Abruzzo and elsewhere, and is used, among other things, to dress little nuggets of handmade pasta known as caratelli. It has a slightly more pungent taste than cultivated spinach. Italians are also fond of stinging nettles, *ortiche*, which are puréed in soup, tossed with pasta, and mixed into gnocchi dough. Many farmers' markets now carry nettles in early spring—they are among the earliest vegetable to come to market—but they can still be hard to find, and I have yet to see them in the supermarket.

Nettles are usually sold in plastic bags. Be careful when handling them. The leaves and stem are covered in fine hairs that harbor an irritating chemical. To neutralize the irritant, plunge the nettles in boiling salted water just for a minute or so, and then drain them. Be sure to use gloves or tongs to do this. Once blanched, the nettles are safe for handling and eating.

In choosing spinach and other tender greens, look for bright green leaves that show no sign of wilting or yellowing. Spinach is perishable and turns slimy pretty quickly, so you should plan on using it soon after buying.

TO CLEAN: Rinse spinach in several changes of water, gently swirling the leaves around to dislodge any dirt. Drain and spin dry.

TO PREPARE: In addition to the simple sauté I mentioned above, you can also sauté spinach with butter and finish with a sprinkle of freshly grated Parmigiano. I often add a handful or two of spinach to chicken or vegetable soups. For spinach pasta, take care to squeeze out as much liquid as possible from the cooked spinach before mixing it into the dough (see page 58).

SUMMER SQUASH AND ZUCCHINI/*ZUCCHINE*
SEASON: LATE SPRING THROUGH FALL; AVAILABLE YEAR-ROUND

The prize for most accommodating vegetable goes to zucchini and her sisters, yellow crookneck, pattypan, and all the other pretty summer squashes that populate farmers' market stalls from mid-May through September. Summer squash is easy to clean—no soaking, no peeling, no blanching—and unless it is overgrown, no seeding is required. It can be sliced or diced easily, and performs well no matter what cooking technique you subject it to, whether the grill, the frying pan, or the roasting pan. Baby summer squashes are adorable and perfect for roasting or sautéing whole, with a sprinkle of cheese on top. And then there are the blossoms—what a bonus! Squash blossoms can be poached in broth, dipped in batter and fried, or shredded and tossed with pasta or stirred into risotto.

I often see summer squash described as bland, but I couldn't disagree more. Toss zucchini into a hot frying pan with olive oil and its flavor quickly turns nutty as it browns. Cooked gently over low heat, the squash's flavor is sweet and mellow. At the same time, it takes on the flavors of whatever else is in the pan, absorbing the aroma of garlic or basil, the bright flavor of tomato or vinegar. Oh, and cheese. Zucchini loves cheese—Asiago, Fontina, goat cheese, mozzarella, Parmigiano, pecorino, and more.

Different summer squash shapes inspire different uses in the kitchen. Right now, one of my favorites is Tondo di Nizza, a light green, round squash about the size of a tennis ball. The large ones can be sliced thickly and grilled. The smaller ones are perfect for hollowing out and stuffing with bread crumbs, cheese, sausage, or rice. Pattypan squashes also make good stuffers because they are so pretty. A few years ago at the farmers' market, I found a variety called Romanesco, striped with prominent ribs. It has a pronounced nutty taste and is especially good grilled.

TO CLEAN: Rinse briefly under running water to remove any grit. Slice off the stem and flower ends. To clean blossoms, pry them open to make sure they are not harboring any little bugs. Rinse them gently and pat dry with paper towels.

TO PREPARE: Slice zucchini into sticks, dip them in batter, and fry. Or cook them in oil over high heat with a little garlic until they are nicely browned and just tender. Sprinkle with salt and pepper and a splash of good wine vinegar. Slice zucchini and summer squash into coins and cook gently with garlic in a little oil and butter, until they are very soft and pulpy. Toss with hot cooked pasta and cheese.

SWISS CHARD/*BIETOLA*
SEASON: LATE SPRING THROUGH WINTER

This versatile green with large ruffled leaves lies somewhere between tender and hearty, and gets plenty of use in the Italian kitchen. Cooking chard in a little olive oil turns it silky and brings out its sweetness.

Chard is in the same family as beets, and like beets you'll find it in a range of colors. Standard Swiss chard has deep green leaves with creamy white ribbing and stems. Rhubarb chard has ruby-red stems and ribs that provide a pretty contrast to the green leaves. There's also golden chard, which has sunny-colored ribs and stems. Multicolored bunches of chard are marketed as "rainbow chard" and are available in many supermarkets. Baby chard, too, is becoming more popular, and it is great tossed raw into salads or cooked quickly like spinach.

When buying chard, look for fresh, firm unbent leaves with succulent stalks. The leaves should be free or mostly free of spots and holes, with no signs of yellowing.

TO CLEAN: Baby chard can be gently rinsed in water. Wash large leaves and stems to remove grit and shake off excess water. Cut the stems at the base of the leaves and set aside. They take longer to cook than the leaves, so when sautéing, start with the stems and then add the leaves.

TO PREPARE: Cut chard stems crosswise into small pieces and coarsely shred the leaves. Sauté the stems with a little olive oil and garlic until they start to soften; then add the leaves and cook until tender. Chard can also be blanched or steamed until tender. Finely minced, cooked chard makes a tasty vegetarian filling for ravioli and other stuffed pasta dishes.

TOMATOES/*POMODORI*
SEASON: MIDSUMMER THROUGH EARLY FALL

Tomatoes may not be native to Italy, but Italians certainly showcase them in the kitchen. The tomatoes of San Marzano, located outside of Naples, are famous for the sauce they produce. Sicilians have turned the making of sundried tomatoes and tomato paste into an art.

A good tomato from the garden or the farmers' market makes my heart beat faster. It might be bright red or reddish brown or striped with green; it might be large and lopsided or uniformly round and the size of tennis ball. It will be juicy and savory, sharply acidic, like a lemon, and yet still mellow and sweet. If it's a sauce tomato, it will be oval in shape and saturated red in color, and its insides will be meaty. Such tomatoes are gifts from nature that only come around once a year. When it's tomato season—from midsummer through early fall, where I live—I eat them every day. I make tomato salad, with or without mozzarella. I put them on pizza. I roast them. I make sauce. I can sauce. When tomato season is over, that's it. Then I turn to what I've preserved myself and good-quality canned tomatoes, which are a much better choice for sauce than the mealy, flavorless tomatoes that you see piled in supermarket bins throughout the year.

Good heirloom tomatoes from the farmers' market are wonderful, but they can be expensive, so it is worth growing your own in summer. If you have one sunny patch in your yard or on your patio, you can grow tomatoes. Some varieties—especially cherry tomatoes—are bred to be compact and are perfect for growing in containers. They have lots of flavor and are great in salads or roasted. Tomatoes should be picked when they are almost ripe, and then allowed to finish ripening over three or four days—I line mine up on my kitchen windowsill. Some scarring around the stem end is not unusual and doesn't mean the tomato isn't good. But do stay away from tomatoes that have gone soft or split.

One area where I am at odds with Italians on the subject of tomatoes concerns salad tomatoes. Italians prefer barely ripe tomatoes—still quite firm and mostly green with a soft pink blush—in their salads. Like the majority of Americans, I prefer my salad tomatoes to be ripe and juicy.

TO CLEAN: Rinse tomatoes gently under running water just before using. Don't store them in the refrigerator; they will lose their flavor and turn mealy.

TO PREPARE: Use thin-skinned juicy tomatoes for salad, bruschetta, and other summery dishes that call for raw tomatoes. Choose somewhat firmer tomatoes for hollowing out and stuffing and baking; and use plum or cherry tomatoes for roasting. Don't use salad tomatoes to make sauce, or you will have to simmer them to death to achieve the right consistency, and your sauce will taste overcooked. Instead, use ripe pear-shaped Roma tomatoes or plum tomatoes; these have less juice and more flesh and make the finest, fresh-tasting sauce. To enjoy the best summer tomatoes, slice off the top and core, and slice thinly or thickly. Arrange the tomatoes on a plate, overlapping them slightly. Dress them with your best olive oil and flaky sea salt. Sprinkle a few baby basil leaves or arugula flowers on top. Serve at room temperature.

WINTER SQUASH AND PUMPKIN/*ZUCCA*
SEASON: FALL THROUGH WINTER

It wasn't that long ago that acorn, butternut, and your basic sugar pumpkin were pretty much the only winter squash varieties available. Now, at grocery stores and farmers' markets alike, we have our choice of so many beautiful specimens—squat, striped, stippled, bumpy, and smooth. I love them all.

Winter squashes are especially popular in northern Italy, where they grow well and are used in soups, to make gnocchi, and as a filling for ravioli. Seeds from Italy has a good selection of Italian winter squash and pumpkin varieties, including butternut Rugosa, a large, ribbed butternut squash that keeps well; and Marina di Chioggia, an old variety from the Veneto with a bumpy gray-green rind and sweet orange flesh (see Sources, page 266). I am also especially fond of bon bon and buttercup, two squat, dark green–striped varieties. Both have dense, intensely orange flesh that is sweet and smooth when cooked. Delicata is another of my favorites; it has thin skin and a lovely golden interior that is sweet and smooth, especially when baked. Butternut is a good all-purpose squash that is relatively easy to peel. Choose squashes that feel heavy for their size.

TO CLEAN: Rinse or wipe the surface of the squash clean with a damp towel. To cut squat, tough-rind squashes, use a large, sharp chef's knife to split the squash in half through the stem end, starting with the knife at a 45-degree angle and slowly applying pressure to slice down through the rind and flesh. Scoop out the seeds with a spoon. For butternut squash, cut the squash cross-wise right where the bulb begins. Cut the bulb end in half lengthwise and scoop out the seeds. Cut the remaining piece in half lengthwise. To peel squash, cut the halves into manageable pieces and use a paring knife to carefully slice off the peel. Use the chef's knife to cut the peeled squash into slices, chunks, or dice.

TO PREPARE: Roast squash halves until tender and scoop out the flesh. Use the purée for soups, gnocchi, sweet or savory tarts, and to make gelato. Or season with butter, salt and pepper, and Parmigiano and serve as a side dish. Sliced or diced winter squash can be baked into gratins and goes well with other vegetables such as potatoes, onions, and fennel.

HERBS

Certain herbs are integral to the regional cooking of Italy. Generally I prefer cooking with fresh herbs, which have a brighter, more genuine flavor than the dried versions in bottles. Here are some notes on herbs used throughout this book:

BASIL/*BASILICO*
Basil is a tender-leaf herb that is sweet, with a hint of licorice and spice. The key ingredient in pesto Genovese, and also an essential seasoning in fresh tomato sauce. Pairs well with many vegetables, including eggplant, peppers, tomatoes, and zucchini.

BAY LEAF/*FOGLIA DI ALLORO*

This fragrant herb has glossy green leaves of medium size that are used either fresh or dried. It is commonly used to flavor sauces, soups, stews, and braises. Bay leaf pairs beautifully with legumes such as lentils and split peas, and goes well with many vegetables, including artichokes, fennel, onions, and tomatoes.

FLAT-LEAF PARSLEY/*PREZZEMOLO*

Flat-leaf parsley is a versatile, fresh-tasting herb that brightens almost any dish. It is used to flavor broths, sauces, stews, and braises; as a finishing herb; and as a garnish. Pairs well with many vegetables but especially artichokes, beans, carrots, eggplant, lentils, mushrooms, peas, peppers, potatoes, and summer squash.

MARJORAM/*MAGGIORANA*

This tender perennial herb with thin branches and small oval leaves is a relative of oregano, but with a sweeter, more flowery perfume. It is an essential flavor in the cooking of Liguria and is excellent with fresh cheeses. Pairs well with fava beans, onions, peas, peppers, and summer squash.

MINT/*MENTA*

Mint is a hardy (invasive) herb with dark stems and dark green leaves and a bright, fresh taste. It is used throughout the Italian peninsula to flavor everything from meatballs to sardines to tripe. It pairs well with just about every vegetable, including artichokes, eggplant, fava beans, fennel, onions, peas, peppers, tomatoes, and winter and summer squash.

OREGANO/*ORIGANO*

A close relative of marjoram, but oregano is sturdier and has a more pronounced flavor. Popular in Italian American cooking. I use it judiciously, and in almost all cases, I stay away from dried oregano from the supermarket, which has an aggressive flavor that tends to overpower other ingredients.

ROSEMARY/*ROSMARINO*

Rosemary is a woodsy herb with thin, needlelike leaves and a resinous fragrance and tackiness. A common seasoning in pork, lamb, and poultry dishes, as well as focaccia. Pairs well with onions and potatoes and is an excellent seasoning for hearty bean and chickpea soups.

SAGE/*SALVIA*

An aromatic, savory herb, sage has pretty silvery-green leaves and a pronounced flavor. The fresh version is almost always preferable to dried. Pairs especially well with carrots, caramelized onions, and roasted or sautéed winter squash.

THYME/*TIMO*

A member of the mint family, thyme has tiny green leaves on tender stems and a slightly pungent, savory flavor. Whole sprigs can be used to flavor broths, soups, and stews. Blends well with other herbs and pairs well with eggplant, mushrooms, onions, peppers, potatoes, and tomatoes.

INGREDIENTS

Following is a list of special ingredients called for in the recipes in this book. You are probably familiar with many of them, and most of them are fairly easy to find.

ANCHOVIES

For recipes that call for anchovies, I almost always use Rizzoli brand *alici in salsa piccante* (anchovies in a spicy olive oil–based sauce). They are expensive but, to me, worth the occasional splurge. They are not easy to find, but can be purchased online (see Sources, page 266). In their absence, use the best-quality imported Italian or Spanish anchovy fillets packed in olive oil that you can find.

BREAD

Good bread is essential to many Italian dishes, such as bruschetta, crostini, and rustic soups. For crostini (toasts) I use a thin baguette called a *ficelle* that produces perfect-size slices. For bruschetta (grilled bread) I use a sturdy country-style loaf. For bread that goes into soup, I use a sturdy country-style loaf, but I either let it sit out for a couple of days to dry out, or I toast it lightly in the oven. Stay away from fine-textured, cottony "Italian"-style loaves stocked by many supermarkets; those don't have enough substance and will turn flabby in soup.

CHEESES

Italy is blessed with a wealth of cheeses, from fresh mozzarella to hard, granular Parmigiano-Reggiano. Here are brief descriptions of cheese used in the recipes in this book.

ASIAGO: a cow's milk cheese produced in the Italian Alps. Fresh Asiago is a semisoft cheese suitable for slicing; aged Asiago has a more pronounced flavor and is a good grating cheese.

AURICCHIO: aged provolone that traditionally was produced in southern Italy. It has a sharp, buttery flavor and is much better than the sliced provolone typically found in a supermarket deli.

BURRATA: the "it" cheese of the moment, originally produced in Puglia. Burrata is a sweet, slightly tangy milky pouch of fresh mozzarella filled with delicate curds and cream. The top is tied to form a little topknot, and the cheese is typically wrapped in the green leaves of the asphodelus plant; the greenness of the leaves is an indication of how fresh the cheese is.

CACIO DI ROMA: a creamy, semifirm sheep's milk cheese from Lazio, the region that encompasses Rome. Substitute manchego or pecorino fresco (following) if you are unable to find it.

CAPRINO: a goat's milk cheese that can range from fresh and spreadable to semihard. The caprino called for in this book is akin to chèvre—fresh goat's milk cheese that is rich and tangy and almost pure white.

FETA: a briny, salty cheese that comes in blocks and is both creamy and crumbly. It is, of course, Greek. But I happen to like it and I use it a lot, especially with green beans and salads.

FONTINA VAL D'AOSTA: a dense, semifirm cheese made in the Italian Alps near the French and Swiss borders. It has a sharp, somewhat pungent aroma and an appealing nutty, slightly mushroomy flavor. Excellent melting cheese.

GRANA PADANO: a hard, granular cheese made from partially skimmed milk that is often compared to Parmigiano-Reggiano (following). Grana Padano is made in several northern regions along the Po River Valley. It is not as nutty or complex as Parmigiano-Reggiano but it is flavorful, especially sliced into thin scales as a garnish for salad.

GORGONZOLA AND BLUE CHEESE: a blue-veined cow's milk cheese produced in Lombardy and Piedmont. Gorgonzola dolce is creamy and soft. Gorgonzola piccante, also known as mountain Gorgonzola, is aged longer, and has a sharper flavor and more crumbly texture. The recipe for Cream of Cauliflower Soup with Pancetta "Croutons" (page 106) calls for Rogue Creamery Smokey Blue, a blue cheese made in Oregon that is cold-smoked over hazelnut shells. The smoky and sharp flavors complement each other beautifully, so if you can find it, do use it (see Sources, page 266).

MOZZARELLA: a name that refers to numerous fresh Italian cheeses that are shaped by spinning and then cutting the curd. The cheese can be made from the milk of cows or water buffalo. Fresh mozzarella is tender, with a rich, milky, slightly tangy flavor. Good domestic cow's milk mozzarella is now available at farmers' markets, cheese shops, gourmet food stores, and many supermarkets. Smoked mozzarella, which is slightly drier than fresh, is also widely available these days. Partially dried, aged mozzarella is known as scamorza and is sold both smoked and unsmoked. Good scamorza is hard to find outside of Italy. A decent substitute is the packaged low-moisture mozzarella available in supermarkets; it shreds and melts well and is good on pizza.

PARMIGIANO-REGGIANO: a type of grana—hard, granular cow's milk cheese. Parmigiano-Reggiano is made in Emilia-Romagna and a small section of Lombardy and is considered the undisputed king of Italian cheeses. Its sharp, rich flavor is essential to many of the recipes in this book. It is sold in craggy wedges and keeps best tightly wrapped in plastic wrap and refrigerated. Look for the words *Parmigiano-Reggiano* stamped on the rind. For the best flavor, grate only as needed. Hold on to that rind. I drop it into soups to enrich their flavor. The rind softens as the soup simmers. You can either discard it when the soup is done or you can cut it up into pieces and enjoy it in your soup; it is deliciously chewy.

PECORINO: a name that refers to numerous sheep's milk cheeses produced throughout Italy. Pecorino fresco is slightly aged and has an appealing nutty and slightly tangy flavor. It is a good slicing and shredding cheese and melts beautifully. Most commonly known is Pecorino Romano, an aged cheese, hard and granular in texture, that is paler in color than Parmigiano-Reggiano. It has a sharp, salty flavor and is an excellent grating cheese. Pecorino Sardo, also known as *fiore sardo*, is made on the island of Sardinia. It is richer and less salty than Pecorino Romano.

RICOTTA: a cheese made from sheep's milk or cow's milk whey, which is a by-product of cheese making. Most ricotta sold in the United States is made from cow's milk whey. It is moister than sheep's milk ricotta and a little tangier. I generally prefer sheep's milk ricotta because it is denser and a bit sweeter. If you are unable to find it, substitute a good-quality cow's milk ricotta. Look for the freshest you can find at well-stocked supermarket cheese departments, cheese shops, and farmers' markets. To be avoided: the mass-produced ricotta (skim-milk, part-skim, and whole milk) sold in tubs in the dairy case of most supermarkets, which has an inferior taste and an unpleasant grainy texture. If you find that the cow's milk ricotta you buy has a lot of moisture, drain it in a colander or sieve lined with cheesecloth.

SOTTOCENERE AL TARTUFO: a semisoft cow's milk cheese produced in the Veneto region. It has a thin ash-coated rind and a smooth paste flecked with bits of black truffle.

TALEGGIO: a semisoft, washed-rind cow's milk cheese from Lombardy. It has a strong aroma and an appealing flavor that is both buttery and meaty, rich and salty.

CURED MEATS

Numerous recipes in this book call for small amounts of *salumi*, or cured Italian meats. In nearly all instances, their use is optional. Here are short descriptions of the salumi used in the recipes in this book.

BRESAOLA: lean, spiced, air-dried beef that is produced in the Valtellina area of Lombardy. Good bresaola is deep red and tender, with a sweet, musty aroma. It is best enjoyed sliced paper-thin.

COPPA: heavily seasoned cured pork that is available either spicy or sweet. The meat, typically pork shoulder, is cut into chunks, rather than ground or left whole, and stuffed into casings and dried. It should be sliced thinly for serving.

PANCETTA: pork belly cured with salt, pepper, and other spices. It is generally rolled up into a sausage shape for curing and then sold sliced, but slab pancetta is also available.

SPECK: dry- and smoke-cured prosciutto (ham) that is produced far north in the Alto Adige region. The ham is dried for several weeks and then smoked at a low temperature, a process that allows the meat to take on a smoky flavor while retaining its natural sweetness.

EGGS

I use organic eggs that I buy from the farmers' market or from an organic grocery store near my house. For most recipes I use large eggs, but for making fresh pasta I use extra-large eggs. Why extra-large? Because three extra-large eggs absorb just the right amount of flour to yield 1 lb/455 g of pasta.

FARRO

Farro is an oval-shaped grain that has been cultivated since Roman times. It is similar to wheat berries and spelt, and has a pleasantly chewy texture and an earthy, nutty flavor. Many recipes call for using pearled farro (*farro perlato*) or for soaking whole farro before using it. I prefer to use the whole grain and have found that soaking it before cooking is unnecessary and turns the grain mushy.

FLOUR

Five different flours are called for in this book. I use a soft wheat Italian flour, known as "00" flour, which is very finely milled, to make Fresh Egg Pasta Dough (page 55) and Spinach Pasta Dough (page 58), though unbleached all-purpose flour may be substituted. For pizza and focaccia dough, I use bread flour, which is high in gluten and also contains small amounts of barley flour and potassium bromide, ingredients that help the yeast work and increase the elasticity of the dough. I also use a small amount of semolina—coarsely milled hard wheat flour—in my pasta dough, in my pizza dough, and for dusting the work surface. I find it adds substance and flavor. For pastry dough and baked goods, I generally use unbleached all-purpose flour, which is made from a blend of high- and low-gluten wheats. Almond meal, or almond flour, which is called for in the recipe for Chocolate Zucchini Cake (page 244), is simply blanched almonds that have been ground to a powder.

GRAPPA

A fragrant, colorless Italian brandy, grappa is distilled from the pulpy mass of grape skins, pits, and stems left in the wine press after the juice has been extracted. It has a high alcohol content (40 percent).

MARSALA

Marsala is an alcohol-fortified wine named for its Sicilian city of origin. It is similar to Madeira, port, and sherry, and is a common flavoring ingredient in southern Italian and Italian American cooking and baking.

NUTMEG

I prefer freshly grated whole nutmeg to ground nutmeg in a jar because it has a fresher, more pronounced flavor. Use a nutmeg grater, a Microplane grater, or the smallest holes on a box grater to grate nutmeg, and grate it judiciously as needed. Store whole nutmeg in a glass jar with a tight-fitting lid and keep it in a cool, dark place.

OLIVE OIL

Nearly all of the recipes in this book call for extra-virgin olive oil, which is made from the first cold pressing of olives and contains less than 1 percent oleic acid. The term *extra virgin* indicates the highest grade of olive oil; however, taste, color, and, for that matter, quality can vary widely. Be sure to look for a date of harvest and/or expiration, and choose oil whose expiration date is at least a year—preferably two—in the future. The letters *DOP* are a government guarantee that the oil is from the area stated on the bottle. Light olive oil is olive oil that has been refined and filtered to yield a pale color and minimal flavor. The quality of light olive oil can vary, so choose a brand you trust. I use light olive oil to fry vegetables and in cakes where I don't want the flavor of the oil to dominate. Store olive oil in a dark bottle in a cool area away from sunlight.

PASTA

Both fresh and dried pasta are called for in recipes in this book. Check the individual fresh pasta recipes for more information on making, storing, and cooking fresh pasta. For dried pasta, choose a reliable brand that does not turn mushy when cooked. High-quality dried pasta is cut with bronze dies; this gives it a rough surface to which sauce clings well.

PUNCH ABRUZZO

This sweet liqueur is produced outside of Chieti. It is made from caramelized sugar and the zest of lemons and oranges. It is not easy to find, but worth knowing about (see Sources, page 206). If you are unable to find it, substitute Cointreau, Grand Marnier, or dark rum mixed with a little lemon and orange zest.

RICE

I use either Arborio or Carnaroli rice for the recipes in this book. Both are pearly white, short-grain varieties with a high starch content that is ideal for risotto. For Insalata di Riso (page 126) I cook the rice without stirring it so that less starch is released during cooking.

SAFFRON

Saffron is the red-gold thread of the dried stigma of a variety of crocus flower. As a spice, saffron is sold either in threads or in packets as a powder. The powder dissolves more easily but it is also more easily tampered with. To be sure you are getting pure saffron, buy the threads and gently pound them to a powder before using.

SALT

I use fine sea salt to season most of the recipes in this book. For salting large pots of water, such as for boiling pasta, I use coarse kosher salt or coarse or fine sea salt. Occasionally I use flaky sea salt, or fleur de sel, to season a dish after it has been cooked. Fleur de sel has a pleasingly crunchy, yet light, texture that makes it an appropriate finishing salt.

VEGETABLE OIL

I use vegetable oil for frying; it has a higher smoking point. My preferred vegetable oil is sunflower oil, which is high in vitamin E and is lighter in flavor than olive oil.

VINEGAR

Red wine vinegar, white wine vinegar, and balsamic vinegar are all used in recipes throughout this book to dress salads, enhance the flavor of grilled vegetables, and in pickling. If possible, choose superior-quality vinegar, preferably one that has been aged naturally in wood and is aromatic and bright, rather than harsh, in flavor.

EQUIPMENT

Here are some tools, many of which you may already own, that are useful for working with vegetables and making the recipes in this book.

BAKING DISHES

I use ceramic and Pyrex ovenproof baking dishes, casseroles, shallow gratin pans, and deep lasagne pans for baking a number of the recipes in this book. I look for dishes that are attractive enough to go from oven to table.

BAKING SHEETS

Rimmed baking sheets have many uses, from toasting bread for crostini and making pizza to serving as a tray to hold just-cut fresh pasta noodles and ravioli. I freeze fresh pasta right on the sheets before transferring it to ziplock freezer bags or lidded containers. I also use rimmed baking sheets to make Slow-Roasted Tomatoes (page 67).

CAKE PANS

I use an 8-in/20-cm square aluminum pan for Carrot Polenta Cake with Marsala (page 246) and Chocolate Zucchini Cake (page 244). I use a 10-by-2-in/25-by-5-cm round aluminum cake pan for focaccia and savory tortes.

CANNING EQUIPMENT

I have a canning set that includes a large canning pot with a rack, tongs, a magnet-tipped wand for removing metal lids and rings from water, and a flat, tapered plastic wand used to release air bubbles trapped in jars (you can also use a clean fork handle or chopstick for this task). I have glass canning jars in a variety of sizes, including pint-size and half-pint–size jars; plus the corresponding lids and rings.

CHEESECLOTH

Use cheesecloth to strain broth and for draining porcini mushrooms that have been reconstituted in hot water.

COLANDER

Use a colander for draining pasta and blanched or boiled vegetables.

CONTAINERS

I keep plastic containers in various sizes with tight-fitting lids for freezing broth, sauce, soup, and cooked beans.

COOLING RACKS

Use these for cooling cakes and tortes, and for drying chile peppers before preserving.

DEEP-FRYING THERMOMETER

This stainless-steel thermometer can be immersed in oil to measure the temperature for frying.

DOUGH SCRAPER

Use a dough scaper to coax dough off the counter and scrape off bits of dried dough from the work surface.

DUTCH OVEN

This big, heavy-bottomed pot is what I use to make many soups and sauces. It has a tight-fitting lid and a flat bottom, which makes it ideal for sautéing chopped onions and other aromatics. It is also good for cooking dried beans. I prefer Dutch ovens made of enameled cast iron, which retains heat well and provides a good surface for browning.

FINE-MESH SIEVE

This tool is used for straining broth, draining porcini mushrooms and straining their liquid, and for draining excess water from ricotta cheese.

FOOD PROCESSOR

This is an essential piece of equipment in my kitchen; it's expensive but I have had mine for nearly two decades. I use it to mix pasta, pizza, and tart doughs, and for making pesto and chopping vegetables.

GRATERS

I use a box grater for grating and shredding cheeses and for grating plum tomatoes for sauce. I use a Microplane grater for zesting citrus and sometimes for grating cheese.

GRILL

I prefer a charcoal grill to gas, and I use hardwood rather than charcoal bri-quettes. I use the grill for numerous recipes in this book, including Grilled Peppers (page 74), Grilled Summer Vegetables alla Parmigiana (page 194), and Grilled Eggplant in Olive Oil (page 261).

ICE CREAM MAKER

A standard home ice cream machine with a 1-qt/960-ml capacity freezer bowl is sufficient for the Pumpkin Gelato (page 250).

IMMERSION BLENDER

I rely on this simple motorized tool for puréeing vegetable soups. A note of caution: The blades on an immersion blender are small but extremely sharp. Be sure you unplug it before you attempt to clean it or remove the blade attach-ment from the motor.

KNIVES

I use a paring knife for trimming and peeling vegetables and fruit; a 7- or 8-in/17- or 20-cm stainless-steel chef's knife for chopping and for lightly crushing garlic; and a serrated bread knife to slice bread, tomatoes, and citrus fruit.

MANDOLINE

This rectangular utensil with a razor-sharp blade makes quick work of cutting potatoes, onions, and other vegetables into uniform paper-thin slices or julienne strips.

MORTAR AND PESTLE

I enjoy using my marble mortar and pestle. I use it to make the anchovy sauce for the Roasted Romanesco with Anchovy Sauce (page 227) and occasionally for Fresh Basil Pesto (page 64).

PASTA MACHINE

I use a basic Marcato Atlas hand-crank pasta machine for stretching pasta dough and cutting the sheets into fettuccine or square-cut maccheroni alla chitarra. As with my mortar and pestle, I enjoy using this low-tech, "unplugged" appliance.

PASTRY CUTTER

I love my Italian-made, two-wheel pastry cutter, which has one straight-edged wheel and one fluted wheel for cutting and shaping strips of pasta dough. I also use it to make the lattice strips for the Buttercup Squash and Ricotta Crostata (page 242).

PIZZA PEEL

This flat, shovel-like tool with a long handle, usually made from wood or steel, is useful for transferring pizza to the grill or onto a pizza stone in the oven.

POTATO MASHER OR RICER

I use a potato masher to mash potatoes and green beans together in the recipe for Smashed Green Beans and Potatoes with Pancetta (page 230) and to mash the baked eggplant for eggplant "meatballs" (see page 202). For potato gnocchi (see page 157), I use a potato ricer, which yields an airy purée that is essential for making light gnocchi.

RAMEKINS

I use 6-oz/180-ml ramekins for cardoon and other vegetable *sformati* (custards).

SALAD SPINNER

This tool comes in handy for drying lettuce and other greens.

SAUCEPANS

I use stainless-steel saucepans in a variety of sizes for blanching vegetables and for making sauces such as tomato sauce and béchamel, and for making custard for panna cotta and gelato.

SERVING BOWLS AND PLATTERS

Not surprisingly, I am partial to hand-painted Italian ceramic serving platters and bowls, and over the years I have collected them in various sizes. After all, glorious Italian vegetables deserve to be served in glorious vessels! I look for platters and serving bowls that can be warmed in the oven without being damaged.

SILICONE SPATULA

I use these heat-proof utensils to stir sauces, soups, and stews, and to scrape batter and dough out of the food processor or mixing bowl. Silicone spatulas, which don't melt when used with hot pans, have virtually replaced rubber ones.

SKILLETS

Many of the recipes in this book call for a skillet for browning, sautéing, and cooking vegetables and aromatics in a small amount of olive oil. In general, I use a 10- or 12-in/25- to 30.5-cm heavy-bottomed stainless-steel skillet for this purpose. I use a 9-in/23-cm well-seasoned cast-iron skillet to make crêpes and to cook diced pancetta. For frittatas, I use a 10-in/25-cm nonstick broiler-proof skillet. I use an old, deep, well-seasoned 10-in/25-cm cast-iron skillet to fry Potato Croquettes (page 94), eggplant "meatballs" (see page 202), and Sweet Potato Frittelle (page 241).

SKIMMER
I use this tool for removing foam from the surface of simmering broths and soups, and for removing blanched vegetables from boiling water.

SLOTTED SPOON
Use this tool for removing blanched vegetables from boiling water and fried vegetables from hot oil.

SPICE GRINDER
This small electric appliance is also known as a coffee grinder. It can be used for grinding fennel seeds and other whole spices.

STEAMER BASKET
Use this tool for steaming cauliflower, broccoli, string beans, and other vegetables over boiling water.

STOCKPOT
I use a tall 12-qt/11.5-L stainless-steel pot for cooking large quantities of pasta.

TART PANS
I use 9-in/23-cm and 11-in/28-cm round aluminum tart pans with removable bottoms for baking both savory and sweet tarts.

TONGS
I use tongs for removing fried foods from blanching oil or water, for tossing salads, and for stirring greens as they wilt in a hot pan.

WHISK
Whisks are useful for salad dressings, béchamel sauce, and custard.

WIDE SPATULAS
These are useful for coaxing pizza off the grill or out of the baking sheet.

WOODEN SPOONS
I use these for stirring sauces and soups, scraping liquids into containers, and mixing batter.

ZIPLOCK FREEZER BAGS
I use these for freezing pasta, gnocchi, and pizza dough.

BASIC RECIPES

The following recipes are building blocks used in other recipes throughout the book. Beyond that, they are useful to have in your basic cooking repertoire. A good Vegetable Broth (page 62) is easy to make and comes in handy not only for making soup, but also for flavoring sautés and stews.

Here you will also find a recipe for Fresh Egg Pasta Dough (facing page)—easier to make than you might think, and worth knowing because fresh pasta tossed with seasonal vegetables is one of life's culinary pleasures. Also included is my recipe for Spinach Pasta Dough (page 58), which is used to make Vegetable Lasagne (page 148) and Spinach Fettuccine with Baby Spinach (page 133).

The basic vegetable recipes in this chapter—Grilled Peppers (page 74), Roasted Fennel (page 68), Roasted Mushrooms (page 69), Slow-Roasted Tomatoes (page 67), and Roasted Winter Squash Purée (page 70)—are employed in recipes throughout the book as stuffings, toppings, and to dress pasta, among other things. But they can also be enjoyed as they are.

This section also contains two tart dough recipes—one savory and one sweet. I rely on them in my day-to-day cooking, and I hope you will do the same, using them not only for the recipes in this book, but also for your own vegetable creations.

FRESH EGG PASTA DOUGH
makes about 1 lb / 455 g

The key to making good fresh pasta is to relax. It's an intuitive process, and the more you touch and handle the dough, the more familiar you will become with what it should feel like—how firm and smooth it should be. You can mix the dough the old-fashioned way on the countertop, or in the food processor. I often use the food processor to save time; it's quick and works beautifully, but if using, just remember to start with the smaller amount of flour listed in the recipe. If the dough is sticky, you can always work in more flour as you knead.

2 TO 2¼ CUPS/255 TO 285 G ITALIAN "00" FLOUR OR UNBLEACHED ALL-PURPOSE FLOUR

1 TBSP SEMOLINA FLOUR, PLUS MORE FOR DUSTING THE WORK SURFACE AND DOUGH

½ TSP FINE SEA SALT

PINCH OF FRESHLY GRATED NUTMEG

3 EXTRA-LARGE EGGS

1 TO 2 TBSP EXTRA-VIRGIN OLIVE OIL

TO MIX THE DOUGH BY HAND: Combine the 2 cups/255 g "00" flour, semolina flour, salt, and nutmeg on a clean, smooth work surface. Form a mound and create a well in the center. Carefully break the eggs into the well. Use a fork to break the yolks and begin mixing the eggs. Drizzle in 1 tbsp of olive oil and work it in as you gently beat the eggs. Slowly begin to incorporate the inner wall of flour as you whisk. When the mixture has thickened, begin using your fingers to incorporate more "00" flour. Continue to mix until a rough dough has formed—you may not need all of the flour. Scrape any excess flour off to the side of your work surface. Sprinkle the work surface lightly with semolina flour and press the dough together to form a rough ball.

TO MIX THE DOUGH IN THE FOOD PROCESSOR: Put 2 cups/255 g of the "00" flour, semolina flour, salt, and nutmeg into the work bowl of a food processor and pulse briefly to combine. Break the eggs into the work bowl and drizzle in 1 tbsp of the olive oil. Process the mixture until it forms crumbs that look like small curds. Pinch together a bit of the mixture and roll it around. It should form a soft ball. If it seems dry, drizzle in the remaining 1 tbsp olive oil and pulse briefly. If it seems too wet and sticky, add more "00" flour, 1 tbsp at a time, and pulse briefly. Turn the mixture out onto a clean work surface sprinkled lightly with semolina flour and press it together with your hands to form a rough ball.

TO KNEAD THE DOUGH: Using the palm of your hand, push the dough gently but firmly away from you, and then fold it over toward you. Rotate the dough

CONTINUED

a quarter turn, and repeat the pushing and folding motion. Continue kneading for several minutes until the dough is smooth and silky. Form it into a ball and wrap it tightly in plastic wrap. Let the dough rest at room temperature for 30 minutes.

TO STRETCH THE DOUGH: Set up your pasta machine with the rollers on the widest setting (#1 on my standard Marcato Atlas hand-crank machine). Scatter a little semolina flour on the work surface around the machine and have more on hand for sprinkling on the dough.

Cut the dough into four equal pieces and rewrap three pieces. Knead the remaining piece briefly. Then, using a rolling pin or patting it with the heel of your hand, form the dough into an oval 3 to 4 in/7.5 to 10 cm long and about 3 in/7.5 cm wide. Feed the dough through the rollers of the pasta machine, and then lay the strip on the work surface. Fold the dough into thirds as you would a business letter, sprinkle with a little semolina flour, and pass it through the rollers again.

Repeat the folding and rolling process a few more times, until the strip of dough is smooth. Move the roller to the next narrower notch and feed the strip through twice, sprinkling it with semolina, if necessary, to keep it from sticking. Continue to pass the dough through the rollers twice on each setting, until it is the desired thickness. Lay the sheet of dough out on a semolina-dusted surface and cover it lightly with plastic wrap while you stretch the remaining three pieces.

TO MAKE RAVIOLI: Stretch the dough to about $1/16$ in/2 mm thick—no thicker—on either the last or second-to-last notch on a standard pasta machine. You should be able to see the shadow of your hand through the dough. Fill and cut the ravioli according to the individual recipe.

TO CUT FETTUCCINE: Stretch the dough to about $1/16$ in/2 mm thick or slightly thicker. Use the wide cutters on the pasta machine to cut the sheets into fettuccine. Sprinkle them liberally with semolina flour to keep them from sticking and wrap them gently around your hand to form nests. Set the nests on a semolina-dusted, rimmed baking sheet.

TO CUT MACCHERONI ALLA CHITARRA: Stretch the dough to about $1/8$ in/ 3 mm thick. Use the narrow cutters on the pasta machine to cut the sheets into chitarra noodles. Sprinkle them liberally with semolina flour to keep them from sticking and wrap them gently around your hand to form nests. Set the nests on a semolina-dusted, rimmed baking sheet.

TO CUT LASAGNE NOODLES: Stretch the dough to about $\frac{1}{16}$ in/2 mm thick—no thicker—on either the last or second-to-last notch on a standard pasta machine. You should be able to see the shadow of your hand through the dough. Use a fluted pastry wheel to cut the sheets into rectangles about 4 by 5 in/10 by 12 cm.

TO STORE THE PASTA: If you don't plan to cook the pasta immediately, I recommend storing it in the freezer. I find this to be more reliable than drying, which can result in cracked or broken noodles. To freeze freshly cut pasta, put the tray of noodles or ravioli in the freezer and freeze for 1 hour or until firm. Carefully transfer the noodle nests or ravioli to a large container with a tight-fitting lid or to ziplock freezer bags. Return the pasta to the freezer until cooking time. You can store uncooked cut pasta in the freezer for up to 1 month. To cook, simply remove the pasta from the freezer and plunge them into a pot of salted boiling water. Cook until al dente, drain, and sauce as you please.

SPINACH PASTA DOUGH

makes 1 lb / 455 g

Here is my tried-and-true recipe for spinach pasta dough, which I always mix in the food processor. In this book I use it to make Vegetable Lasagne (page 148) and Spinach Fettuccine with Baby Spinach (page 133).

9 OZ/255 G FRESH BABY SPINACH LEAVES

2 EXTRA-LARGE EGGS

2 TO 2¼ CUPS/255 TO 285 G "00" FLOUR OR UNBLEACHED ALL-PURPOSE FLOUR

2 TBSP SEMOLINA FLOUR, PLUS MORE FOR DUSTING THE WORK SURFACE

¾ TSP FINE SEA SALT

PINCH OF FRESHLY GRATED NUTMEG

Put the spinach and 2 tbsp water in a saucepan and set over medium-high heat. Cover and cook for 3 to 5 minutes, or until the spinach is wilted and tender. Drain in a colander. When cool enough to handle, use your hands to squeeze out as much liquid as possible from the spinach.

Put the cooked spinach and 1 egg in the work bowl of a food processor and process to a smooth purée. With a spatula, scrape the purée into a small bowl, and wash and dry the processor bowl and blade.

Put 2 cups/255 g of the "00" flour, semolina flour, salt, and nutmeg into the work bowl of a food processor and pulse briefly to combine. Scrape in the spinach mixture and add the remaining egg. Pulse the mixture until it forms crumbs that look like small curds. Pinch together a bit of the mixture; it should form a soft ball. If it seems dry, drizzle in a few drops of water and pulse briefly. If it seems too wet and sticky, add more "00" flour, 1 tbsp at a time, and pulse briefly. Turn the mixture out onto a clean work surface dusted lightly with semolina flour and press it together with your hands to form a rough ball.

To knead the dough, using the palm of your hand, push the dough gently but firmly away from you, and then fold it over toward you. Rotate the dough a quarter turn, and repeat the pushing and folding motion. Continue kneading for several minutes until the dough is smooth and silky. Form it into a ball and wrap it tightly in plastic wrap. Let the dough rest at room temperature for 30 minutes.

To stretch and cut the dough, follow the instructions for Fresh Egg Pasta Dough (page 56).

spinaci, uova, farina,
semolina, sale, noce moscato

FLAKY PASTRY DOUGH

makes one 9- or 10-in / 23- or 25-cm tart shell

I use this versatile all-butter dough for savory tarts, quiches, and even fruit piecrusts.

1⅓ CUPS/155 G UNBLEACHED
ALL-PURPOSE FLOUR, PLUS MORE
FOR DUSTING THE WORK SURFACE

¼ TSP FINE SEA SALT

¼ TSP SUGAR

8 TBSP/115 G COLD UNSALTED BUTTER,
CUT INTO ½-IN/12-MM PIECES

¼ CUP/60 ML ICE-COLD WATER

Combine the flour, salt, and sugar in the work bowl of a food processor. Pulse to combine. Distribute the butter around the bowl and pulse until incorporated. With the motor running, drizzle the water through the feed tube and process just until a ball of dough begins to form.

Turn the dough out onto a lightly floured work surface and pat it into a disk. Wrap tightly in plastic wrap and refrigerate for at least 1 hour or up to overnight. Remove the dough from the refrigerator about 20 minutes before rolling it out.

SWEET PASTRY DOUGH

*makes enough Dough for one 9-in / 23-cm
or 10-in / 25-cm lattice-crust tart*

Pasta frolla is a sweet dough that is typically used as a base for crostata—rustic tarts filled with jam, custard, or fruit. In this book, I use it for the sweet Buttercup Squash and Ricotta Crostata (page 242). When baked, it has a rich buttery flavor and a crumbly shortbread texture. Be sure to let the dough chill after mixing it—at least 1 hour and up to overnight.

3 CUPS/385 G UNBLEACHED ALL-PURPOSE FLOUR, PLUS MORE FOR DUSTING THE WORK SURFACE

1 CUP/100 G CONFECTIONERS' SUGAR

1/4 TSP FINE SEA SALT

ZEST OF 1 LEMON OR 1 SMALL ORANGE—OR A LITTLE OF BOTH, FINELY GRATED

1 CUP/225 G COLD UNSALTED BUTTER, CUT INTO 1/2-IN/12-MM PIECES

1 LARGE EGG

2 LARGE EGG YOLKS

Put the flour, sugar, salt, and lemon zest in the work bowl of a food processor. Pulse to combine. Distribute the butter around the bowl and pulse until the mixture is crumbly. Add the egg and egg yolks and process until the dough just begins to clump together.

Turn the dough out onto a lightly floured work surface and pat it into a disk. Wrap tightly in plastic wrap and refrigerate at least 1 hour or up to overnight. Remove the dough from the refrigerator about 45 minutes before rolling it out.

VEGETABLE BROTH

makes about 2 qt / 2 L

Homemade vegetable broth takes a lot less time to make than meat broth, and this one is every bit as hearty. Roasting the vegetables before simmering them in water concentrates their flavors. Here is my favorite basic recipe, with two variations, one flavored with tomato and the other with mushrooms.

4 CARROTS, CUT INTO 2-IN/5-CM PIECES

3 RIBS CELERY, CUT INTO 2-IN/5-CM PIECES

2 LEEKS, WHITE AND LIGHT GREEN PARTS ONLY, THOROUGHLY WASHED TO REMOVE GRIT, HALVED LENGTHWISE AND CUT INTO 2-IN/5-CM PIECES

1 MEDIUM YELLOW ONION, CUT INTO WEDGES

1 FENNEL BULB, CUT INTO WEDGES, PLUS SOME OF THE STEMS AND FRONDS

1 TSP FINE SEA SALT, PLUS MORE FOR SEASONING

FRESHLY GROUND BLACK PEPPER

SMALL HANDFUL OF PARSLEY SPRIGS, INCLUDING STEMS

SMALL HANDFUL OF THYME SPRIGS, INCLUDING STEMS

3 TBSP EXTRA-VIRGIN OLIVE OIL

ONE 2-IN/5-CM PIECE PARMIGIANO-REGGIANO CHEESE RIND (OPTIONAL)

¼ CUP/60 ML DRY WHITE WINE OR DRY SHERRY

Heat the oven to 450°F/230°C/gas 8.

Put all of the vegetables in a large roasting pan. Add the salt, a generous grinding of pepper, and the parsley and thyme sprigs. Drizzle the olive oil over the vegetables and toss to coat well. Roast the vegetables for 45 minutes, turning them every 15 minutes, until they are tender and browned in spots.

Tip the vegetables into a large pot and pour in 10 cups/2.4 L cold water. Toss in the Parmigiano rind, if using. Bring the water to a boil over medium-high heat. Cover partially, reduce the heat to medium-low, and cook at a gentle simmer for 30 minutes. Pour in the wine and simmer for 15 more minutes. The broth is done when it has reduced slightly and has a full flavor. Taste and adjust the seasoning with salt.

Strain the broth through a fine-mesh sieve lined with damp cheesecloth into a clean container. Use the back of a wooden spoon to press down on the solids, extracting as much broth as possible. Discard the solids. Let the broth cool to room temperature, then cover and refrigerate for up to 3 days or freeze for up to 3 months.

TOMATO-VEGETABLE BROTH VARIATION: Add 4 ripe plum tomatoes, peeled, seeded, and coarsely chopped, or 4 canned plum tomatoes, coarsely chopped, to the vegetables in the roasting pan. Follow the recipe as directed.

MUSHROOM BROTH VARIATION: Omit the Parmigiano rind. Add 4 large portobello mushrooms, sliced, to the vegetables in the roasting pan. While the vegetables are roasting, place 1/2 oz/15 g dried porcini mushrooms in a small heat-proof bowl and pour 1 cup/240 ml boiling water over them. Let the porcini steep for 20 minutes, until softened. Drain the porcini in a fine-mesh sieve lined with damp paper towels or cheesecloth, reserving the liquid. Chop the mushrooms coarsely. Add both the mushrooms and their liquid to the pot when you add the roasted vegetables. Follow the recipe as directed.

FRESH BASIL PESTO

Makes about 1 cup/240 ml

This classic lively sauce from Liguria is now famous all over the world. In this book, I use it to dress potato gnocchi (see page 157). But of course you can use it to sauce pasta, as a topping for crostini, or as an accompaniment to simple boiled vegetables.

2 FIRMLY PACKED CUPS/55 G YOUNG FRESH BASIL LEAVES

1 GARLIC CLOVE, CUT INTO PIECES

2 TBSP PINE NUTS OR BLANCHED SLIVERED ALMONDS

½ TSP COARSE SEA SALT

½ CUP/120 ML EXTRA-VIRGIN OLIVE OIL

½ CUP/60 G FRESHLY GRATED PARMIGIANO-REGGIANO OR PECORINO ROMANO CHEESE, OR A MIX OF THE TWO

Put the basil, garlic, pine nuts, and salt in the work bowl of a food processor and pulse until roughly chopped. With the motor running, dribble in the olive oil through the feed tube until the mixture forms a loose paste. Using a spatula, scrape the pesto into a small bowl and stir in the cheese. If not using immediately, transfer the pesto to a small container with a tight-fitting lid and press a piece of plastic wrap onto the surface on the pesto to prevent discoloration. Cover the container with the lid and store the pesto in the refrigerator for up to 1 day.

To freeze the pesto, omit the cheese and freeze in a plastic container for up to 6 months. To use, let the pesto thaw to room temperature and stir in the cheese.

FRESH TOMATO SAUCE

*makes 3 to 3½ cups /
720 to 840 ml, enough to dress 1 lb / 455 g pasta*

Nothing compares to fresh tomato sauce, made with local sun-ripened tomatoes. To prepare tomatoes for sauce, you can either blanch them in boiling water, peel off their skins, and then clean and chop them; or you can use my preferred method, which is to cut them in half, scoop out the seeds, and grate them against the large holes of a box grater. It takes a bit of elbow grease but it produces a perfectly textured pulp that requires no extra chopping or milling. Give it a try!

2½ TO 3 LB/1.2 TO 1.4 KG RIPE PLUM TOMATOES

¼ CUP/60 ML EXTRA-VIRGIN OLIVE OIL

¼ CUP/30 G DICED RED ONION (OPTIONAL)

2 GARLIC CLOVES, LIGHTLY CRUSHED

FINE SEA SALT

5 LARGE FRESH BASIL LEAVES, SHREDDED OR TORN

Cut the tomatoes in half lengthwise and scoop out the seeds with your fingers. I do this over the sink to minimize mess. Place a box grater on a cutting board with a moat to catch the tomato juice as you grate. Hold the cut side of a tomato flat against the large holes of the grater and grate the tomato, pressing gently, until only the skin is left in your palm. Continue until you have grated all the tomato halves. As you work, transfer the pulp and any juice that collects to a glass or stainless-steel bowl to prevent too much from accumulating on the cutting board. Collect the tomato skins in a separate bowl as you work. When you have collected them all, put them in a colander and squeeze them hard over the bowl with the tomato pulp to catch any residual juice. Discard the squeezed skins.

Warm the oil, onion (if using), and garlic in a large saucepan set over medium-low heat. Cook, stirring, until the onions are softened but not browned, 7 to 8 minutes. Carefully pour in the tomatoes and stir to coat them with the oil. Season with 1 tsp salt, raise the heat to medium, and bring the tomatoes to a simmer. When the juices start bubbling, return the heat to medium-low and let the tomatoes simmer, uncovered, for 25 to 30 minutes, until thickened to a nice sauce consistency. Stir from time to time to prevent the sauce from burning.

Remove the sauce from the heat and stir in the basil. Taste and adjust the seasoning with salt, if you like. If not using immediately, transfer the sauce to a container with a tight-fitting lid and refrigerate for up to 3 days or freeze for up to 3 months.

SIMPLE TOMATO SAUCE
makes about 5 cups / 1.2 L

Even though I preserve batches of tomato sauce to use through winter, I still rely on sauce made from good canned tomatoes from time to time. Using excellent-quality canned tomatoes and good olive oil is important to the integrity of this simple, everyday sauce. Look for canned diced tomatoes packed in their natural juice rather than in heavy, pasty purée.

2 GARLIC CLOVES, LIGHTLY CRUSHED

1/4 CUP/60 ML EXTRA-VIRGIN OLIVE OIL

TWO 28-OZ/800-G CANS DICED TOMATOES, WITH THEIR JUICE

FINE SEA SALT

5 LARGE FRESH BASIL LEAVES, SHREDDED OR TORN

Warm the garlic in the olive oil in a large saucepan over medium heat. Use a wooden spoon to press down on the garlic to release its flavor. Cook for about 2 minutes, or until the garlic begins to sizzle. Don't let it brown. Carefully pour in the tomatoes and their juice (the oil will spatter) and stir to coat with the oil. Season with 1 tsp salt and raise the heat to medium-high. Bring the sauce to a simmer, reduce the heat to medium-low, and simmer gently, stirring from time to time, for 30 to 35 minutes, or until the sauce has thickened and the oil is pooling on the surface.

Remove from the heat and stir in the basil. Taste and add more salt if you like. If not using immediately, transfer the sauce to a container with a tight-fitting lid and refrigerate for up to 3 days or freeze for up to 3 months.

SLOW-ROASTED TOMATOES

makes 1½ lb / 680 g (4 packed cups)

Over the years, I have used these slow-roasted tomatoes in pastas, risotto, soups, and stews. They also make an excellent topping for bruschetta (see page 86), as well as an accompaniment to roast chicken, grilled steaks or sausages, and baked polenta (see page 160). If plum tomatoes are not in season, use cherry tomatoes instead (see recipe variation). They will need less time in the oven than larger tomatoes.

2½ LB/1.2 KG PLUM TOMATOES, HALVED LENGTHWISE

½ CUP/120 ML EXTRA-VIRGIN OLIVE OIL

3 LARGE GARLIC CLOVES, SLICED PAPER-THIN

1 TBSP FENNEL SEEDS, LIGHTLY CRUSHED

FINE SEA SALT

FRESHLY GROUND BLACK PEPPER

OLIVE OIL (OPTIONAL)

Heat the oven to 275°F/135°C/gas 1.

Arrange the plum tomato halves, cut-side up, on a large rimmed baking sheet. Drizzle the olive oil over them. Scatter the garlic slices and fennel seeds over the tomatoes and season with salt and pepper.

Roast the tomatoes for 3 to 4 hours, or until they are partially collapsed and caramelized but not dry. They should look somewhat shriveled but still be juicy.

Scrape the tomatoes, along with any juices from the pan, into a container with a tight-fitting lid. If you're not using the tomatoes within 2 days, top them off with olive oil so they are submerged, and refrigerate for up to 2 weeks.

COOK'S NOTE: You can omit the fennel seeds, if you like, and instead season the tomatoes with some chopped fresh herbs, such as oregano or thyme, or season them simply with salt and black pepper.

SLOW-ROASTED CHERRY TOMATO VARIATION: Slice the cherry tomatoes in half and arrange them, cut-side up, on a large rimmed baking sheet so that they are just touching one another. Proceed with the recipe. Roast for about 1½ hours, or until they are somewhat shriveled but still juicy.

ROASTED FENNEL

makes 4 to 6 servings

Crunchy, licorice-flavored fennel turns mellow and sweet when you roast it. Serve this as a simple fall side dish, toss with pasta, or turn it into a topping for pizza (see page 168).

2 OR 3 LARGE FENNEL BULBS, QUARTERED, CORED, AND CUT INTO THIN SLICES

3 TO 4 TBSP EXTRA-VIRGIN OLIVE OIL

FINE SEA SALT

FRESHLY GROUND BLACK PEPPER

Heat the oven to 400°F/200°C/gas 6.

Mound the fennel on a large rimmed baking sheet and drizzle the olive oil over it, starting with 3 tbsp and adding more as necessary. Season with a little salt and pepper. Toss everything together with your hands or a silicone spatula, then spread the fennel out on the baking sheet.

Roast for 15 minutes. Toss and roast for another 5 to 10 minutes, until the fennel is golden and lightly caramelized with some brown edges.

VARIATION: After roasting, toss the fennel with a little lemon juice or balsamic vinegar and serve warm or at room temperature.

ROASTED MUSHROOMS

makes 2½ cups / 310 g

I used to always sauté mushrooms before using them any number of ways—in pasta sauces or baked pasta dishes, in frittatas, as a side dish, and so on. A couple of years ago, I tried roasting them and have never looked back. Roasting mushrooms on high heat in the oven concentrates their flavor. Frankly, I love them because they taste like steak. Look for a variety of mushrooms of different sizes and textures. You can serve these plain as a side dish, or use them in recipes such as Vegetable Lasagne (page 148) and as a filling for calzoni (page 174).

6 TBSP/90 ML EXTRA-VIRGIN OLIVE OIL

1 LARGE GARLIC CLOVE, LIGHTLY CRUSHED

1½ LB/680 G MIXED FRESH MUSHROOMS, SUCH AS PORTOBELLO, CHANTERELLE, CREMINI, SHIITAKE, AND OYSTER

½ TSP FINE SEA SALT, OR TO TASTE

FRESHLY GROUND BLACK PEPPER

1 TBSP MINCED FRESH FLAT-LEAF PARSLEY (OPTIONAL)

Heat the oven to 425°F/220°C/gas 7.

Measure the oil into a small bowl and add the garlic clove. Let the oil sit for about 1 hour or until it is nicely infused with the flavor of the garlic. Remove the garlic and discard or save it for another use.

Cut the mushrooms into big pieces or thick slices. Combine all of the mushrooms in a large bowl and drizzle with the garlic-infused oil. Toss them well to coat them with the oil. Season with the salt and a generous grinding of pepper, and sprinkle the parsley over them, if using. Toss again.

Spread the mushrooms out in one layer on a large rimmed baking sheet. Roast the mushrooms for 15 minutes, then toss with a spatula. Roast them for 10 minutes more, or until they are tender and browned, and the ones around the edges of the pan are lightly crisped.

Remove the mushrooms from the oven and scrape them into a bowl. Serve immediately or reserve for another use. Store the mushrooms in a container with a tight-fitting lid and refrigerate for up to 5 days or freeze for up to 3 months.

ROASTED WINTER SQUASH PURÉE

makes 2½ to 3 cups / 570 to 680 g

Roasting winter squash intensifies its sweet, vegetal flavor and yields a dense purée that is perfect for soups, mashes, and as a foundation for desserts. In this book, I use puréed winter squash in several recipes, including Cream of Bon Bon Squash and Fennel Soup (page 104) and Winter Squash Panna Cotta (page 248). The best squashes for roasting and puréeing are the squat ones with a hard dark green rind and sweet dense golden or orange flesh, including buttercup, Autumn Cup, Bon Bon, and kabocha. Many farmers' markets carry at least one of these in the fall. They are worth seeking out, not only for their flavor but also because their smooth flesh purées easily with a fork or potato masher—no need to pull out the food processor or blender!

1 BUTTERCUP, AUTUMN CUP, BON BON, OR KABOCHA SQUASH (ABOUT 2 LB/910 G)

1 TBSP SUNFLOWER OR OTHER VEGETABLE OIL

Heat oven to 375°F/190°C/gas 5.

Use a large, sturdy chef's knife to split the squash in half through the stem end. Scoop out and discard the seeds (or, if you like, reserve them for roasting and snacking on).

Rub the flesh with a small amount of oil and set the halves, cut-side down, on a rimmed baking sheet. Bake for 45 to 60 minutes, or until you can easily pierce through the rind with a fork. Remove from the oven and let cool. Scoop the flesh into a large bowl and discard the rind. Use a fork or a potato masher to mash the cooked squash into a smooth purée.

If not using the squash immediately, store it in a covered container and refrigerate for up to 5 days or freeze for up to 3 months.

BASIC BEANS IN A POT
makes 6 cups / 1.4 kg cooked beans

While freshly shelled beans cook fairly quickly, dried beans need soaking time to soften and then additional time on the stovetop to cook. This method, in which the beans are briefly boiled in water and then left to sit for a couple of hours before cooking, cuts down on the soaking time. Once the beans are cooked, you can use them in soups, salads, stews, or however you like.

1 LB/455 G CANNELLINI BEANS, CHICKPEAS, OR OTHER DRIED BEANS

1 SMALL CARROT, CUT INTO 2 OR 3 PIECES

1 RIB CELERY, WITH LEAVES, CUT INTO 2 OR 3 PIECES

½ YELLOW ONION, HALVED

1 BAY LEAF

3 OR 4 FRESH SAGE LEAVES

3 OR 4 FRESH THYME SPRIGS

HANDFUL OF FRESH FLAT-LEAF PARSLEY SPRIGS

FINE SEA SALT

Put the beans in a large heavy-bottomed pot with water to cover by 2 in/5 cm. Set the pot over high heat and bring to a boil. Boil for 2 minutes; then turn off the heat, cover, and let the beans steep for 2 hours. Unless they were fairly fresh to begin with, they will need more time on the stove to cook.

Add more water to the pot, so that the beans are covered by 2 in/5 cm. Add the carrot, celery, onion, and the bay leaf, sage, thyme, and parsley—you can use any or all of the herbs—and bring the beans to a boil over medium-high heat. Reduce the heat to medium-low and let the beans simmer for 1 hour or more, until they are tender. Season with salt toward the end of the cooking time.

If not using immediately, transfer the beans to a large container with a tight-fitting lid and refrigerate for up to 5 days or freeze for up to 3 months.

finocchio infornuto

peperoni arrostiti

rapini saltati

GRILLED PEPPERS
makes 4 servings

Nothing evokes Italy more than the aroma of grilled peppers. To me, it is magical, conjuring families at the dinner table and the clatter of plates and cutlery. It is the scent that wafts along the breeze at lunchtime in every seaside town, the perfume that fills the side streets of every hilltop village. A platter of grilled peppers lifts everything around it by association, whether a roast chicken, some grilled sausages, or a fried egg. Serve these classic grilled peppers as a side dish, in a panino or frittata, or on top of pizza.

4 LARGE RIPE BELL PEPPERS—RED, YELLOW, AND ORANGE

3 TBSP EXTRA-VIRGIN OLIVE OIL

1/2 TSP FINE SEA SALT

2 TSP MINCED FRESH FLAT-LEAF PARSLEY

1 GARLIC CLOVE, SLICED PAPER-THIN

Prepare a medium-hot charcoal grill or preheat a gas grill to medium-high. Lay the whole peppers right on the grate and grill, turning them with tongs every so often, until their skins are blistered and blackened on all sides—about 15 minutes total. They will soften as they cook, so take care to turn them gently.

Transfer the grilled peppers to a bowl and cover tightly with plastic wrap. Let the peppers steam for about 10 minutes.

Lay a pepper on a cutting board near the sink and slice or gently pull off the stem. Let any juice from the pepper drain into the sink. Cut the pepper in half and lay the halves out, skin-side up on the cutting board. Use a paring knife to gently scrape away all of the charred skin—it should come away easily. Scrape off and discard the seeds and any white pith. Slice the pepper halves length-wise into thin strips and put them in a bowl. Repeat with the remaining three peppers until you have skinned and sliced them all.

Drizzle the olive oil over the peppers, season with salt, and sprinkle with parsley. Toss gently until the peppers are well coated. Transfer the peppers to a serving platter and tuck the garlic slivers here and there among them. Cover loosely and let sit for approximately 30 minutes before serving.

SAUTÉED RAPINI
makes 4 generous servings

This is the traditional Neapolitan way of preparing rapini—sautéed with lots of garlic and hot pepper. Serve these spicy, pungent greens as an accompaniment to grilled sausages, on pizza, or as a filling for calzone. You can also toss them with cooked pasta—orecchiette is the traditional pasta shape of choice—or stir them into eggs for a tasty frittata.

2 LB/910 G RAPINI, TOUGH STEMS DISCARDED

1/3 CUP/75 ML EXTRA-VIRGIN OLIVE OIL, OR MORE TO TASTE

4 GARLIC CLOVES, SLICED PAPER-THIN, OR MORE TO TASTE

2 CHILE PEPPERS IN OLIVE OIL (PAGE 259), MINCED, OR A GENEROUS PINCH OF RED PEPPER FLAKES

1 TSP FINE SEA SALT, OR TO TASTE

Bring a large pot of water to a boil over high heat. Immerse the rapini in the water and cook for 3 to 5 minutes, until wilted. Drain the greens in a colander.

In a large skillet, warm the olive oil, garlic, and *peperoncini* over medium-low heat. Cook, stirring frequently, for about 3 minutes, or until the garlic begins to soften. Don't let it brown. Add the rapini to the pan and sprinkle with the salt. Use tongs to toss the greens in the oil so they are well coated. Raise the heat to medium and cook, tossing often, for 15 to 20 minutes or until the greens are tender.

chapter 2

APPETIZERS

antipasti

APPETIZERS
antipasti

For many of us, the word *antipasto* calls to mind unappealing images of rolled-up deli meat and leathery, dull green pickled hot peppers. Now is the time to banish such images permanently. Italian cooking is really about letting ingredients speak for themselves, and that philosophy starts with the appetizers.

Pane, olio, e pomodoro. Bread, olive oil, and tomatoes. This recipe begins this chapter. It could not be easier to make, but what matters is the integrity of the ingredients; they must be impeccable for the dish to succeed. That's why I make it only in late summer, when tomatoes have had nearly a full season to ripen in the sun.

When I cook for friends, I often start with a platter of crostini, or simple toasts with savory toppings. Fresh fava bean purée, grilled peppers, tomato marmalade, and caramelized onions are among my regular toppings. In late summer, when farmers' market stalls are teeming with tomatoes, it gives me a thrill to set out a beautiful ruby-red tomato crostata. And in winter, a batch of potato croquettes, with their melted cheese centers, are one of my favorite ways to start a dinner party.

PANE, OLIO E POMODORO

makes 2 servings

This recipe could not be simpler—just slices of good bread lightly rubbed with garlic and anointed with juicy, ripe tomatoes, good olive oil, and coarse sea salt. Yet it is one of the first ones that came to mind when I started thinking about this book. *Pane, olio e pomodoro* was something my Italian aunts used to prepare for my sister and me in the late afternoon in summer, and to this day it remains a treat that I enjoy immensely. It is a perfect marriage of flavors and textures—the chewy crumb of the bread that so readily absorbs the sharp, acidic juice of the tomatoes, the crunch of the salt, and the rich gloss of olive oil. The quality of the ingredients is everything here. Make this dish when local tomatoes are at their sun-ripened best. I use really good artisan bread and the best olive oil and sea salt in my pantry.

4 THICK SLICES RUSTIC ITALIAN BREAD WITH A LARGE CRUMB AND CRUNCHY CRUST

1 LARGE GARLIC CLOVE, LIGHTLY CRUSHED

2 MEDIUM SUMMER TOMATOES, HALVED

BEST-QUALITY EXTRA-VIRGIN OLIVE OIL FOR DRIZZLING

COARSE SEA SALT

Set the bread slices on a plate. Rub the garlic clove gently over the surface of each slice. Rub a tomato half, cut-side down, on each slice, squeezing some of the flesh out of the tomato onto the bread. Drizzle the olive oil, as much or as little as you please, over the bread slices, and sprinkle with salt. Serve immediately.

CROSTINI
makes 24 to 30 crostini

Crostini (toasts) are simply thin slices of baguette, or *ficelle* in Italy. They are often, but not always, grilled or toasted, and garnished with any number of savory toppings. Here is my basic recipe for toasted crostini, followed by some of my favorite toppings.

1 THIN BAGUETTE (*FICELLE*), CUT ON THE BIAS INTO THIN SLICES

EXTRA-VIRGIN OLIVE OIL

Heat the oven to 400°F/200°C/gas 6. Arrange the bread slices on a rimmed baking sheet and brush the tops with olive oil. Bake for 8 to 10 minutes, or until the edges are lightly browned and the tops are beginning to turn golden. Store the crostini in a large ziplock bag or plastic container with a tight-fitting lid for up to 3 days.

CROSTINI WITH FONTINA AND TOMATO MARMALADE
makes 6 to 8 servings

It is a good feeling, in the middle of winter, to open the pantry and retrieve a jar of something lovely that you preserved the previous summer. It's even better if that something is sweet and savory tomato marmalade which, when paired with pungent Fontina Val d'Aosta, makes a superb crostini topping.

ABOUT ½ CUP/115 G TOMATO MARMALADE (PAGE 264)

1 THIN BAGUETTE (*FICELLE*), CUT ON THE BIAS INTO THIN SLICES

8 OZ/227 G GRATED FONTINA VAL D'AOSTA CHEESE

Position an oven rack 4 in/10 cm from the broiler and turn the broiler on.

Spread the tomato marmalade on the *ficelle* slices and top each with a mound of shredded cheese. Arrange the slices on a rimmed baking sheet. Broil for 1 to 2 minutes, or until bubbly and browned.

Transfer the crostini to a platter and serve immediately.

CROSTINI WITH FRESH FAVA BEAN PURÉE
makes 6 to 8 servings

I can't think of a dish that better expresses spring than this bright mash of favas and herbs garnished with shavings of Pecorino Romano cheese. It's lush and buttery and just assertive enough to banish any traces of the winter doldrums. Serve it as an appetizer for guests, or as a side dish for simple roast chicken.

2 TBSP EXTRA-VIRGIN OLIVE OIL, PLUS MORE FOR DRIZZLING

2 SMALL GARLIC CLOVES, MINCED (ABOUT 2 TSP)

2 LB/910 G FRESH FAVA BEANS, SHELLED, BLANCHED, AND PEELED (SEE PAGE 28)

2 TSP MINCED FRESH HERBS (I USE A MIX OF MINT AND OREGANO)

2 TBSP HEAVY CREAM

2 TSP FRESHLY SQUEEZED LEMON JUICE

1/4 TSP FINE SEA SALT, OR TO TASTE

FRESHLY GROUND BLACK PEPPER

1 BATCH CROSTINI (FACING PAGE) OR 1 THIN BAGUETTE (*FICELLE*), CUT ON THE BIAS INTO THIN SLICES

THINLY SHAVED PECORINO ROMANO CHEESE FOR GARNISH

Warm the olive oil and minced garlic in a small skillet over low heat. Cook, stirring from time to time, until the garlic is soft and fragrant but not browned, about 7 minutes.

Set aside 2 tbsp of the peeled fava beans and add the remaining ones to the skillet. Raise the heat to medium and cook until the beans are tender enough to break apart easily with a wooden spoon but are still bright green, about 5 minutes. Dribble in the heavy cream and using a potato masher, gently mash the beans to a coarse paste. Add the lemon juice, salt, and several grindings of pepper, and mash everything together. Remove from the heat and fold in the reserved fava beans.

Scoop the purée into a decorative bowl and drizzle with olive oil. Serve with the crostini and Pecorino Romano shavings. Alternatively, you can spread the purée on the crostini and top each one with a shaving of Pecorino Romano. Arrange on a platter and drizzle with a little olive oil. Serve immediately.

crostini con peperoni e tonno

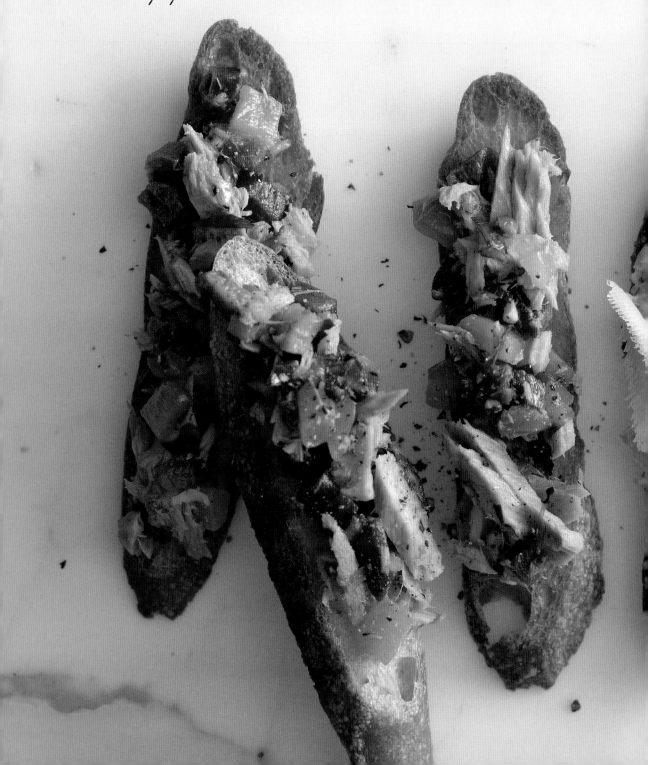

crostini con purea di fave fresche

crostini con fontina
e marmellata di pomodoro

CROSTINI WITH GRILLED PEPPERS AND TUNA

makes 6 to 8 servings

I have brought these crostini to backyard barbecues, pool picnics, and other potluck gatherings. There must be something about the combination of assertive flavors—the sweet, sharp peppers and vinegar, the briny capers, the rich tuna and salty anchovies—because I always come home with an empty platter.

1 BATCH GRILLED PEPPERS (PAGE 74)

1 GARLIC CLOVE, PRESSED

¼ TSP FINE SEA SALT

1 TBSP BALSAMIC VINEGAR

ONE 5-OZ/140-G CAN BEST-QUALITY TUNA IN OLIVE OIL, PLUS SOME OF THE OIL

2 TBSP MINCED FRESH FLAT-LEAF PARSLEY, PLUS A SPRIG FOR GARNISH

1 TBSP CAPERS, RINSED, DRAINED, AND FINELY CHOPPED

2 BEST-QUALITY IMPORTED ITALIAN OR SPANISH ANCHOVY FILLETS IN OLIVE OIL, MINCED

1 BATCH CROSTINI (PAGE 80)

EXTRA-VIRGIN OLIVE OIL FOR DRIZZLING

Cut the grilled peppers into ¼-in/6-mm dice. Place in a large bowl.

In a small bowl, mix together the garlic and salt to form a paste. Add it to the peppers and drizzle in the vinegar. Fold everything together and let stand for 15 to 30 minutes. Add the tuna and a little of the oil from the can, taking care to gently break up any large chunks of fish. Add the parsley, capers, and anchovies and toss gently to combine.

Spoon the mixture onto the crostini and arrange them on a serving platter. Drizzle a little olive oil over the crostini and place the sprig of parsley in the center of the platter as a garnish.

CROSTINI WITH TALEGGIO AND CARAMELIZED ONIONS

makes 6 to 8 servings

I am not the world's most patient person, but I know that if I give my onions the time they need to caramelize properly, I will be richly rewarded with a sweet, velvety topping for crostini. To get a head start, I cook the onions a day ahead of time and store them in a lidded container in the refrigerator.

2 TBSP UNSALTED BUTTER

2 TBSP EXTRA-VIRGIN OLIVE OIL

2 LB/910 G YELLOW ONIONS, HALVED LENGTHWISE AND VERY THINLY SLICED INTO HALF-RINGS

1 TSP MINCED FRESH THYME

1/2 TSP FINE SEA SALT, OR TO TASTE

2 TBSP DRY MARSALA

8 OZ/227 G TALEGGIO CHEESE

1 THIN BAGUETTE (*FICELLE*), CUT ON THE BIAS INTO THIN SLICES

Heat the butter and oil in a large, deep skillet over medium heat. When the butter is melted and begins to sizzle, add the onions and stir to coat them with the butter and oil. Sprinkle in the thyme and salt, reduce the heat to medium-low, and cover. Let the onions cook for 15 to 20 minutes, or until they have begun to turn soft. Reduce the heat to low, uncover, and continue to cook, stirring from time to time, for about 1 hour, or until the onions are soft and silky and deep gold in color.

When the onions are beautifully caramelized, raise the heat slightly and stir in the Marsala. Cook for 1 to 2 minutes, until the wine has been absorbed. Remove from the heat.

Position an oven rack 4 in/10 cm from the broiler and turn the broiler on.

Spread the Taleggio on the slices of bread and top each with a spoonful of onions. Arrange the slices on a rimmed baking sheet. Broil for 1 to 2 minutes, or until bubbly and browned.

Transfer the crostini to a platter and serve immediately.

BRUSCHETTA WITH SLOW-ROASTED TOMATOES AND BURRATA

makes 8 servings

I generally believe that less is more when it comes to bruschetta. The bread slices are bigger and thicker than those used for crostini; if you go overboard with toppings, bruschetta becomes unwieldy, not to mention messy. Usually I do nothing more than rub the grilled bread with garlic, top with a little sliced tomato or diced roasted peppers, and garnish with good coarse sea salt and a drizzle of olive oil. Then there is this recipe, which calls for topping the bread with oozy Burrata cheese and juicy roasted tomatoes in oil. Grab a napkin and all will be well.

16 SLICES ITALIAN COUNTRY BREAD, CUT ½ IN/12 MM THICK (IF THE BREAD IS SQUAT AND THE SLICES ARE LONG, USE 8 SLICES AND CUT THEM IN HALF)

EXTRA-VIRGIN OLIVE OIL FOR BRUSHING

TWO 8-OZ/225-G BALLS BURRATA CHEESE OR OTHER FRESH SPREADABLE CHEESE SUCH AS SHEEP'S MILK OR COW'S MILK RICOTTA

1 BATCH SLOW-ROASTED TOMATOES (PAGE 67), COARSELY CHOPPED

Position an oven rack 4 in/10 cm from the broiler and turn the broiler on. Arrange the bread slices on a large rimmed baking sheet and brush the tops with olive oil. Broil for 1 to 2 minutes or until the edges are lightly charred and the tops are golden. Remove from the heat and let cool slightly.

Spoon some Burrata and then some tomatoes on top of each slice of bread. Arrange the bruschetta on a platter and serve.

CHERRY TOMATO AND RED ONION FOCACCIA

makes one 10-inch / 25-cm focaccia; 6 servings

It took me some time to warm up to the idea of no-knead bread. I've always thought knead-ing to be an integral part of the bread-making experience, a meditative act that I enjoy. But this recipe changed my mind. It is adapted from one by my friend Nancy Baggett. Nancy is an expert baker and the author of numerous acclaimed cookbooks, including *Kneadlessly Simple: Fabulous, Fuss-Free, No-Knead Breads*. Her method for making focaccia is foolproof. And it turns out a loaf that is as close to perfect as you can get—with a light, crispy crust and a wonderfully chewy, yeasty interior. Feel free to improvise with toppings, switching out rosemary for oregano or sage, or using roast peppers in place of the tomatoes. Or keep it classic, with a simple topping of olive oil, rosemary, and coarse sea salt.

DOUGH:

2¾ CUPS/350 G BREAD FLOUR

¾ TSP SEA SALT

1 TSP INSTANT OR RAPID-RISE YEAST

1⅓ CUPS/315 ML ICE WATER

2 TBSP EXTRA-VIRGIN OLIVE OIL
PLUS MORE FOR BRUSHING

TOPPINGS:

3 OZ/85 G PANCETTA, CUT INTO
¾-IN/2-CM DICE (OPTIONAL)

1 TBSP MINCED FRESH ROSEMARY

2 TBSP EXTRA-VIRGIN OLIVE OIL

8 CHERRY TOMATOES, CUT IN HALF

¼ CUP/30 G DICED RED ONION

1 TSP COARSE SEA SALT

TO MAKE THE DOUGH: Whisk together the flour, salt, and yeast in a large bowl. Pour in the ice water, stirring vigorously as you pour and mixing until thoroughly incorporated. Add 1 tbsp olive oil and stir vigorously. The dough should be slightly stiff but still wet enough to stir and slightly sticky. Brush the top with a little olive oil and cover the bowl with plastic wrap. Refrigerate the dough for several hours—anywhere from 3 to 10. Then remove the bowl from the refrigera-tor and let the dough rise, covered, at room temperature for 12 to 18 hours. Stir it once partway through the rise.

Generously coat a 10-by-2-in/25-by-5-cm round baking pan (I use a straight-sided cake pan) with olive oil. Using a silicone spatula, scrape the dough into the pan, taking care not to deflate it more than necessary. Drizzle 1 tbsp olive oil over the top, and with your fingers, gently press the dough out to the rim of the pan. Cover the pan loosely with plastic wrap. Refrigerate the dough for several hours—anywhere from 4 to 24. I recommend closer to 24 if you can, since the extra time allows the dough to develop a wonderful yeasty flavor. Then remove the pan from the refrigerator and let it rise at room temperature until puffy and almost doubled in size, 2 to 3 hours.

CONTINUED

CONTINUED

TO MAKE THE TOPPINGS: Prepare the toppings while the dough is in its final rise. If using pancetta, put the pancetta cubes in a dry nonstick skillet (I use a small cast-iron skillet) over medium heat. When the pancetta begins to sizzle, lower the heat to medium-low and sauté, stirring from time to time, for 12 to 15 minutes, or until the pancetta has rendered some of its fat and is browned and crispy. Use a slotted spoon to remove the pancetta to a paper towel-lined bowl and set aside.

Combine the rosemary and the 2 tbsp olive oil in a small bowl. Let the oil sit until the dough is ready.

Place an oven rack in the lowest position in the oven and heat the oven to 475°F/240°C/gas 9.

When the dough has risen, remove the plastic wrap. Arrange the cherry tomatoes on top of the dough, pressing them in lightly. Then press in the diced onion, and finally the pancetta cubes. Gently brush the rosemary-oil mixture over the top of the dough and sprinkle with sea salt.

Bake the focaccia for 20 minutes; rotate the pan in the oven and bake for another 10 to 12 minutes, until the top is beautifully browned. Set the pan on a wire rack to cool for 10 minutes. Then, using an angled spatula, carefully lift the focaccia out of the pan and set it on the rack. To serve, slice the focaccia into wedges or rectangular pieces.

COOK'S NOTE: Focaccia is best served fresh, still warm from the oven or at room temperature.

PLAIN FOCACCIA VARIATION: To make plain focaccia, omit the tomatoes, pancetta, and red onion. Use oiled fingers to form dimples in the risen dough, and brush with the rosemary-oil mixture. Sprinkle sea salt on top and proceed with baking.

pancetta, pomodoro,
cipolla, olio, sale

TOMATO CROSTATA WITH FRESH CAPRINO

makes one 9-in / 23-cm crostata; 8 servings

Every summer I make at least one tomato and cheese tart. I never make it the same way twice. I might use a different crust or change the type of cheese, and I always look for those wonderful, colorful, misshapen heirloom tomatoes to layer in the tart shell. Last summer I happened to have some slow-roasted cherry tomatoes in my fridge, so on impulse I added them to the mix, along with some fresh goat cheese and a layer of freshly sliced tomatoes. What emerged from the oven was the most tomatoey tomato tart I have ever had the pleasure of sinking my teeth into. It will be tough to top this summer. Serve this luscious tart as a first course, with a mound of lightly dressed arugula alongside.

FLOUR FOR DUSTING THE WORK SURFACE

1 BATCH FLAKY PASTRY DOUGH (PAGE 60), READY TO STRETCH OUT

1 CUP/170 G SLOW-ROASTED TOMATOES (PAGE 67), COARSELY CHOPPED, OR SLOW-ROASTED CHERRY TOMATOES (SEE PAGE 142)

5 OZ/140 G CAPRINO (FRESH GOAT CHEESE), CRUMBLED

2 TO 3 MEDIUM-SIZE RIPE SUMMER TOMATOES, SLICED 1/4 IN/6 MM THICK

1/4 TSP FINE SEA SALT

1 TSP MINCED FRESH BASIL

1/2 TSP MINCED FRESH THYME

1 TBSP EXTRA-VIRGIN OLIVE OIL

Heat the oven to 425°F/220°C/gas 7.

On a lightly floured work surface, roll the dough out into an 11-in/28-cm circle. Carefully wrap the dough around the rolling pin and drape it over a 9-in/23-cm round fluted tart pan with a removable bottom. Gently press the dough into the bottom and up the sides of the pan. Trim the overhang to about 1/2 in/12 mm and fold it in, pressing it against the inside rim to reinforce the sides of the tart shell. Use the rolling pin or the palm of your hand to press around the perimeter to cut off any excess dough. Place the dough-lined tart pan on a rimmed baking sheet. Press a piece of aluminum foil or parchment over the crust and fill it with pie weights or dried beans. Bake for 10 minutes. Remove the foil and pie weights and bake another 5 minutes, or until the crust is pale golden. Remove from the oven and let cool slightly.

Reduce the oven temperature to 375°F/190°C/gas 5.

Spoon the slow-roasted tomatoes into the bottom of the tart crust and crumble the goat cheese over them. Arrange the tomato slices on top in a circular pattern. Sprinkle with the salt, basil, and thyme and drizzle with the olive oil. Bake the crostata for 30 to 40 minutes, until the crust is golden and the fresh tomatoes are slightly shriveled around the edges. Let rest for 5 to 10 minutes before serving.

CHICKPEA SALAD WITH RED ONIONS AND LEMON ZEST

makes 6 servings

This summer salad features bright colors and equally bright flavors. It also welcomes improvisation. Add diced bell peppers or Kalamata olives if you like. Serve it with crispy flatbread crackers or Plain Focaccia (page 88).

2 CUPS/340 G COOKED CHICKPEAS (SEE PAGE 71)

1 MEDIUM TOMATO, CUT INTO CHUNKS

1 SMALL MIDDLE EASTERN CUCUMBER, HALVED, SEEDED, AND SLICED

1 SMALL GARLIC CLOVE, MINCED

¼ CUP/60 ML CHOPPED RED ONION

3 TBSP EXTRA-VIRGIN OLIVE OIL

FINELY GRATED ZEST OF 1 SMALL LEMON PLUS 2 TBSP FRESHLY SQUEEZED LEMON JUICE

2 TBSP MINCED FRESH FLAT-LEAF PARSLEY

½ TO 1 TSP MINCED FRESH MINT

¼ TSP FINE SEA SALT

FRESHLY GROUND BLACK PEPPER

Combine the chickpeas, tomato, cucumber, garlic, and red onion in a bowl. Add the olive oil, lemon zest and juice, parsley, mint, and salt. Season with pepper, and toss gently but thoroughly. Let the salad sit for 30 minutes before serving.

SWEET-AND-SOUR EGGPLANT SALAD

makes 8 to 10 servings

Eggplant takes on a soft, almost melting, texture when cooked slowly in a pan. Though I usually don't peel eggplant, I do here just to emphasize that silky quality. Spoon this piquant salad onto crackers or bread, and serve it with good cheese and a bowl of olives.

⅓ CUP/75 ML EXTRA-VIRGIN OLIVE OIL

1 GARLIC CLOVE, SLICED PAPER-THIN

2 MEDIUM EGGPLANTS (ABOUT 1½ LB/680 G), PEELED AND CUT INTO ½-IN/12-MM DICE

½ TO 1 TSP FINE SEA SALT

3 TSP AGED BALSAMIC VINEGAR

1 TBSP MINCED FRESH HERBS (I USE A MIX OF MINT, BASIL, AND OREGANO)

CROSTINI (PAGE 80), OR SLICED BREAD, FOR SERVING

SHEEP'S MILK CHEESE SUCH AS CACIO DI ROMA (PAGE 44) FOR SERVING

In a large skillet, heat the oil and garlic over medium-low heat. Cook, stirring frequently, for 7 to 8 minutes or until the garlic is soft and translucent but not browned. Add the eggplant and ½ tsp salt and stir well to coat the eggplant with the oil. Cook, stirring occasionally, for 10 minutes or until the eggplant is just tender but not mushy.

Spoon the eggplant, along with the garlic slices and any juices, into a bowl. Sprinkle in the vinegar and herbs and toss gently to combine. Taste and add more salt if you like. Cover and let the eggplant sit for at least 30 minutes, preferably longer, before serving.

Serve the eggplant with the crostini and cheese.

WARM CITRUS-SCENTED OLIVES
WITH RICOTTA SALATA
makes 8 to 10 servings

Warm, fragrant olives make a welcoming appetizer or snack, especially in fall and winter. Serve them straight from the baking dish, or in a pretty bowl. Their dark, glossy colors look beautiful set out next to a wedge of pure white ricotta salata.

2 CUPS/340 G MIXED OLIVES (I USE A MIX OF GREEN, PURPLE, AND BLACK OIL-CURED)

ZEST OF 1 SMALL LEMON, CUT INTO STRIPS

ZEST OF 1 SMALL ORANGE, CUT INTO STRIPS

3 GARLIC CLOVES, LIGHTLY CRUSHED

3 TBSP EXTRA-VIRGIN OLIVE OIL

3 TBSP DRY WHITE WINE OR DRY SHERRY

1 BAY LEAF

1 SMALL FRESH ROSEMARY SPRIG

ONE 8-OZ/225-G WEDGE OF RICOTTA SALATA CHEESE

FLATBREAD CRACKERS FOR SERVING

Heat the oven to 325°F/165°C/gas 3.

Combine the olives, lemon and orange zest, and garlic in a small ovenproof ceramic baking dish in which they fit snugly in one layer. Drizzle in the oil and wine and toss gently. Tuck in the bay leaf and rosemary sprig.

Bake, uncovered, for 10 minutes; toss and bake for another 10 minutes, until the olives are heated through. Remove from the oven and toss gently.

Serve the olives with the ricotta salata and flatbread crackers.

POTATO CROQUETTES

makes 8 to 10 servings

Elsa, one of my mom's older sisters, was the official croquette maker in the family. This was a bit out of character, since Elsa wasn't as fond of cooking as my mom and their other two sisters, Gilda and Adriana. But every now and again she would emerge from the kitchen with a beautiful platter of golden croquettes—either rice or potato—and that, together with a selection of salumi and a salad, would be lunch. My version of Elsa's croquettes is a little dolled up with diced speck and smoked cheese, but I'm pretty sure she would approve.

2 LB/910 G YELLOW OR RED POTATOES

KOSHER SALT FOR COOKING THE POTATOES

5 LARGE EGGS

2 CUPS/85 G FRESHLY GRATED PARMIGIANO-REGGIANO CHEESE

1 TSP FINE SEA SALT

FRESHLY GROUND BLACK PEPPER

2 OZ/55 G IMPORTED ITALIAN SPECK, DICED

1/2 CUP/60 G UNBLEACHED ALL-PURPOSE FLOUR

1 1/2 CUPS/170 G DRIED BREAD CRUMBS

4 OZ/115 G SCAMORZA OR SMOKED MOZZARELLA CHEESE, CUT INTO 20 EQUAL PIECES

VEGETABLE OIL FOR FRYING

Put the potatoes in a large pot with cold water to cover by 1 to 2 in/2.5 to 5 cm. Salt generously. Set the pot over medium-high heat and bring to a boil. Cook the potatoes for 25 to 30 minutes, or until they are tender. Drain the potatoes in a colander and let them sit until they are cool enough to handle but still warm. Peel them, cut them into big pieces, and force them through a ricer into a large bowl.

Lightly beat 2 of the eggs and pour them into the bowl with the potatoes. Add the Parmigiano, salt, and season with pepper. Scatter the speck into the bowl. With a wooden spoon or silicone spatula, mix together gently but thoroughly until well blended.

Measure the flour into a shallow bowl. In another shallow bowl, lightly beat the remaining 3 eggs. Measure the bread crumbs into a third shallow bowl.

Scoop up a small handful of the potato mixture and press a piece of scamorza into it. Form into a log about 3 in/7.5 cm long and 1 1/2 in/4 cm wide, with the piece of cheese at the center.

Roll the croquette in flour, gently shaking off the excess. Transfer the croquette to the bowl of beaten eggs and, using a fork, gently roll it around to coat it thoroughly. Finally, move the croquette to the bowl of bread crumbs and roll it around several times until it is thoroughly coated. Place the croquette on a platter or rimmed baking sheet. Continue to shape and roll the remaining croquettes. You should have 20 croquettes.

Pour enough vegetable oil into a deep frying pan or straight-sided sauté pan to measure 1 in/2.5 cm. Heat the oil over medium-high heat until it registers 350°F/180°C on a deep-frying thermometer. Carefully lower 5 croquettes into the pan and fry them, turning them several times for even browning, for 3 to 4 minutes, until they are a deep golden brown. Using a slotted spoon, remove the croquettes to a paper towel–lined platter to drain. Repeat until all the croquettes have been fried.

Arrange the croquettes on a warmed, decorative serving platter and serve immediately.

VEGETABLE FRITTO MISTO

makes 12 or more servings

It may not be the most convenient appetizer, but a big platter of beautiful, crisp, golden-fried artichokes, zucchini and their flowers, and savory sage leaves is without a doubt one of the most welcoming. For best results, serve the vegetables soon after frying, because they lose their crispness fairly quickly. Should you be blessed with leftovers, consider yourself lucky. They are delicious sandwiched, together with fresh mozzarella and tomatoes, in a panino (see page 176). This recipe makes a generous amount; use half the batter to fry fewer vegetables, or just one vegetable—up to 24 zucchini blossoms, for example, or 12 baby artichokes—to serve 6 to 8.

2 CUPS/255 G UNBLEACHED ALL-PURPOSE FLOUR

2 CUPS/480 ML SPARKLING SPRING WATER, SUCH AS SAN PELLEGRINO

2 LARGE EGGS, LIGHTLY BEATEN

1 TSP FINE SEA SALT

6 BABY ARTICHOKES

12 ZUCCHINI BLOSSOMS, WITH STEMS, RINSED AND PATTED DRY

12 LARGE FRESH SAGE LEAVES, WITH STEMS, RINSED AND PATTED DRY

2 SMALL ZUCCHINI, EACH CUT LENGTHWISE INTO 8 WEDGES

VEGETABLE OIL FOR FRYING

1 OR 2 LEMONS, CUT INTO WEDGES, FOR SERVING

COARSE SEA SALT FOR SERVING

In a medium bowl, whisk together the flour, water, eggs, and fine sea salt to make a smooth batter about the consistency of heavy cream. Cover loosely with plastic wrap and let it rest for 20 to 30 minutes.

To prepare the artichokes (do this right before frying to avoid discoloration), using your fingers or a small paring knife, strip any tough outer leaves from the artichokes. Slice off the top third. Cut the artichokes lengthwise into quarters.

Pour enough oil into a medium skillet to reach a depth of $1/2$ to $3/4$ in/12 mm to 2 cm. Place over medium-high heat and heat the oil to 375°F/190°C on a deep-frying thermometer. To test the oil temperature, drop a small amount of batter into the hot oil. It should sizzle and float to the surface immediately, and quickly turn golden.

Have ready a paper towel-lined baking sheet for draining.

Dip the artichoke pieces in the batter and then transfer them immediately to the hot oil. Fry the artichokes in batches, taking care not to crowd the skillet, for 2 minutes; use a fork to turn and fry another 2 minutes, until golden brown and crispy. With a slotted spoon, transfer the artichokes to the prepared baking sheet. Fry the zucchini blossoms, zucchini wedges, and sage leaves in the same way, turning them once as they cook.

When all the vegetables have been fried, transfer them to a large decorative serving platter and sprinkle a little coarse sea salt over them. Arrange the lemon wedges on the platter and serve immediately.

zucchine, carciofi, olio, salvia
sale, uova, farina

chapter 3

GARDEN SOUPS AND SALADS
minestre, zuppe, e insalate

GARDEN SOUPS AND SALADS
minestre, zuppe, e insalate

Count me among the soup lovers of the world. We have soup for dinner once a week if not more, and nine times out of ten it is a vegetable soup.

The array of vegetable soups across Italy is nothing short of astounding; every region—every *village*, it seems, has a way of bringing together local vegetables and grains (or rice or pasta or bread) in a comforting soup. Tuscany is famous the world over for its Ribollita, a twice-cooked soup of vegetables, beans, and bread (page 113). But in the northern corner of that region, you are more likely to see Zuppa di Farro alla Garfagnana (page 110), with hearty grains taking the place of the bread.

There are elegant, creamy soups, like Cream of Bon Bon Squash and Fennel Soup (page 104), and hearty, wintry soups like Garlicky Lentil Soup (page 102). Some soups are meant to be served hot, and others at room temperature, brightened with a drizzle of good olive oil.

At our house, soup is usually accompanied by salad. Our go-to salad, like the standard trattoria salad in Italy, is what Italians refer to as *insalatina* or "little salad"; nothing more than lettuce, maybe with a little arugula and radicchio mixed in, and a dressing of olive oil and red wine vinegar or freshly squeezed lemon juice. If it's summer, there will be a couple of sliced tomatoes tossed in, too.

But as you look through this chapter, you'll see that the definition of salad is broad. It can mean anything from that simple mix of greens to a crunchy toss of cauliflower, olives, and sundried tomatoes (see page 120); or a hearty grain salad (see page 118); or my Aunt Gilda's appealingly old-fashioned rice salad with hard-boiled eggs and chopped pickled vegetables (see page 126).

PAPPA AL POMODORO

makes 4 servings

This humble soup is composed of little more than tomatoes and bread, and yet it is elegant in its simplicity and luxurious in its flavor. The quality of ingredients is paramount here, so don't skimp. Use your best olive oil, good country bread, and garden tomatoes that have spent the summer basking in the sun.

3 TBSP EXTRA-VIRGIN OLIVE OIL, PLUS MORE FOR DRIZZLING

1/3 CUP/45 G FINELY DICED RED ONION

2 GARLIC CLOVES, LIGHTLY CRUSHED

2 LARGE RIPE SUMMER TOMATOES (ABOUT 1 LB/455 G), PEELED, SEEDED, AND COARSELY CHOPPED

1 OR 2 MINCED CHILE PEPPERS IN OLIVE OIL (PAGE 259) OR A GENEROUS PINCH OF RED PEPPER FLAKES

1 TSP FINE SEA SALT, OR TO TASTE

10 LARGE FRESH BASIL LEAVES, CUT CROSSWISE INTO FINE STRIPS (CHIFFONADE)

8 OZ/225 G SLIGHTLY STALE STURDY ITALIAN COUNTRY BREAD (CRUSTS REMOVED), TORN INTO LARGE PIECES, OR IF NOT STALE, LIGHTLY TOASTED (SEE COOK'S NOTE)

3 TO 4 CUPS/720 TO 960 ML VEGETABLE BROTH (PAGE 62), TOMATO-VEGETABLE BROTH (PAGE 63), BEST-QUALITY COMMERCIAL VEGETABLE BROTH, OR WATER

ONE 2-IN/5-CM PIECE PARMIGIANO-REGGIANO CHEESE RIND

In a Dutch oven or other heavy-bottomed pot, warm the 3 tbsp olive oil, the onion, and the garlic over medium-low heat. Cook, stirring often, for 7 to 8 minutes, or until the onion and garlic are softened but not browned.

Tip in the tomatoes and their juices, the chile peppers, salt, and half of the basil chiffonade. Stir, raise the heat to medium-high, and bring to a simmer. Reduce the heat to medium-low and cook at a gentle simmer until the tomatoes have broken down into a pulp and deepened in color.

Add the bread pieces and stir to combine them with the tomatoes. Stir in the broth, starting with 3 cups/720 ml and adding more if the soup is too thick. Toss in the Parmigiano rind. Raise the heat to medium-high and bring the soup to a simmer. Reduce the heat to medium-low and cook at a gentle simmer for 30 to 40 minutes, or until the bread has been reduced to a thick porridge. Turn off the heat and stir in the remaining basil. Taste and adjust the seasoning if you like. Cover the soup and let it rest for 5 to 10 minutes before serving.

Ladle the soup into shallow bowls and drizzle a little olive oil over each serving.

COOK'S NOTE: To toast the bread, spread the pieces on a rimmed baking sheet and bake in a 350°F/180°C/gas 4 oven for 15 to 20 minutes, or until lightly golden.

GARLICKY LENTIL SOUP

makes 4 servings

My sister and I loved our mother's lentil soup when we were kids. It was thick and hearty, with colorful pieces of carrot and a full garlicky flavor (hence the name). But what really made the soup appealing were her homemade croutons, which we piled on top of our portions. To this day, I adore lentil soup topped with crunchy croutons. In fall and winter, I often serve it for dinner on weeknights because it is so easy to make and comes together in less than an hour.

¼ CUP/60 ML EXTRA-VIRGIN OLIVE OIL, PLUS MORE FOR DRIZZLING

4 GARLIC CLOVES, LIGHTLY CRUSHED

3 MEDIUM CARROTS, SLICED OR DICED

1 MEDIUM YELLOW ONION, DICED

1 SMALL FENNEL BULB, DICED

1 RIB CELERY, DICED

1 MEDIUM YELLOW POTATO, PEELED AND DICED

1 TURNIP, PEELED AND DICED

3 FRESH THYME SPRIGS

1 BAY LEAF

8 OZ/225 G TUSCAN KALE, COARSELY CHOPPED (SUBSTITUTE FRESH SPINACH IF YOU CAN'T FIND THE KALE)

1 TSP SEA SALT

1 PEPERONCINO, CHILE PEPPER IN OLIVE OIL (PAGE 259), MINCED, OR A GENEROUS PINCH OF RED PEPPER FLAKES (OPTIONAL)

2 CUPS/480 G BROWN LENTILS, RINSED AND DRAINED

4 CUPS/960 ML VEGETABLE BROTH (PAGE 62), TOMATO-VEGETABLE BROTH (PAGE 63), OR BEST-QUALITY COMMERCIAL VEGETABLE OR CHICKEN BROTH

4 CUPS/960 ML WATER

1 RECIPE CROUTONS (SEE COOK'S NOTE, PAGE 107)

Heat the olive oil in a large Dutch oven or other heavy-bottomed pot over medium heat. Add the garlic, carrots, onion, fennel, and celery, and stir to coat with oil. Cook, stirring occasionally, for 7 minutes, or until the onion is softened and pale gold and the carrots are bright orange. Add the potato, turnip, thyme, bay leaf, and kale (if using spinach, reserve and add later). Sprinkle in the salt and *peperoncino*, if using, and stir gently but thoroughly. Cook, stirring frequently, until the kale is wilted. Stir in the lentils.

Pour in the broth and the water and raise the heat to medium-high. Bring the soup to a simmer, reduce the heat to medium-low, and cover partially. Let the soup simmer gently, stirring from time to time, for 45 minutes or until the lentils are tender. (If using spinach, toss the leaves into the pot when the lentils are done cooking. Simmer an additional 5 minutes, or until the spinach leaves are completely wilted.) Discard the bay leaf and thyme sprigs (you can look for pieces of garlic to discard, too, but I find that by this point most of it has melted into the soup). Taste and adjust the seasoning with additional salt if you like.

Ladle the soup into shallow bowls, drizzle a little olive oil over each serving, and top with a handful of croutons.

BREAD SOUP WITH SUMMER SQUASH

makes 4 to 6 servings

Cooking doesn't get more resourceful than this—day-old bread softened in broth or water, simply seasoned with garlic and fresh basil, and made more nourishing with summer squash and a Parmigiano rind. This soup was a specialty of my Zia Gilda, and over the years I have made many variations, mixing up the herbs, adding pancetta, or stirring in a dollop of tomato sauce, as I do here.

3 TBSP EXTRA-VIRGIN OLIVE OIL, PLUS MORE FOR SERVING

1 MEDIUM WHITE SPRING ONION, THINLY SLICED (ABOUT 1 CUP/115 G)

2 GARLIC CLOVES, SLICED PAPER-THIN

1 LB/455 G GREEN AND YELLOW SUMMER SQUASH, SLICED INTO THIN COINS

1 TSP FINE SEA SALT

FRESHLY GROUND BLACK PEPPER

4 CUPS/960 ML VEGETABLE BROTH (PAGE 62), BEST-QUALITY COMMERCIAL VEGETABLE OR CHICKEN BROTH, OR WATER

ONE 2-IN/5-CM PIECE OF PARMIGIANO-REGGIANO CHEESE RIND

4 OZ/115 G SLIGHTLY STALE STURDY ITALIAN COUNTRY BREAD (CRUSTS REMOVED), TORN INTO LARGE PIECES; OR IF NOT STALE, LIGHTLY TOASTED (SEE COOK'S NOTE, PAGE 107)

1/2 CUP/120 ML FRESH TOMATO SAUCE (PAGE 65) OR SIMPLE TOMATO SAUCE (PAGE 66)

2 LARGE EGGS

1 CUP/115 G FRESHLY GRATED PARMIGIANO-REGGIANO CHEESE

HANDFUL OF FRESH BASIL LEAVES, COARSELY CHOPPED OR TORN INTO PIECES

In a Dutch oven or other heavy-bottomed pot, heat the oil, onion, and garlic over medium heat. Cook, stirring frequently, for 7 to 8 minutes, or until the onion and garlic are softened but not browned. Stir in the squash, the salt, and a generous grinding of pepper. Cook, stirring occasionally, for about 20 minutes, or until the squash is tender and browned in spots but still holds its shape.

Pour in the broth and raise the heat to medium-high. Toss in the Parmigiano rind and bring the soup to a simmer. Add the bread pieces and tomato sauce and stir. Reduce the heat to medium-low and cook at a gentle simmer for about 10 minutes, until nicely thickened.

In a bowl, lightly beat the eggs with the grated Parmigiano cheese. Pour the mixture into the soup pot and stir until the egg forms ragged strands. Cook for 5 more minutes, and then remove from the heat. Stir in the basil and let the soup sit for 5 to 10 minutes. Ladle the soup into shallow bowls and drizzle a little olive oil over each serving.

CREAM OF BON BON SQUASH AND FENNEL SOUP

makes 8 servings

Winter squash soup may not seem particularly Italian, but it is! None other than Pellegrino Artusi, Italy's revered authority on nineteenth-century gastronomy, included a recipe for *Zuppa di Zucca Gialla* (Yellow Squash Soup) in his famous book, *La Scienza in Cucina e L'Arte di Mangiare Bene*.

The plain fact is, we (meaning just about everybody) love winter squash soup, whether made with the ubiquitous butternut squash, or with one of the lesser known varieties. For soup, I always go for those squat squashes with hard, dark green rinds, like Bon Bon and Buttercup. They are most similar to the varieties grown in northern Italy, with candy-sweet, rich, dense flesh.

I wanted a soup that was different from so many others out there, so I turned to fennel. Fennel becomes mellow-sweet and silky when roasted. How could the combination of roasted winter squash and fennel not be spectacular? And the pancetta croutons? They take it over the top.

2 FENNEL BULBS, EACH CUT INTO 8 WEDGES

1 LARGE YELLOW ONION, CUT LENGTHWISE INTO THIN WEDGES

1 LONG FRESH ROSEMARY SPRIG, SNIPPED INTO 3 PIECES

4 OR 5 SHORT FRESH THYME SPRIGS

3 TBSP COARSELY CHOPPED FRESH FLAT-LEAF PARSLEY

1 TBSP COARSELY CHOPPED FRESH SAGE

1 TSP FINE SEA SALT

FRESHLY GROUND BLACK PEPPER

1/4 CUP/60 ML EXTRA-VIRGIN OLIVE OIL

5 TO 6 CUPS/1.2 TO 1.4 L VEGETABLE BROTH (PAGE 62), OR BEST-QUALITY COMMERCIAL VEGETABLE OR CHICKEN BROTH

2 3/4 CUPS/625 G ROASTED WINTER SQUASH PURÉE (PAGE 70), PREFERABLY MADE WITH BON BON SQUASH

PANCETTA "CROUTONS" (PAGE 106) OR BREAD CROUTONS (SEE COOK'S NOTE, PAGE 107) FOR SERVING

Heat the oven to 400°F/200°C/gas 6.

Place the fennel, onion, rosemary, thyme, parsley, and sage in a roasting pan large enough to hold everything in one snug layer. Sprinkle on the salt and a generous grinding of pepper. Drizzle the oil over the vegetables and toss to coat thoroughly. Roast for about 45 minutes, tossing once or twice, until the fennel and onions are soft and golden. Remove from the oven and pick out and discard any herb sprigs or stems.

Tip the roasted vegetables and their juices into a Dutch oven or heavy-bottomed pot. Add 4 cups/960 ml of the broth and the squash purée. Bring to a simmer over medium-high heat, reduce the heat to medium-low, and simmer gently for 10 minutes. Remove from the heat and let cool briefly.

Purée the soup with an immersion blender, or in batches using a standard blender; if you are using a standard blender, return the puréed soup to the pot. Stir in another 1 to 2 cups/240 to 480 ml broth to thin the soup to a creamy consistency. Taste the soup and season with additional salt or pepper, if you like. Return the soup to a simmer over medium-low heat.

Ladle the soup into shallow bowls, drizzle a little olive oil over each serving, and top with a few croutons.

CREAM OF CAULIFLOWER SOUP WITH PANCETTA "CROUTONS"

makes 4 to 6 servings

Rarely am I able to pass a display of snowy cauliflower heads at the farmers' market without scooping one into my shopping bag. I love cauliflower for its versatility. It is at home whether immersed with peppers in pickling brine, slow-roasted with onions, or puréed in this creamy soup and enhanced with crumbled blue cheese.

Awhile back I tried my hand at curing my own pancetta from pork belly and was delighted with how easy the process was, not to mention the delicious results. I turned some of the pancetta into "croutons" by cutting it into fat cubes and frying them in a skillet. You don't need to make your own pancetta to make the "croutons"; indeed, you don't need to use pancetta at all. You can substitute bread croutons (see Cook's Note) and still have a delicious, warming, winter soup.

8 OZ/225 G PANCETTA, CUT INTO 3/4-IN/2-CM DICE

1 TBSP UNSALTED BUTTER (OPTIONAL)

2 MEDIUM LEEKS, WHITE AND LIGHT GREEN PARTS, THOROUGHLY WASHED, HALVED LENGTHWISE, AND SLICED THINLY CROSSWISE (ABOUT 2 CUPS/ 140 G)

2 RIBS CELERY, CHOPPED (ABOUT 3/4 CUP/73 G)

1 LARGE HEAD CAULIFLOWER (ABOUT 1 1/2 LB/680 G), TRIMMED AND CUT INTO SMALL FLORETS (I CUT THE TENDER PART OF THE CORE INTO CHUNKS AND ALSO USE THAT)

1/4 CUP/30 G UNBLEACHED ALL-PURPOSE FLOUR

3 TO 4 CUPS/720 ML TO 960 ML VEGE-TABLE BROTH (PAGE 62) OR BEST-QUALITY COMMERCIAL VEGETABLE OR CHICKEN BROTH

1 CUP/240 ML HEAVY CREAM OR WHOLE MILK

3 OZ/85 G SMOKED BLUE CHEESE, SUCH AS ROGUE CREAMERY SMOKEY BLUE, OR IMPORTED GORGONZOLA PICCANTE, CRUMBLED

Put the pancetta in a Dutch oven or other heavy-bottomed pot and set it over medium heat. When the pancetta begins to sizzle, reduce the heat to medium-low and cook, stirring from time to time, for 12 to 15 minutes, or until the pancetta has rendered some of its fat and is browned and crispy. Use a slotted spoon to remove the pancetta to a paper towel–lined bowl and set aside.

Pour out all but 3 tbsp of the rendered pancetta fat; add the butter to the pot, if using, and cook over medium heat. When the butter is melted, add the leeks and celery, and toss well to coat with the fat. Cook the vegetables for 8 to 10 minutes, stirring occasionally, until the leeks are wilted and the celery has softened a bit. Stir in the cauliflower and toss well to coat. Cover the pot, reduce the heat to medium-low, and cook for about 15 minutes, until the cauliflower begins to soften. Stir the vegetables occasionally as they cook.

Uncover the pot and sprinkle in the flour, mixing well to incorporate into the vegetables. Cook for 2 to 3 minutes, until the flour has been absorbed. Pour in 3 cups/720 ml of the broth, raise the heat to medium, and bring the soup to a simmer. Reduce the heat to medium-low or low to maintain a gentle simmer, cover the pot, and simmer for 25 to 30 minutes, until the cauliflower is completely tender and breaks apart easily when pierced with a fork.

Remove the pot from the heat and use an immersion blender to purée the soup until it is completely smooth and creamy. If it seems too thick, add a little more broth and purée again. Return the pot to the heat and pour in the cream. Cook on medium-low heat for 10 minutes more, or until the soup is heated through.

Ladle the soup into shallow bowls and top each serving with some crumbles of blue cheese and pancetta "croutons." Or, if you prefer, you can stir the blue cheese into the soup until it is melted, and serve topped with the pancetta "croutons."

COOK'S NOTE: To make bread croutons, spread 2 cups/60 g cubed Italian country bread on a rimmed baking sheet and drizzle 1 to 2 tbsp extra-virgin olive oil over them. Toss well with a wooden spoon or spatula. Season with salt and freshly ground pepper, if you like, and toss again. Spread the bread cubes out in a single layer. Bake at 400°F/200°C/gas 6 for 15 to 20 minutes, or until they are evenly browned and crisp. Let cool before using.

MINESTRONE VERDE

makes 6 to 8 servings

Have you ever tried making color-coordinated minestrone? I know, it sounds silly, but think of the delicious possibilities—a golden version featuring yellow summer squash, yellow bell peppers, and roasted corn, or a purple version with eggplant, purple onion and peppers, and purple basil as a garnish. No doubt green would yield the most possible variations, and here is one of them, a bold-flavored, summery soup with spinach, zucchini, peas, and a fresh basil pesto.

3 TBSP EXTRA-VIRGIN OLIVE OIL, PLUS MORE FOR SERVING

1 OZ/30 G PANCETTA, DICED (OPTIONAL)

2 MEDIUM LEEKS, WHITE AND LIGHT GREEN PARTS, THOROUGHLY WASHED, HALVED LENGTHWISE, AND SLICED THINLY CROSSWISE (ABOUT 2 CUPS/140 G)

2 SMALL ZUCCHINI, QUARTERED LENGTHWISE AND THEN CUT CROSSWISE INTO SMALL WEDGE-SHAPED PIECES

1/4 TSP FINE SEA SALT

FRESHLY GROUND BLACK PEPPER

6 TO 7 CUPS/1.4 TO 1.7 L VEGETABLE BROTH (PAGE 62) OR BEST-QUALITY COMMERCIAL VEGETABLE OR CHICKEN BROTH

2 CUPS/230 G TUBETTINI, DITALINI, OR OTHER SMALL SOUP PASTA

2 CUPS/230 G FRESH OR FROZEN PEAS, THAWED IF FROZEN

4 HANDFULS (ABOUT 4 OZ/115 G) OF FRESH BABY SPINACH LEAVES

1/2 CUP/60 G FRESHLY GRATED PARMIGIANO-REGGIANO CHEESE (OPTIONAL)

3 TO 4 TBSP FRESH BASIL PESTO (PAGE 64), LOOSENED WITH 1 OR 2 DROPS OF OLIVE OIL

Put the oil, pancetta, if using, and leeks in a large Dutch oven or other heavy-bottomed pot and place over medium heat. Cook, stirring frequently, until the oil and pancetta begin to sizzle, then lower the heat to medium-low and cook for 7 to 8 minutes, until the leeks are softened and the pancetta is just beginning to turn crisp.

Stir in the zucchini and season with the salt and a generous grinding of pepper. Cook, stirring frequently, for about 15 minutes, or until the zucchini is tender but still holds its shape. Pour in 6 cups/1.4 L of the broth and raise the heat to medium-high. Bring the broth to a boil and slowly pour in the pasta, taking care not to let the broth boil over. Reduce the heat to medium-low to maintain a gentle simmer and cook the pasta for 1 to 2 minutes. Stir in the peas and spinach and cook until the pasta is al dente or even a little bit more tender; cooking time will depend on the shape and brand of pasta you use. Add more broth to thin the soup, if you like.

Remove from the heat and stir in the Parmigiano cheese, if using. Ladle the soup into shallow bowls, top with a dollop of pesto—no more than 1/2 tbsp—and drizzle a little olive oil over each serving.

tubettini, pancetta, spinaci, pis
basilico, cipolle, zucchin

ZUPPA DI FARRO ALLA GARFAGNANA

makes 4 servings

Garfagnana is located in northwestern Tuscany, at the foot of the Apuan Alps. The landscape is one of craggy hills and mountains rather than gentle slopes for which the rest of the region is famous. The food, appropriately, is hearty and rustic and makes the most of the area's native ingredients, especially legumes and grains. This soup, featuring cannellini beans and farro, is one of my favorite dishes from this dramatic and picturesque corner of Italy.

2 OZ/55 G PANCETTA, DICED (SEE COOK'S NOTE)

2 MEDIUM CARROTS, DICED

1 SMALL YELLOW ONION, FINELY CHOPPED

1 TBSP MINCED FRESH FLAT-LEAF PARSLEY

2 GARLIC CLOVES, LIGHTLY CRUSHED

1 TO 2 CHILE PEPPERS IN OLIVE OIL (PAGE 259) OR FRESH CHILE PEPPERS, MINCED

2 TBSP EXTRA-VIRGIN OLIVE OIL, PLUS MORE FOR DRIZZLING

8 OZ/225 G TUSCAN KALE, COARSELY SHREDDED

2 CUPS/455 G COOKED CANNELLINI BEANS (SEE PAGE 71)

1 1/2 CUPS/315 G FARRO, RINSED AND DRAINED

4 TO 6 TBSP TOMATO PURÉE

4 CUPS/960 ML VEGETABLE BROTH (PAGE 62), BEST-QUALITY COMMERCIAL VEGETABLE BROTH, OR WATER

ONE 2-IN/5-CM PIECE OF PARMIGIANO-REGGIANO CHEESE RIND, PLUS FRESHLY GRATED PARMIGIANO-REGGIANO CHEESE FOR SERVING (OPTIONAL)

1 TSP FINE SEA SALT

Put the pancetta in a large Dutch oven or other heavy-bottomed pot and place over medium heat. Sauté for 5 to 6 minutes, or until the pancetta has rendered some of its fat and is beginning to crisp. Stir in the carrots, onion, parsley, garlic, and chile peppers, and cook, stirring often, until the onion is softened and translucent and the carrot is bright orange, about 7 minutes. Add the 2 tbsp olive oil and the kale, cover the pot, and cook for about 5 minutes, until the kale is wilted. Add the cannellini beans and cook for 2 minutes, and then add the farro and tomato purée. Stir to combine thoroughly.

Pour in the broth, toss in the Parmigiano rind, if using, and raise the heat to medium-high. Bring the soup to a simmer, reduce the heat to medium-low, cover partially, and cook at a gentle simmer for 30 to 40 minutes, or until the farro is tender but still pleasantly chewy. Add the salt.

Ladle the soup into shallow bowls and drizzle a little olive oil over each serving. Sprinkle with grated Parmigiano, if you like.

COOK'S NOTE: You can omit the pancetta; just use 3 tbsp olive oil to sauté the vegetables.

CONCHIGLIETTE WITH CANNELLINI BEANS AND BRAISED RADICCHIO

makes 6 servings

Round, compact radicchio di Chioggia is the most common variety of this member of the chicory family. If you've encountered it, it has probably been in a salad. What you may not know, however, is that radicchio has another, secret identity. It is delicious cooked and can be grilled, sautéed, stewed, or braised. What happens is a wonderful transformation: it loses its crunch and its bright color, turning a rich shade of brown and taking on a satisfying pulpy texture and a mellow nutty flavor. One of my favorite ways to feature cooked radicchio is in a twist on the classic Italian dish *pasta e fagioli* (pasta and bean soup). It adds a pleasing complementary flavor to the beans, as well as body to the soup itself.

2 TBSP EXTRA-VIRGIN OLIVE OIL, PLUS MORE FOR DRIZZLING

2 OZ/55 G PANCETTA, DICED (SEE COOK'S NOTE)

1/2 CUP/55 G DICED RED ONION

2 GARLIC CLOVES, MINCED

1 TBSP MINCED FRESH HERBS (I USE A MIX OF OREGANO, ROSEMARY, AND SAGE)

1 HEAD RADICCHIO (8 OZ/225 G), QUARTERED, CORED, AND SHREDDED

ONE 14 1/2-OZ/415-G CAN DICED TOMATOES, WITH THEIR JUICE

2 CUPS/455 G COOKED CANNELLINI BEANS (SEE PAGE 71) OR ONE 15-OZ/430-G CAN CANNELLINI BEANS, WITH THEIR LIQUID

5 TO 6 CUPS/1.2 TO 1.4 L VEGETABLE BROTH (PAGE 62) OR BEST-QUALITY COMMERCIAL CHICKEN BROTH

1 1/2 CUPS/215 G DRIED MEDIUM-SIZE CONCHIGLIETTE (SHELL-SHAPED PASTA)

FRESHLY GRATED PARMIGIANO-REGGIANO CHEESE FOR SERVING

Heat the 2 tbsp of olive oil and pancetta in a large Dutch oven or other heavy-bottomed pot over medium heat. Cook for about 5 minutes, or until the pancetta has rendered some of its fat and is slightly crisp. Stir in the onion, garlic, and herbs and sauté for 5 minutes, until the onion begins to soften. Add the radicchio to the pot and stir to combine. Reduce the heat to medium-low, cover, and cook for about 15 minutes, until the radicchio has completely wilted. Uncover and stir occasionally while the radicchio cooks. Pour in the tomatoes and simmer, uncovered, for 20 minutes, or until the mixture thickens to a sauce.

Stir in the beans. Pour in 5 cups/1.2 L of the broth, raise the heat to medium-high, and bring to a boil. Add the pasta and stir gently. Cook according to the manufacturer's instructions until the pasta is al dente or a bit more tender. Add more broth to thin the soup, if you like.

Ladle the soup into warmed shallow bowls, drizzle a little olive oil over each serving, and sprinkle with a little cheese. Serve immediately.

RIBOLLITA
makes 6 main-dish servings

This Tuscan specialty is enjoyed year-round at my house. In warmer months, when hearty greens such as kale and cabbage are not in season, I substitute fresh spinach leaves. Ribollita translates to "twice-boiled" and refers to the way the soup is cooked. First, the medley of vegetables is simmered in tomatoes and broth; then bread is added and the soup is brought to a second simmer to finish cooking. What this long-simmered soup lacks in vibrant color it more than makes up for in hearty flavor.

¼ CUP/60 ML EXTRA-VIRGIN OLIVE OIL, PLUS MORE FOR DRIZZLING

4 GARLIC CLOVES, LIGHTLY CRUSHED

8 OZ/225 G TUSCAN KALE, COARSELY SHREDDED

8 OZ/225 G SAVOY CABBAGE, COARSELY SHREDDED

½ TSP FINE SEA SALT, PLUS MORE FOR SEASONING (OPTIONAL)

2 OZ/55 G PANCETTA, DICED

2 MEDIUM CARROTS, CUT INTO BITE-SIZE PIECES (ABOUT 1 CUP/225 G)

2 SMALL RIBS CELERY, CUT INTO BITE-SIZE PIECES (ABOUT ½ CUP/115 G)

½ CUP/55 G DICED RED OR YELLOW ONION

1 TBSP MINCED FRESH FLAT-LEAF PARSLEY

2 RED BLISS OR YUKON GOLD POTATOES, PEELED AND CUT INTO ½-IN/12-MM DICE

GENEROUS PINCH OF RED PEPPER FLAKES

ONE 14½-OZ/415-G CAN DICED TOMATOES

2 CUPS/455 G COOKED CANNELLINI BEANS OR CHICKPEAS, OR ONE 15-OZ/430-G CAN CANNELLINI BEANS OR CHICKPEAS, WITH THEIR LIQUID

4 CUPS/960 ML VEGETABLE BROTH (PAGE 62) OR BEST-QUALITY COMMERCIAL CHICKEN BROTH

ONE 2-IN/5-CM PIECE PARMIGIANO-REGGIANO CHEESE RIND (OPTIONAL)

4 TO 6 CUPS/120 TO 200 G BREAD CROUTONS (SEE COOK'S NOTE, PAGE 107)

In a large sauté pan, heat 3 tbsp of the oil with 2 cloves of garlic over medium-low heat. Cook until the garlic is fragrant but not browned, about 3 minutes. Add the kale and cabbage in batches, covering the pan after each addition and letting the greens cook until they begin to wilt, about 5 minutes. Cook, stirring occasionally, until the greens are completely wilted and tender, about 20 minutes. Season with the salt. Remove from the heat and set aside.

CONTINUED

CONTINUED

In a Dutch oven or other heavy-bottomed pot, heat the remaining 1 tbsp oil over medium-low heat and add the pancetta. Cook, stirring occasionally, until the pancetta is lightly browned but not too crisp and has rendered its fat, 7 to 8 minutes. Add the carrots, celery, onion, and parsley and toss to coat well with the oil. Cook until the vegetables are shiny and beginning to soften, 7 to 8 minutes. Add the potatoes, toss, and cook until they begin to soften, about 10 minutes.

Stir in the wilted greens and sprinkle with the red pepper flakes. Cook for about 5 minutes, until the greens are heated through. Pour in the tomatoes and the beans and stir to combine all the ingredients. Add the vegetable broth and raise the heat to medium-high. Toss in the Parmigiano rind, if using. Bring the soup to a simmer, lower the heat to medium-low or low, and let the soup simmer until all the vegetables are cooked through and tender, about 30 minutes.

Add the bread croutons and stir them into the soup. Let simmer for another 15 to 20 minutes, until all of the ingredients have had a chance to meld. Taste and add additional salt if you like. Turn the heat off and cover the soup. Let it sit for about 5 minutes to bring the flavors together.

Ladle the ribollita into shallow rimmed bowls and drizzle each serving with a little olive oil.

ARUGULA, FENNEL, AND ORANGE SALAD

makes 4 to 6 servings

A confession: I am not big on presentation. I don't have the patience for plating, and frankly, I don't like dabs or smears or other fussy garnishes on my plate. This salad is one of the few exceptions because I pay attention to placement. The arrangement is simple, and the composed salad looks like a beautiful flower or sunburst. It's a great dish to serve at a dinner party. Cara Cara oranges, used in this recipe, have pink flesh and are juicy and sweet—substitute regular navel oranges if you can't find them. Make sure you use a top-notch olive oil and good, flaky sea salt, because those are the only two ingredients used to dress the salad.
4 OZ/115 G ARUGULA

2 BLOOD ORANGES

1 CARA CARA OR NAVEL ORANGE

1/2 RED ONION, THINLY SLICED

1 SMALL FENNEL BULB, QUARTERED, CORED, AND THINLY SLICED, PLUS A SMALL HANDFUL OF THE FRONDS

BEST-QUALITY EXTRA-VIRGIN OLIVE OIL FOR DRIZZLING

1/2 TSP FLEUR DE SEL

FRESHLY GROUND BLACK PEPPER (OPTIONAL)

Use a large, round serving platter for the salad. Spread the arugula out on the platter to make a bed.

Using a sharp paring knife, cut off the tops and bottoms of the oranges. Stand the oranges up and slice around them to remove the peel as well as the membrane. Then slice the oranges crosswise into thin wheels.

Arrange the blood oranges in an outer ring on top of the arugula, overlapping the slices slightly. Use the Cara Cara orange slices to form an inner ring, overlapping the slices. Scatter the onion slices on top of the oranges. Then arrange the fennel slices on top of the oranges in a pattern of rays. Mound any extra slices in the center.

Drizzle several tbsp olive oil on the salad, and sprinkle with the fleur de sel. Season with pepper, if using.

CHICORY SALAD WITH ANCHOVY DRESSING
makes 6 to 8 servings

Every now and then I like a salad with attitude. This one has it, with its mix of assertive, crunchy radicchio, pungent anchovy-lemon dressing, and crispy croutons. Serve it with a rich main course such as Vegetable-Stuffed Pasta Shells (page 192) or Crêpe Cannelloni with Mushrooms and Zucchini (page 189).

1 TSP FINE SEA SALT

1 GARLIC CLOVE, PRESSED

4 RIZZOLI-BRAND *ALICI IN SALSA PICCANTE* (SEE PAGE 43) OR BEST-QUALITY IMPORTED ITALIAN OR SPANISH ANCHOVY FILLETS IN OLIVE OIL, COARSELY CHOPPED, PLUS 1 TBSP OF THE OIL

1 TBSP SMOOTH DIJON MUSTARD

1 TBSP MAYONNAISE

2 DASHES OF WORCESTERSHIRE SAUCE

JUICE OF 1 SMALL LEMON

1/3 TO 1/2 CUP/75 TO 120 ML EXTRA-VIRGIN OLIVE OIL

1 LARGE HEAD RADICCHIO DI CHIOGGIA (8 OZ/225 G), TORN INTO LARGE PIECES

1 HEAD RADICCHIO DI CASTELFRANCO (8 OZ/225 G), CURLY ENDIVE, OR FRISÉE, TORN INTO LARGE PIECES

1/2 CUP/60 G FRESHLY GRATED PARMIGIANO-REGGIANO CHEESE

2 CUPS/60 G BREAD CROUTONS (SEE COOK'S NOTE, PAGE 107)

In a small bowl, mix together the salt and garlic to form a paste. Whisk in the anchovies and 1 tbsp of their oil, and then whisk in the mustard, mayonnaise, and Worcestershire sauce. Whisk in the lemon juice. Drizzle in the olive oil, whisking constantly, until the dressing is thick and emulsified.

Place the radicchios in a large bowl and toss together. Pour the dressing over and toss to combine. Sprinkle the cheese on top and toss again. Transfer the salad to a decorative bowl and top with the croutons. Serve immediately.

alici in salsa piccante, o.
radicchio di chiozzia, parmigian
aglio, sale

HEARTY SALAD WITH ALMONDS, ARTICHOKES, BRESAOLA, AND GRANA PADANO

makes 6 to 8 servings

My sister, Maria, is the best salad maker in the family. She is always finding unusual ingredients to toss into the mix. She came up with this robust combination a few years ago, and I have been making variations of it ever since. If you prefer a meatless salad, simply substitute an equal quantity of sun-dried tomatoes for the bresaola (page 46).

2 HEADS (ABOUT 12 OZ/340 G) BUTTER LETTUCE, TORN INTO LARGE PIECES

4 OZ/115 G BABY ARUGULA

1/2 SMALL FENNEL BULB, CUT INTO THIN SLICES

1 CUP/225 G BOTTLED MARINATED ARTICHOKE HEARTS, DRAINED AND CUT INTO QUARTERS

6 THIN SLICES (ABOUT 2 OZ/55 G) BRESAOLA, CUT INTO THIN STRIPS

1/3 CUP/30 G SLICED RAW ALMONDS

1 1/2 OZ/45 G SHAVED GRANA PADANO CHEESE, PLUS MORE FOR GARNISH

2 TO 4 TBSP EXTRA-VIRGIN OLIVE OIL

JUICE OF 1 SMALL LEMON (ABOUT 2 TBSP)

FINE SEA SALT

FRESHLY GROUND BLACK PEPPER

Combine the lettuce, arugula, fennel, artichoke hearts, bresaola, almonds, and cheese in a large salad bowl and toss gently. Drizzle enough olive oil over the salad to thoroughly coat but not saturate the greens. Sprinkle the lemon juice over the salad, then season with salt and pepper. Toss gently.

Divide among individual plates and garnish with additional shavings of Grana Padano.

BIRD EGG BEAN SALAD

makes 6 to 8 servings

How can you pass up a bean named "bird egg"? I couldn't, so when I came across a bin of these scarlet-splashed shell beans at a Washington, DC, farmers' market, I scooped up several handfuls. They are similar to the more common maroon-streaked cranberry or borlotti beans, with easy-to-open pods nestling the oval, speckled beans. The pretty pink speckles fade as the beans cook, but no matter. The beans themselves are full-flavored with a creamy texture, so they are the star of the show in this salad. Look for bird egg beans, or their easier-to-find cousins, in late summer and into fall.

1 LB/455 G SHELLED FRESH BIRD EGG BEANS OR CRANBERRY BEANS (2 LB/910 G IN THE POD)

2 BAY LEAVES

3 GARLIC CLOVES, LIGHTLY CRUSHED

1 SMALL RED ONION, CUT IN HALF

HANDFUL OF FRESH FLAT-LEAF PARSLEY SPRIGS

SEA SALT

FRESHLY SQUEEZED JUICE OF 1 LEMON

3 TO 4 TBSP EXTRA-VIRGIN OLIVE OIL

GENEROUS PINCH OF RED PEPPER FLAKES

5 OZ/140 G ARUGULA OR RADICCHIO, OR A MIX OF BOTH, TORN INTO BITE-SIZE PIECES

Put the beans in a large, heavy-bottomed saucepan with cold water to cover by 1 in/2.5 cm. Toss in the bay leaves, 2 of the garlic cloves, ½ onion, and the parsley. Bring to a boil over medium-high heat. Reduce the heat to medium-low and simmer gently, uncovered, until the beans are tender but not mushy, about 30 minutes. Season with salt and simmer another 1 or 2 minutes. Drain the beans and remove the bay leaves, garlic, onion, and parsley.

Place the beans in a medium bowl. Pour half the lemon juice over the beans and drizzle in 2 tbsp of the olive oil. Add the remaining garlic clove, ½ tsp salt, and the red pepper flakes. Thinly slice the remaining ½ onion and add it to the beans. Toss gently to combine.

In a separate medium bowl, toss the arugula with the remaining lemon juice and 1 to 2 tbsp olive oil. Season with salt and toss.

Arrange the arugula in a shallow serving bowl and spoon the beans over them. Serve immediately.

WINTER CAULIFLOWER SALAD

makes 6 to 8 servings

Although you can enjoy this salad at any time of year, I find that its refreshing crunch is especially welcome in winter, when the foods we (or at least I) eat tend to be of the rich, stick-to-your-ribs sort, such as stews and braises, or oozy baked pasta dishes.

1 MEDIUM HEAD CAULIFLOWER (1 LB/ 455 G), TRIMMED AND CUT INTO FLORETS

1 LARGE RIB CELERY, SLICED ON THE BIAS

1 CUP/115 G COARSELY CHOPPED PITTED OLIVES (I USE A MIX OF GREEN AND PURPLE, SUCH AS CERIGNOLA AND GAETA OR KALAMATA)

1 TBSP COARSELY CHOPPED FRESH FLAT-LEAF PARSLEY

2 GARLIC CLOVES, MINCED

¼ CUP/30 G DICED RED ONION

2 TBSP COARSELY CHOPPED SLOW-ROASTED TOMATOES (PAGE 67) OR BOTTLED SUN-DRIED TOMATOES

1 FRESH CHILE PEPPER, VERY HOT OR MILDLY HOT, YOUR PREFERENCE, MINCED

FINELY GRATED ZEST OF 1 LEMON, PLUS 2 TBSP LEMON JUICE

1 TSP FINE SEA SALT

¼ TO ½ CUP/60 TO 120 ML EXTRA-VIRGIN OLIVE OIL

3 TO 4 OZ/85 TO 115 G GORGONZOLA PICCANTE, CRUMBLED

Place a steamer basket in a large saucepan and fill the pan with water up to but not touching the bottom of the basket. Bring the water to a boil over high heat. Arrange the cauliflower in the steamer basket, cover, and steam until just tender, about 5 minutes.

Transfer the cauliflower to a large bowl. Add the celery, olives, parsley, garlic, onion, roasted tomatoes, and chile pepper and toss gently but thoroughly. Sprinkle the lemon zest and lemon juice over the salad. Season with the salt and toss again. Drizzle in the olive oil, starting with ¼ cup/60 ml and adding more if you like. Cover the salad and let it marinate at room temperature for 30 minutes, or refrigerate until chilled if you prefer it cold. Right before serving, fold in the cheese.

COOK'S NOTE: Any or all of the following items would make good additions to the salad: sliced carrots, sliced fennel bulb, roasted peppers, or diced salami.

cavolfiore, sedano, folia d
prezzemolo,
gorgonzola piccante

ROASTED BEET AND CARROT SALAD
WITH TOASTED FENNEL SEEDS

makes 6 servings

I'd never thought of putting carrots and beets in the same dish until I brought them both home in the same bag from the farmers' market. Then it seemed like they belonged together. Roasting these colorful root vegetables brings out their natural sweetness.

1 LB/455 G MEDIUM BEETS, ENDS TRIMMED

4 TBSP/60 ML EXTRA-VIRGIN OLIVE OIL

1 LB/455 G CARROTS, CUT INTO 1-IN/2.5-CM CHUNKS

FINE SEA SALT

FRESHLY GROUND BLACK PEPPER

1 TSP FENNEL SEEDS

1 TBSP AGED BALSAMIC VINEGAR

1 TBSP RED OR WHITE WINE VINEGAR

2 TSP HONEY

1 CUP/120 G THINLY SLICED RED ONION

Heat the oven to 425°F/220°C/gas 7.

Set the beets upright in a small roasting pan or baking dish. Drizzle 1 tbsp olive oil over them. Cover with aluminum foil.

Put the carrots in a separate roasting pan or baking dish and drizzle 1 tbsp olive oil over them. Season with 1/4 tsp salt and a grinding of pepper.

Place the carrots and beets in the oven separately. Bake the carrots, uncovered, for 20 minutes, until just tender but not too soft. Bake the beets, covered, for 40 to 45 minutes, until tender; you should be able to pierce through them with a cake tester. Remove the foil and set them aside until cool enough to handle. Reserve any beet juices in the baking dish for the dressing.

Meanwhile, make the dressing. Heat a small, dry skillet over medium-high heat. Pour in the fennel seeds and toast, shaking the pan frequently, until the seeds have turned a shade darker and are fragrant, about 3 minutes. Pour the seeds onto a plate to cool briefly. Grind them in a spice grinder until finely ground. Put the ground fennel seeds into a small bowl. Whisk in the juices reserved from baking the beets, 2 tbsp olive oil, the vinegars, the honey, and 1 tsp salt.

Peel the beets and cut them into chunks about the same size as the carrots. Put the beets and carrots in a medium bowl and add the sliced onion. Pour the dressing over the vegetables. Cover and let the vegetables marinate for at least 30 minutes and up to 2 hours. Serve at room temperature.

POTATO SALAD
makes 6 to 8 serving

Living in Virginia for most of the year, I have come to love Southern-style potato salads, many of which feature a good dose of mayonnaise, chunks of hard-boiled eggs, and chopped sweet pickles. But my heart belongs to this simple Italian preparation, which calls for little more than good potatoes and great olive oil, with a handful of parsley tossed in. Taking a cue from my mom, I also add some chopped spring onions or scallions, and a grinding of black pepper. The arugula flowers are a new flourish that I've added since coming across them recently in a local farmers' market. They are as delicate and perishable as cherry blossoms, but they contribute a spicy kick. If you can't find them, toss in a handful of baby arugula leaves.

2½ LB/1.2 KG MEDIUM RED POTATOES

KOSHER OR SEA SALT

½ CUP/60 G CHOPPED RED SCALLIONS OR RED SPRING ONIONS

2 TBSP MINCED FRESH FLAT-LEAF PARSLEY

⅓ CUP/75 ML EXTRA-VIRGIN OLIVE OIL

FLAKY SEA SALT, SUCH AS FLEUR DE SEL, FOR SPRINKLING

FRESHLY GROUND BLACK PEPPER

HANDFUL OF ARUGULA FLOWERS (SEE PAGE 16), IF AVAILABLE, OR A HANDFUL OF BABY ARUGULA LEAVES

Put the potatoes in a large pot with water to cover by 1 to 2 in/2.5 to 5 cm. Salt generously. Set the pot over medium-high heat and bring to a boil. Cook the potatoes for 20 to 25 minutes, until just tender. You should be able to poke through them with a cake tester, meeting with just a little resistance. Drain the potatoes in a colander and let them sit until they are cool enough to handle but still quite warm.

Peel the potatoes and cut them into slices about ¼ in/6 mm thick. Put them in a bowl and sprinkle the scallions and parsley over them. Drizzle the olive oil over the potatoes and fold everything together gently but thoroughly. Sprinkle a generous pinch of sea salt over the potatoes and sprinkle with a generous grinding of black pepper. Toss again. Transfer to a decorative serving bowl and cover with plastic wrap or a plate. Let sit for about 30 minutes.

Right before serving, scatter a handful of arugula flowers on top of the potato salad. Serve while still warm or at room temperature.

FARRO SALAD WITH GORGONZOLA
makes 6 to 8 servings

This may sound silly, but I still remember the first time I had farro, at a restaurant in Lucca more than two decades ago. This nutritious grain is reputed to have nourished the Roman army and has long been a staple in the cuisine of Garfagnana, the rugged northern portion of Tuscany. The dish I had back then was a delicious rustic soup (see page 110 for my version). Nowadays, thanks to its ever-growing popularity, farro is featured in everything from salads, such as this one, to desserts.

DRESSING:

2 TBSP FRESHLY SQUEEZED MEYER LEMON JUICE, OR 1 TBSP EACH FRESHLY SQUEEZED LEMON JUICE AND ORANGE JUICE

1 TBSP AGED BALSAMIC VINEGAR

3/4 TSP FINE SEA SALT

FRESHLY GROUND BLACK PEPPER

1/3 CUP/75 ML EXTRA-VIRGIN OLIVE OIL

1 SMALL GARLIC CLOVE, LIGHTLY CRUSHED

SALAD:

1½ CUPS/315 G FARRO, RINSED AND DRAINED

3 CUPS/720 ML VEGETABLE BROTH (PAGE 62), BEST-QUALITY COMMERCIAL VEGETABLE BROTH, OR WATER

FINE SEA SALT

1/2 CUP/85 G DICED FENNEL BULB (USE THE STEMS TO FLAVOR THE VEGETABLE BROTH IF MAKING THE BROTH FROM SCRATCH)

1/2 CUP/85 G DICED GRILLED PEPPERS (PAGE 74)

1/2 CUP/85 G SLICED CANNED HEARTS OF PALM

1/4 CUP/30 G DICED RED ONION

1/3 CUP/70 G PITTED OIL-CURED BLACK OLIVES, HALVED

1/4 CUP/10 G MINCED FRESH FLAT-LEAF PARSLEY

3 OZ/85 G GORGONZOLA PICCANTE CHEESE, CRUMBLED

FRESHLY GROUND BLACK PEPPER (OPTIONAL)

TO MAKE THE DRESSING: In a small bowl, whisk together the Meyer lemon juice, balsamic vinegar, salt, and a generous grinding of pepper. Slowly whisk in the olive oil until the dressing has emulsified. Drop in the garlic clove and let the dressing sit while you make the salad.

TO MAKE THE SALAD: Put the drained farro in a large saucepan and add the broth. If using water, season with 1 tsp salt. Bring to a boil over high heat. Reduce the heat to medium-low, cover partially, and simmer for 20 minutes, or until the farro is tender but still pleasantly chewy. Turn off the heat, cover completely, and let the farro sit for 10 minutes. Fluff with a fork.

Transfer the cooked farro to a large mixing bowl. Add the fennel, grilled peppers, hearts of palm, onion, olives, parsley, and half of the Gorgonzola. Gently fold all the ingredients together.

Remove the garlic clove from the dressing and discard. Pour the dressing over the salad and gently fold to mix. Taste and season with salt and pepper if you like. Spoon the salad into a decorative serving bowl, cover, and let rest for 30 minutes to allow the flavors to mingle. Just before serving, toss gently and sprinkle the remaining Gorgonzola on top.

You can make the farro salad several hours ahead of time and refrigerate it. Remove from the refrigerator 30 to 60 minutes before serving.

COOK'S NOTE: This recipe welcomes improvisation, so feel free to add or omit ingredients to your liking. Use ricotta salata cheese or good Greek Feta in place of the Gorgonzola. Try adding some Grilled Eggplant in Olive Oil (page 261) or Slow-Roasted Tomatoes (page 67), or hard-boiled eggs and good tuna in olive oil.

INSALATA DI RISO

makes 8 servings

Whenever I make this appealingly old-fashioned salad, I feel as though my Zia Gilda were standing right beside me in the kitchen. Rice salad was one of her specialties and her version—a tangy, savory mix of pickled vegetables, hard-boiled eggs, tuna, and more—was the best. She didn't have a recipe and she never made it the same way twice, letting herself be guided by what was in her pantry, but it still always tasted like her *insalata*. Even to my young palate there was something irresistible about the colors, textures, and blend of mellow and assertive of flavors. There still is.

KOSHER OR COARSE SEA SALT

1½ CUPS/315 G ARBORIO, CARNAROLI, OR OTHER SHORT-GRAIN RICE

¼ CUP/60 ML EXTRA-VIRGIN OLIVE OIL

3 HARD-BOILED EGGS, 2 COARSELY CHOPPED AND 1 QUARTERED LENGTHWISE

4 RIZZOLI-BRAND *ALICI IN SALSA PICCANTE* (SEE PAGE 43) OR 4 BEST-QUALITY IMPORTED ITALIAN OR SPANISH ANCHOVY FILLETS IN OLIVE OIL, COARSELY CHOPPED

ROUNDED ½ CUP/70 G FROZEN PEAS, THAWED

ROUNDED ½ CUP/70 G BLANCHED ASPARAGUS SPEARS, CUT CROSSWISE INTO ½-IN/12-MM PIECES; RESERVE TIPS SEPARATELY

½ CUP/85 G COARSELY CHOPPED GIARDINIERA (SEE PAGE 256) OR BOTTLED *GIARDINIERA*

½ CUP/85 G COARSELY CHOPPED SWEET-AND-SOUR CIPOLLINE (PAGE 255) OR BOTTLED COCKTAIL ONIONS

½ CUP/70 G PITTED GAETA OR KALAMATA OLIVES, HALVED CROSSWISE

2 TBSP MINCED FRESH FLAT-LEAF PARSLEY

1 TBSP CAPERS, RINSED, DRAINED, AND COARSELY CHOPPED

¼ CUP/55 G MAYONNAISE

JUICE OF ½ LEMON

1 TBSP WHITE WINE VINEGAR

FINE SEA SALT

FRESHLY GROUND BLACK PEPPER

Bring a medium pot of water to a boil over high heat and salt generously. Pour in the rice and let it come to a boil. Cover and reduce the heat to medium-low or low, and cook the rice at a gentle simmer for 20 minutes or until it is al dente. Drain the rice in a colander and rinse it under cold water to stop the cooking and to cool it. Drain thoroughly and transfer to a large mixing bowl. Add the olive oil and gently toss.

Add the 2 chopped eggs, anchovies, peas, asparagus spear pieces, *giardiniera*, cipolline, olives, parsley, and capers to the bowl. Gently fold until well combined. Add the mayonnaise, and sprinkle in the lemon juice and vinegar. Toss gently but thoroughly. Season with salt, if you like, and a generous grinding of pepper. Toss again.

Transfer the rice to a decorative serving bowl. Arrange the egg quarters and asparagus tips in a decorative pattern on top of the salad. Cover with plastic wrap and let sit for up to 30 minutes to allow the flavors to mingle. If you are not ready to serve the salad at that point, store it in the refrigerator. Remove it 20 minutes before serving.

COOK'S NOTE: You can vary this salad in an infinite number of ways. Italians often add protein to their rice salad in the form of good canned tuna in olive oil, baby shrimp, or sliced hot dogs—which is, believe it or not, a common ingredient in *insalata di riso*! Try sliced cornichons, chopped Grilled Peppers (page 74), or Grilled Eggplant in Olive Oil (page 261).

If you feel like getting fancy, spoon the rice into a deep round mold or mixing bowl and let it chill in the refrigerator for about an hour. To serve, invert the mold onto a serving plate and tap gently to release the mounded rice salad. Decorate the top with the reserved egg wedges and asparagus tips.

chapter 4

PASTA, RISOTTO, GNOCCHI, AND POLENTA

pasta, risotto, gnocchi, e polenta

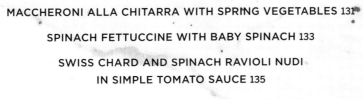

PASTA, RISOTTO, GNOCCHI, AND POLENTA
pasta, risotto, gnocchi, e polenta

Pasta in Italy is not heavily doused with red sauce; in fact, quite the opposite is true. Plenty of sauces contain no tomato at all, but instead are simple sautés of seasonal vegetables and herbs, which are tossed with freshly cooked noodles.

These are the types of pasta dishes that I cook at home and that you will find in this chapter. Maccheroni alla Chitarra with Spring Vegetables (facing page) pays tribute to spring with baby onions, peas, and grassy green fava beans, all tossed with fresh egg pasta. In summer, when tomatoes are in season, I make Ricotta Ravioli (page 137), delicate ricotta-filled ravioli, and spoon a little—not a lot!—of fresh tomato sauce over them.

My mother's spinach lasagne with Bolognese ragù is one of my all-time favorite recipes. Here, the extravagant party dish gets a meatless makeover, with roasted mushrooms, sautéed greens, and cheese layered between thin sheets of spinach noodles.

My daughter, Adriana, adores risotto, so I've included four recipes here—one for each season. And I had to give a shout-out to my son Nick's favorite gnocchi (page 157)—after all, they are made out of potatoes. You can dress them with tomato sauce, or with classic basil pesto—my personal preference.

MACCHERONI ALLA CHITARRA
WITH SPRING VEGETABLES

makes 4 to 5 servings

This dish is an unabashed celebration of spring, with young onions, baby artichokes, grassy green fava beans, and fresh peas front and center. Feel free to bring other young spring vegetables into the fold—asparagus tips or baby spinach leaves, for example. Do take the time to make the fresh chitarra noodles; their light texture really showcases this delicate sauce.

1 LEMON, HALVED

4 BABY ARTICHOKES

KOSHER SALT

1 TBSP UNSALTED BUTTER

1 TBSP EXTRA-VIRGIN OLIVE OIL

3 RED SPRING ONIONS, THINLY SLICED (INCLUDING SOME OF THE GREEN STEMS)

2 TBSP FINELY CHOPPED FRESH HERBS, SUCH AS A MIX OF PARSLEY, MARJORAM, AND MINT

1/4 CUP/60 ML DRY WHITE WINE

1/4 CUP/60 ML VEGETABLE BROTH (PAGE 62) OR BEST-QUALITY COMMERCIAL VEGETABLE BROTH

1 CUP/140 G FRESH OR FROZEN PEAS, THAWED IF FROZEN

4 OZ/115 G ROMAINE LETTUCE, SHREDDED

2 CUPS/280 G SHELLED, BLANCHED, AND PEELED FRESH FAVA BEANS (2 LB/910 G IN THE POD; SEE PAGE 28 FOR INSTRUCTIONS)

1/2 CUP/120 ML HEAVY CREAM

1/2 TSP FINE SEA SALT

FRESHLY GROUND BLACK PEPPER

1 BATCH FRESH EGG PASTA DOUGH (PAGE 55), CUT INTO MACCHERONI ALLA CHITARRA

1/2 CUP/60 G FRESHLY GRATED PECORINO ROMANO CHEESE, PLUS MORE FOR SERVING

Squeeze the lemon halves into a medium bowl filled with cold water. Remove any tough outer leaves from the artichokes. Cut them into quarters and plunge them into the lemon water.

Bring a large pot of water to a boil over high heat and salt generously.

CONTINUED

In a large skillet, warm the butter and olive oil over medium-low heat. When the butter is melted, stir in the onions. Reduce the heat to low and cook slowly for 10 minutes, until the onions are softened. Drain the artichokes and add them to the skillet along with the herbs. Cook, stirring frequently, for about 5 minutes, or until the artichokes are just beginning to turn tender. Reduce the heat to medium-high and pour in the wine. Let it bubble for a minute or so and then pour in the broth. Add the peas and lettuce and toss to combine with the onions and broth. Reduce the heat to medium-low, cover partially, and cook for about 5 minutes, until the lettuce is wilted and the peas are bright green. Add the fava beans and the cream and bring the sauce to a simmer. Season with sea salt and pepper.

Drop the pasta into the pot of boiling water and stir to separate the strands. Cover the pot briefly until the water returns to a boil. Uncover and cook the pasta for about 2 minutes, or until the noodles are al dente (taste one to check for doneness).

Drain the pasta in a colander, reserving about ½ cup/120 ml of the cooking water. Return the pasta to the pot and spoon about two-thirds of the vegetable sauce over it. Toss gently to combine. Add the Pecorino Romano and 1 tbsp of the cooking water and toss again. Transfer the dressed pasta to a warmed serving bowl or individual bowls, and spoon the remaining sauce on top. Serve with additional cheese if you like.

SPINACH FETTUCCINE WITH BABY SPINACH
makes 4 servings

This recipe is my answer to anyone who believes that pasta must be doused in "red sauce"—fresh, emerald-green spinach noodles tossed with baby spinach leaves, butter, and a whisper of nutmeg. Sauce, after all, is a condiment and should enhance the noodles, not obliterate them. If red sauce *is* your thing, you can toss these noodles with a little Fresh Tomato Sauce (page 65) and top with grated Parmigiano—but no dousing!

FINE SEA SALT

4 TBSP/55 G UNSALTED BUTTER

1 SMALL SHALLOT, MINCED

1½ LB/680 G FRESH BABY SPINACH LEAVES

1 BATCH SPINACH PASTA DOUGH (PAGE 58), CUT INTO FETTUCCINE

1 CUP/115 G FRESHLY GRATED PARMIGIANO-REGGIANO CHEESE

SMALL PINCH OF FRESHLY GRATED NUTMEG

FRESHLY GROUND BLACK PEPPER

Bring a large pot of water to a boil over high heat and salt generously.

While the water is heating, melt the butter in a large, deep skillet over medium-low heat. Add the shallot to the skillet and cook, stirring, for 7 minutes, or until softened but not browned. Add the spinach to the skillet by the handful and use tongs to toss and coat the leaves with the butter. Cook briefly—no more than about 2 minutes—until the leaves are just beginning to wilt. Remove from the heat.

Drop the fettuccine into the boiling water and stir to separate the strands. Cover the pot briefly until the water returns to a boil. Uncover and cook the pasta for about 2 minutes, or until the noodles are al dente (taste one to check for doneness).

Drain the pasta in a colander, reserving 1 cup/240 ml of the cooking water. Return the pasta to the pot and pour the spinach–butter sauce over it. Toss gently to combine. Add half of the Parmigiano and the nutmeg, and 1 to 2 tbsp of the cooking water, if necessary, to loosen the sauce, and toss gently. Transfer the dressed pasta to individual shallow bowls and sprinkle a little of the remaining cheese on top of each. Serve immediately.

bietola, spinaci,
farina, pomodori, ricotta, parmi
reggiano, noce moscato

SWISS CHARD AND SPINACH RAVIOLI NUDI IN SIMPLE TOMATO SAUCE

makes 4 to 6 servings

Tender and delicate, these nudi—essentially, ravioli without the pasta covering—make an elegant first course for an early spring or fall dinner, dressed with a simple tomato sauce. They are also delicious served in soup; just boil the nudi as directed, then ladle hot vegetable or chicken broth over them and sprinkle with freshly grated Parmigiano cheese. For some reason, maybe because of their fluffy texture and gentle flavor, these nudi are a hit with children—no cajoling or bribing necessary.

1 LB/455 G SWISS CHARD, STEMS REMOVED AND RESERVED FOR ANOTHER USE (SEE COOK'S NOTE), LEAVES SHREDDED

8 OZ/225 G FRESH SPINACH LEAVES

12 OZ/340 G FRESH SHEEP'S MILK OR WELL-DRAINED COW'S MILK RICOTTA CHEESE

FINE SEA SALT

FRESHLY GROUND BLACK PEPPER

PINCH OF FRESHLY GRATED NUTMEG

3/4 CUP/85 G FRESHLY GRATED PARMIGIANO-REGGIANO CHEESE, PLUS MORE FOR SERVING

2 LARGE EGG YOLKS, LIGHTLY BEATEN

1/4 CUP/30 G FLOUR, PLUS MORE FOR COATING THE NUDI

3 CUPS/720 G FRESH TOMATO SAUCE (PAGE 65), SIMPLE TOMATO SAUCE (PAGE 66), OR SMALL-BATCH TOMATO SAUCE (PAGE 263), HEATED TO A SIMMER

Rinse the shredded chard leaves in cold water. Place the leaves, with the water still clinging to them, into a large saucepan, cover, and set the pan over medium heat. Cook the chard, tossing it from time to time, for 12 to 15 minutes, until tender and most of the water has evaporated. Turn off the heat, and using tongs, transfer the chard to a colander and let it cool. Rinse out the saucepan and return it to the stove.

Rinse the spinach leaves in cold water. Place the leaves, with the water still clinging to them, into the saucepan, cover, and set the pan over medium heat. Cook the spinach, tossing it from time to time with tongs, for 5 minutes, until tender. Remove from the heat and transfer to the colander with the chard to cool.

When the greens are cool enough to handle, squeeze as much excess water from them as you can. Transfer them to a cutting board and chop finely. You should end up with about 1 packed cup of freshly chopped greens weighing between 7 and 8 oz/200 and 225 g.

CONTINUED

CONTINUED

Place the greens in a large bowl and add the ricotta, $\frac{1}{2}$ tsp salt, a generous grinding of pepper, the nutmeg, the Parmigiano, and the egg yolks. Mix together gently but thoroughly. Sprinkle in the flour, and gently fold it into the mixture.

Pour some flour into a small shallow bowl. Have ready a large rimmed baking sheet lined with waxed paper or dusted with flour. With your hands, pinch off a piece of the greens mixture, form it into a ball about the size of a chestnut, roll it in the flour, and set it on the baking sheet. Continue to form the nudi until you have used all of the greens mixture.

Bring a large pot of water to a boil over high heat and salt generously. Carefully drop in 8 to 10 nudi. Within 1 or 2 minutes, they will begin to float to the surface. Continue to cook the nudi for another 5 to 6 minutes, until they have floated to the surface and are puffed up. With a large skimmer, remove the nudi and transfer them to a warmed serving bowl. Spoon about 1 cup of the tomato sauce over the nudi and mix very gently. Continue to cook the nudi until you have cooked them all. When they have all been added to the serving bowl, spoon additional sauce over the top and sprinkle with Parmigiano. Serve immediately.

COOK'S NOTE: I love chard stems, so if the chard I purchase has tough stems, rather than discard them I slice them crosswise, sauté the pieces in a little olive oil until they are softened, and then stir them into the tomato sauce.

RICOTTA RAVIOLI

makes about 50 ravioli; 4 to 6 servings

In Italian, these ravioli are known as *ricotta di magro*. The word *magro* translates to "lean" or "skinny," but what it usually refers to in Italian cooking is a recipe that contains no meat. If you follow Italian blogs or cooking sites, you might see the term *magro* pop up around Lent, a period when many Italian Catholics traditionally refrain from eating meat. I happen to love these pretty, delicate ravioli, dressed simply with tomato sauce, at any time of year, and I'm pretty sure you will, too.

8 OZ/225 G FRESH SHEEP'S MILK OR WELL-DRAINED COW'S MILK RICOTTA CHEESE

3 OZ/85 G FRESH MOZZARELLA CHEESE, DICED

1 CUP/115 G FRESHLY GRATED PARMIGIANO-REGGIANO CHEESE, PLUS MORE FOR SERVING

1 LARGE EGG, LIGHTLY BEATEN

1/4 TSP FINE SEA SALT

SEMOLINA FLOUR FOR DUSTING THE WORK SURFACE

1 BATCH FRESH EGG PASTA DOUGH (PAGE 55)

3 CUPS/720 G FRESH TOMATO SAUCE (PAGE 65), SIMPLE TOMATO SAUCE (PAGE 66), OR SMALL-BATCH TOMATO SAUCE (PAGE 263), HEATED TO A SIMMER

In a medium bowl, stir the ricotta with a fork until smooth. Add the mozzarella, Parmigiano, egg, and salt, and mix thoroughly. Cover the bowl with plastic wrap and refrigerate until ready to use.

Cover a large work surface, such as a kitchen table, with a clean tablecloth and sprinkle the cloth with a light coating of semolina flour: This is where you will put the ravioli once you have made them. Sprinkle a separate work surface with a light coating of semolina flour: This is where you will shape your ravioli. Have on hand a fluted pastry wheel for cutting out the ravioli, a glass of water for wetting your fingers, and a fork for sealing the ravioli.

Cut the ball of pasta dough into four equal pieces and rewrap three pieces. Stretch out the first piece into a long, thin strip about 28 in/71 cm long, 5 in/12 cm wide, and 1/16 in/2 mm thick (see page 56). Carefully lay the dough strip out on the semolina-dusted work surface. Mound about 1 1/2 tsp of the filling at 2-in/5-cm intervals along the length of the center of the strip. Dip a finger in the water and moisten along the bottom edge of the strip and the area around each mound of filling. Carefully fold the strip over lengthwise, gently nudging the mounds as you go so that the dough completely covers the mounds when the top and bottom edges meet. With your fingers, press around

CONTINUED

the mounds to separate and seal them. Use the pastry cutter to cut a square around each mound to make individual square-shaped ravioli (one side will be the folded side of the dough strip).

Once you have finished cutting the ravioli, gather up the dough scraps, press them into a ball, and put them in a plastic bag. Using the fork, press along the open edges of each raviolo to seal securely. Transfer the ravioli to the semolina-dusted tablecloth. Continue to stretch out, fill, and shape the remaining dough pieces, collecting the scraps as you go. Reroll the scraps once to form additional ravioli. You should end up with 50 to 60 ravioli.

Bring a large pot of water to a boil over high heat and salt generously. When the water is boiling, carefully drop the ravioli into the pot—you may need to cook them in two batches to avoid crowding. Cover the pot until the water returns to a boil and then uncover and cook the ravioli for 3 to 5 minutes, until they are just tender. Gently stir the water once or twice to make sure the ravioli do not stick together.

Spoon a little of the heated tomato sauce into the bottom of a warmed serving bowl. Using a skimmer or a large slotted spoon, transfer the cooked ravioli to the bowl. Take care to let the excess water drain off the ravioli before you place them in the bowl. (If you have cooked the ravioli in batches, top the first batch with a little sauce and cover to keep them warm.) Once all the ravioli have been cooked and transferred to the serving bowl, spoon more sauce over them (you may not use it all) and sprinkle Parmigiano cheese on top. Serve immediately.

COOK'S NOTE: The ravioli may be prepared over 2 days. Mix the filling on the first day and store it in the refrigerator overnight, then make the dough and assemble the ravioli the next day. The uncooked ravioli may be frozen for up to 1 month: freeze the ravioli on a large baking sheet in a single layer until firm, then transfer them to ziplock plastic bags or a container with a tight-fitting lid, and return to the freezer.

CARROT-RICOTTA RAVIOLI WITH HERBED BUTTER
makes about 50 ravioli; 4 to 6 servings

I enjoy playing around with traditional Italian recipes—while staying true to the spirit of tradition, of course! This is a riff on classic spinach and cheese ravioli, with puréed carrot filling in (literally) for spinach. The resulting ravioli are beautiful—tender half-moon pillows with a bright orange-gold interior. They are sweet and delicate and need no further adornment than the herbed butter sauce that accompanies them in this recipe. Making homemade ravioli is a project for sure, but I would never call it a chore. Watching the ravioli take shape and multiply as you cut them out is a rewarding experience, though the reward of eating them is even better.

FILLING:

3 LARGE CARROTS (3/4 LB/340 G), PEELED AND CUT INTO 1-IN/2.5-CM CHUNKS

1 TBSP EXTRA-VIRGIN OLIVE OIL

SEA SALT

FRESHLY GROUND BLACK PEPPER

2 TSP UNSALTED BUTTER

1 TBSP MINCED SHALLOT

1 TBSP HEAVY CREAM

5 OZ/140 G FRESH SHEEP'S MILK OR WELL-DRAINED COW'S MILK RICOTTA CHEESE

6 TBSP/45 G FRESHLY GRATED PARMIGIANO-REGGIANO CHEESE

PINCH OF FRESHLY GRATED NUTMEG

1 LARGE EGG YOLK

SEMOLINA FLOUR FOR DUSTING THE WORK SURFACE

1 BATCH FRESH EGG PASTA DOUGH (PAGE 55)

HERBED BUTTER:

1/2 CUP/115 G UNSALTED BUTTER

2 TBSP MIXED MINCED FRESH HERBS, SUCH AS PARSLEY, SAGE, AND MARJORAM

FINE SEA SALT

1/4 CUP/30 G FRESHLY GRATED PARMIGIANO-REGGIANO CHEESE

Heat the oven to 400°F/200°C/gas 6.

TO MAKE THE FILLING: In a baking dish, toss the carrots with the olive oil and season with salt and pepper. Cover with foil and bake for about 30 minutes, until tender and lightly browned. Let cool slightly.

CONTINUED

In a small skillet over medium heat, melt the 2 tsp butter. Add the shallot and cook until softened, about 3 minutes. Remove from the heat and let cool slightly.

In a food processor, combine the carrots, shallot, and cream and purée until smooth. Transfer the purée to a medium bowl. Stir in the ricotta, Parmigiano, and nutmeg and season with salt and pepper. Stir in the egg yolk until thoroughly combined. Cover and refrigerate until needed.

Cover a large work surface, such as a kitchen table, with a clean tablecloth and sprinkle the cloth with a light coating of semolina flour: This is where you will put the ravioli once you have made them. Sprinkle a separate work surface with a light coating of semolina flour: This is where you will shape your ravioli. Have on hand a fluted pastry wheel for cutting out the ravioli, a glass of water for wetting your fingers, and a fork for sealing the ravioli.

Cut the ball of pasta dough into four equal pieces and rewrap three pieces. Stretch out the first piece into a long, thin strip about 28 in/71 cm long, 5 in/12 cm wide, and $\frac{1}{16}$ in/2 mm thick (see page 56). Carefully lay the dough strip out on the semolina-dusted work surface. Mound about $1\frac{1}{2}$ tsp of the filling at 2-in/5-cm intervals along the length of the center of the strip. Dip a finger in the water and moisten along the bottom edge of the strip and the area around each mound of filling. Carefully fold the strip over lengthwise, gently nudging the mounds as you go so that the dough completely covers the mounds when the top and bottom edges meet. With your fingers, press around the mounds to separate and seal them. Use the pastry cutter to cut a half-circle around each mound to make individual half-moon–shaped ravioli (the straight side of the half-moon will be the folded side of the dough strip).

Once you have finished cutting the ravioli, gather up the dough scraps, press them into a ball, and put them in a plastic bag. Using the fork, press along the open edge of each raviolo to seal it securely. Transfer the ravioli to the semolina-dusted tablecloth. Continue to stretch out, fill, and shape the remaining dough pieces, collecting the scraps as you go. Reroll the scraps once to form additional ravioli. You should end up with 50 to 60 ravioli.

TO MAKE THE BUTTER: Bring a large pot of water to a boil over high heat and salt generously. While the water is heating, melt the butter in a small skillet placed over medium-low heat. When the butter begins to sizzle, stir in the herbs and a pinch or two of salt and cook, stirring, for 2 minutes, or until the butter has taken on the flavor of the herbs. Turn off the heat and cover to keep warm.

When the water is boiling, carefully drop the ravioli into the pot—you may need to cook them in two batches to avoid crowding. Cover the pot until the water returns to a boil and then uncover and cook the ravioli for 3 to 5 minutes, until they are just tender. Gently stir the water once or twice to make sure the ravioli do not stick together.

Spoon a little of the herbed butter sauce into the bottom of a warmed serving bowl. Using a skimmer or a large slotted spoon, transfer the cooked ravioli to the bowl. Take care to let the excess water drain off the ravioli before you place them in the bowl. (If you have cooked the ravioli in batches, top the first batch with a little sauce and cover to keep them warm.) Once all the ravioli have been cooked and transferred to the serving bowl, drizzle the remaining herbed butter sauce over them and sprinkle Parmigiano cheese on top. Serve immediately.

COOK'S NOTE: The ravioli may be prepared over 2 days. Mix the filling on the first day and store it in the refrigerator overnight, then make the dough and assemble the ravioli the next day. The uncooked ravioli may be frozen for up to 1 month: Freeze on a large baking sheet in a single layer until firm, then transfer the ravioli to ziplock plastic bags or a container with a tight-fitting lid and return to the freezer.

CAPRICCI WITH SLOW-ROASTED CHERRY TOMATOES AND CREAM

makes 4 servings

In summer, when cherry tomatoes abound at the farmers' market, I almost always have a batch that I have roasted and stored in a container in the fridge. They can be used as a topping for bruschetta, a side dish to grilled chops, or as a sauce for pasta, as I've done here. The cream adds a touch of luxury—and who doesn't deserve a little of that now and then? Capricci is one of the many whimsical pasta shapes now on the market. It isn't always easy to find, and I've seen a couple of different variations. They are either tight coils or tight ruffles, and in either case are excellent at trapping sauce. If you are unable to find them, substitute another short, coiled pasta shape, such as fusilli or gemelli.

1½ LB/680 G CHERRY TOMATOES, HALVED	2 OR 3 FRESH THYME SPRIGS
2 TBSP EXTRA-VIRGIN OLIVE OIL	¾ CUP/180 ML HEAVY CREAM
FINE SEA SALT	1 TBSP COARSELY CHOPPED FRESH BASIL
FRESHLY GROUND BLACK PEPPER	1 LB/455 G DRIED CAPRICCI
2 TBSP UNSALTED BUTTER	1 CUP/115 G FRESHLY GRATED PARMIGIANO-REGGIANO CHEESE
1 SHALLOT, MINCED	

Heat the oven to 275°F/135°C/gas 2.

Arrange the cherry tomatoes cut-side up on a large rimmed baking sheet. Drizzle the oil over them and sprinkle with ½ tsp salt and a grinding of pepper. Roast the tomatoes for 1½ hours, until they are somewhat puckered and shriveled but still juicy.

Bring a large pot of water to a boil over high heat and salt generously.

Heat the butter in a large, deep sauté pan set over medium-low heat. When the butter is melted and has just begun to foam, stir in the shallot. Cook, stirring frequently, until softened but not browned, about 7 minutes. Scrape in the tomatoes and any juices that have collected on the baking sheet. Add the thyme sprigs and pour in the cream. Heat gently to a simmer over low to medium-low heat. Right before dressing the pasta, turn off the heat and stir in the basil.

Add the pasta to the boiling water and cook according to the manufacturer's instructions until al dente. Drain the pasta in a colander, reserving about 1 cup/240 ml of the pasta water. Return the pasta to the pot and spoon two-thirds of the sauce over it. Add ½ cup/60 g of the Parmigiano. Toss gently to combine. Add 1 tbsp of the reserved pasta water, if necessary, to loosen the sauce, and toss again.

Spoon the dressed pasta into a warmed serving bowl or individual bowls. Sprinkle the remaining Parmigiano on top and serve immediately, with the remaining sauce passed at the table.

pomodorini, olio d'oliva, pane
basilico, timo

PENNE RIGATE WITH BLISTERED GREEN PEPPERS

makes 4 servings

I have often used sweet red and yellow peppers, sautéed with onion or garlic, to dress pasta. But a few summers ago, I happened upon a basket of green peppers set out by a vendor at my local farmers' market. Even from several feet away I could smell their sharp, spicy scent. Right then I imagined them already sliced, sautéed until lightly blistered, and tossed with hot cooked pasta and grated sharp cheese. And so a new pasta sauce was born.

2 GARLIC CLOVES, LIGHTLY CRUSHED

1/4 CUP/60 ML EXTRA-VIRGIN OLIVE OIL

1 1/2 LB/680 G GREEN BELL PEPPERS, TRIMMED, SEEDED, AND CUT LENGTHWISE INTO 1/2-IN/12-MM STRIPS

1 TO 2 TSP MINCED FRESH OREGANO

FINE SEA SALT

3 TBSP GOOD-QUALITY AGED BALSAMIC VINEGAR

1 LB/455 G DRIED PENNE

4 OZ/115 HARD, SHARP CHEESE, SUCH AS AGED ASIAGO, AURICCHIO (SEE PAGE 44), OR PECORINO ROMANO, PLUS MORE FOR SERVING

Warm the garlic in the olive oil in a large frying pan over medium-low heat until the garlic is fragrant, about 2 minutes. Press down on the garlic with a wooden spoon or silicone spatula and stir it around briefly in the oil to release its flavor. At this point, you can discard the garlic or leave it in (I generally leave it in). Add the peppers and stir to coat them with the oil. Raise the heat to medium-high and cook, without stirring, for 3 to 4 minutes, until the pepper strips are blistered in places where they are in contact with the bottom of the pan. Stir and continue to cook the peppers until they are softened and blackened in spots, about 20 minutes. Keep the flame lively but take care not to let the peppers burn.

When the peppers are nicely blackened and tender, reduce the heat to medium-low and sprinkle in the oregano and 1/2 tsp salt. Add the vinegar and cook for 2 to 3 minutes, until most of the vinegar has been absorbed.

While the peppers are cooking, bring a large pot of water to a boil over high heat and salt generously. Add the penne rigate and cook according to the manufacturer's instructions until al dente. Drain the pasta in a colander, reserving about 1 cup/240 ml of the pasta water.

Transfer the pasta to a warmed serving bowl and spoon the sauce over it. Toss gently but thoroughly to combine. Sprinkle in the cheese and toss again, adding 1 to 2 tbsp of the pasta water, if necessary, to loosen the sauce and toss again. Serve immediately, with additional cheese on the side.

RICCIOLI WITH PEAS AND PORCINI

makes 4 servings

Riccioli (curls) are a whimsical pasta shape I came across in a wonderful Italian market called Piazza, on Maryland's Eastern Shore. The pasta is tightly coiled like a spring and does a great job of capturing sauce. Classic *pasta e piselli* (pasta with peas) calls for a little bit of prosciutto or pancetta to punch up the flavor, but I find that porcini mushrooms, with their intense, woodsy-smoky taste and meaty texture, fill the role just fine.

1 OZ/30 G DRIED PORCINI MUSHROOMS

1 CUP/240 ML BOILING WATER

2 TBSP EXTRA-VIRGIN OLIVE OIL

1 TBSP UNSALTED BUTTER

3 RED SPRING ONIONS, THINLY SLICED

2 FRESH THYME SPRIGS

¼ CUP/60 ML VEGETABLE BROTH (PAGE 62), OR BEST-QUALITY COMMERCIAL VEGETABLE OR CHICKEN BROTH

2 CUPS/455 G FRESH OR FROZEN PEAS, THAWED IF FROZEN

FRESHLY GROUND BLACK PEPPER

2 TBSP MINCED FRESH FLAT-LEAF PARSLEY

1 LB/455 G DRIED RICCIOLI OR FUSILLI

4 OZ/115 G FRESH SHEEP'S MILK OR WELL-DRAINED COW'S MILK RICOTTA CHEESE, AT ROOM TEMPERATURE

½ CUP/60 G FRESHLY GRATED PARMIGIANO-REGGIANO CHEESE, PLUS MORE FOR SERVING

Put the dried porcini in a small heatproof bowl and pour the boiling water over them. Let stand for 20 to 30 minutes, or until softened. Drain the porcini in a fine-mesh sieve lined with a damp paper towel, reserving the liquid. Chop the mushrooms coarsely and set the mushrooms and liquid aside separately.

In a large skillet, heat the oil and butter over medium heat until the butter begins to foam. Stir in the onions and thyme and cook 7 to 8 minutes, until the onions are softened and translucent but not browned. Add the reserved porcini mushrooms and their liquid and bring to a simmer. Cook until most of the liquid is absorbed, about 3 minutes. Stir in the broth and peas and cook until the peas are bright green and just tender, about 5 minutes. Season with salt and pepper, remove the thyme sprigs, and stir in the parsley.

Bring a large pot of water to a boil over high heat and salt generously. Cook the pasta according to the manufacturer's instructions until al dente. Drain in a colander, reserving about 1 cup/240 ml of the cooking water. Return the pasta to the pot and spoon about two-thirds of the pea and porcini sauce over it. Add the ricotta and Parmigiano and 1 to 2 tbsp of the pasta water, if necessary, to loosen the sauce.

Transfer the dressed pasta to a warmed serving bowl or individual bowls. Serve immediately, with additional Parmigiano, and the remaining sauce passed at the table.

PASTA AL FORNO WITH ROASTED VEGETABLES
makes 6 to 8 servings

The Italian word *ortolana* means someone who grows and sells vegetables, and that is where the inspiration for this recipe derives. Think of a farmers' market in full summer, with bins of colorful summer squashes, eggplants, and tomatoes, all at their peak of flavor. This version is just one of many; in fact, baked pasta is one of those dishes I never seem to make the same way twice. There are just too many tasty variations to play around with. Two ingredients I almost always include, though, are eggplant, for its meaty texture and ability to absorb flavor, and a stretchy cheese such as mozzarella or scamorza. Feel free to improvise with what you find in the market—or in your own garden.

¼ CUP/60 ML PLUS 2 TBSP EXTRA-VIRGIN OLIVE OIL, PLUS MORE FOR THE BAKING DISH

3 MEDIUM ZUCCHINI OR MIXED SUMMER SQUASHES (ABOUT 1 LB/455 G), QUARTERED LENGTHWISE AND THEN CUT CROSSWISE INTO SMALL WEDGE-SHAPED PIECES

1 DARK PURPLE EGGPLANT, SUCH AS VIOLETTA LUNGA, CUT INTO ¾-IN/2-CM DICE

1 RED ONION, HALVED LENGTHWISE AND VERY THINLY SLICED INTO THIN HALF-RINGS

2 GARLIC CLOVES, LIGHTLY CRUSHED

FINE SEA SALT

FRESHLY GROUND BLACK PEPPER

1 LB/455 G DRIED ZITI OR OTHER SHORT STURDY DRIED PASTA SHAPE

3 CUPS/680 G GRATED TOMATOES (SEE PAGE 65) OR CANNED DICED TOMATOES

JUICE OF ½ LEMON

1 LB/455 G ITALIAN SAUSAGES, COOKED AND SLICED INTO COINS (OPTIONAL)

1 LB/455 G ROASTED MUSHROOMS (PAGE 69)

8 OZ/225 G SCAMORZA OR LOW-MOISTURE MOZZARELLA CHEESE, SLICED

½ CUP/60 G FRESHLY GRATED PARMIGIANO-REGGIANO CHEESE

Heat the oven to 425°F/220°C/gas 7. Lightly coat a 9-by-13-in/23-by-33-cm baking dish with olive oil.

Combine the zucchini, eggplant, onion, and garlic in a large roasting pan. Pour ¼ cup/60 ml olive oil over the vegetables and toss to coat them thoroughly. Season with 1 tsp salt and a generous grinding of pepper. Roast the vegetables, stirring them every 15 minutes, for 45 minutes, or until they are tender and nicely browned in spots. Scrape the vegetables into a large mixing bowl.

Reduce the oven temperature to 400°F/200°C/gas 6.

While the vegetables are roasting, bring a large pot of water to a boil over high heat and salt generously. Add the pasta, stir to separate, and cook according to the manufacturer's instructions until not quite al dente. (It should be slightly underdone, because it will finish cooking in the oven.) Drain the pasta in a colander, reserving about 1 cup/240 ml of the cooking water.

Put the tomatoes in a medium bowl and mix in the lemon juice, 1/2 tsp salt, and 2 tbsp olive oil.

Transfer the pasta to a large bowl and toss with the roasted vegetables, the sausage, if using, and the roasted mushrooms. Add 2 cups/480 g of the tomato-lemon mixture and gently toss to combine thoroughly.

Spoon half of the pasta mixture into the prepared baking dish. Spread half of the sliced scamorza over the pasta. Spoon the remaining pasta on top, and cover with the remaining scamorza. Spoon the remaining tomatoes over the scamorza. Sprinkle the Parmigiano on top.

Cover the dish with foil and bake for 20 minutes; uncover and bake 20 minutes more, until the cheese is melted and bubbly and the top is nicely browned and crisp around the edges. Let stand for 5 minutes before serving.

VEGETABLE LASAGNE

makes 8 to 10 servings

Lasagne made from scratch is a labor of love, no question. It requires making numerous components: the sauce, the noodles, the filling—in this case, sautéed greens and roasted mushrooms—and then assembling everything and baking it. Phew! The beauty is that most of the labor can be done ahead of time (see Cook's Note). And then there is the reward. For there is no better feeling than sitting down to a "nice dish" of your own homemade lasagne, as my mother might say. And of course, she is right.

2 TBSP EXTRA-VIRGIN OLIVE OIL, PLUS MORE FOR THE BAKING DISH

2 GARLIC CLOVES, SLICED PAPER-THIN

1 LB/455 G MIXED GREENS, SUCH AS TUSCAN KALE, SWISS CHARD, OR SPINACH

1/2 TSP FINE SEA SALT, PLUS MORE FOR THE PASTA WATER

1 BATCH SPINACH PASTA DOUGH (PAGE 58), CUT INTO LASAGNE NOODLES

1 BATCH SIMPLE TOMATO SAUCE (PAGE 66), HEATED TO A SIMMER

12 OZ/340 G FRESH MOZZARELLA CHEESE, THINLY SLICED

2 CUPS/480 G WELL-DRAINED FRESH COW'S MILK RICOTTA CHEESE

1 CUP/115 G FRESHLY GRATED PARMIGIANO-REGGIANO CHEESE

1 BATCH ROASTED MUSHROOMS (PAGE 69)

4 OZ/115 G FONTINA VAL D'AOSTA, SHREDDED OR THINLY SLICED

Heat the olive oil and garlic in a 10-in/25-cm nonstick skillet placed over low to medium-low heat (I use a well-seasoned cast-iron skillet). Cook, stirring once or twice, for 3 minutes, or until the garlic is softened and fragrant but not browned. Add the kale and chard to the skillet by the handful, using tongs to toss and coat the leaves with the oil. Cover and cook, stirring from time to time, for 15 minutes or until the greens are wilted. Then add the spinach, if using, and salt and toss with tongs. Cook for 5 minutes, or until the spinach is wilted. Raise the heat and cook until the liquid in the pan has evaporated. Transfer the cooked greens to a bowl.

Spread a clean tablecloth on a clean, flat surface near the stove. Have ready the uncooked lasagne noodles, tomato sauce, cooked greens, cheeses, and roasted mushrooms. Place a large bowl filled with ice water near the stove for briefly immersing the cooked lasagne noodles to stop the cooking and to remove excess starch.

Heat the oven to 375°F/190°C/gas 5. Lightly coat a 9-by-13-in/23-by-33-cm baking dish with olive oil.

Bring a large pot of water to a boil over high heat and salt generously. Carefully drop in 4 or 5 lasagne noodles, taking care not to crowd the pot. Boil the pasta for about 1 minute; fresh pasta cooks quickly and the lasagne noodles should be slightly underdone. Use a large skimmer to remove the lasagne noodles from the pot and gently immerse them in the bowl of ice water. Use the skimmer to remove the noodles; let them drip and then spread them on the clean tablecloth. Continue to cook, cool, and spread out the lasagne noodles until you have cooked and cooled all of them.

Spread a thin layer of tomato sauce in the bottom of the prepared baking dish. Arrange a single layer of the lasagne noodles over the sauce. Spread half of the greens over the noodles and dot with half the mozzarella slices and ½ cup/115 g of the ricotta. Sprinkle with 1 tbsp of the Parmigiano.

Then spread a second thin layer of sauce and a second layer of noodles. Spread half the roasted mushrooms over the pasta and dot with half of the Fontina and ½ cup/115 g of the ricotta. Sprinkle with 1 tbsp of the Parmigiano.

Spread a third layer of sauce and noodles. Spread the remaining greens over the pasta and dot with the remaining mozzarella and ½ cup/115 g of the ricotta. Sprinkle with 1 tbsp of the Parmigiano.

Cover with a fourth layer of sauce and noodles. Spread the remaining mushrooms over the noodles and dot with the remaining Fontina and the remaining ricotta. Sprinkle with 1 tbsp of the Parmigiano.

Make one more layer of sauce and noodles. Spread another layer of sauce over the noodles and sprinkle the remaining Parmigiano on top. Cover the dish with aluminum foil.

Bake the lasagne for 20 minutes. Uncover and bake for an additional 20 minutes, or until it is bubbling and the top is nicely browned. Remove the lasagne from the oven and let it sit for 10 minutes before cutting. Cut the lasagne into individual portions, and transfer to shallow rimmed bowls. Serve immediately.

COOK'S NOTE: The lasagne noodles and sauce may be made in advance and frozen for up to 1 month. The greens and the roasted mushrooms may be made in advance and refrigerated for up to 3 days. The assembled lasagne may be stored, unbaked, in the refrigerator for up to 2 days or in the freezer for up to 1 month. If frozen, let it thaw overnight in the refrigerator, and bring to room temperature before baking.

If you do not want to make homemade noodles, you can substitute fresh spinach or egg pasta lasagne noodles, available at gourmet food shops, Italian food stores, and well-stocked supermarkets.

asparagi, olio d'oliva,
vino, cipolle, arborio, sottocenere
foglia di prezzemolo

SPRING RISOTTO WITH
GREEN AND WHITE ASPARAGUS

makes 6 servings

I am not hugely fond of white asparagus, which I have always taken to be a paler version—in color and flavor—of the bright, assertive green variety. But I've started to come around. Good, fresh white asparagus is mild and sweet. Broiling it, as I've done in this recipe, helps to bring out its flavor. The mix of white and green makes for a pretty springtime risotto. You can, of course, use all green or all white asparagus. Either goes nicely with the truffle-scented cheese that is stirred in at the last minute.

8 OZ/225 G GREEN ASPARAGUS

8 OZ/225 G WHITE ASPARAGUS (PEEL OFF ANY TOUGH OUTER SKIN)

3 TBSP EXTRA-VIRGIN OLIVE OIL

FINE SEA SALT

FRESHLY GROUND BLACK PEPPER

1 TBSP UNSALTED BUTTER

1 RED SPRING ONION, DICED (INCLUDING SOME OF THE GREEN STEM)

3 CUPS/645 G ARBORIO, CARNAROLI, OR OTHER SHORT-GRAIN RICE

1/2 CUP/120 ML DRY WHITE WINE

7 TO 8 CUPS/1.7 TO 2 L VEGETABLE BROTH (PAGE 62) OR BEST-QUALITY COMMERCIAL VEGETABLE OR CHICKEN BROTH, HEATED TO A SIMMER

1/2 CUP/60 G FRESHLY GRATED PARMIGIANO-REGGIANO CHEESE

1/2 CUP/60 G SHREDDED SOTTOCENERE AL TARTUFO OR FONTINA VAL D'AOSTA CHEESE

1 TBSP MINCED FRESH FLAT-LEAF PARSLEY

Position an oven rack 4 in/10 cm below the broiler and turn the broiler on.

Arrange the asparagus on a rimmed baking sheet to fit snugly in one layer. Drizzle 2 tbsp of the olive oil over them. Sprinkle a little salt and pepper over them and use your fingers to rotate the spears so they get coated with the oil and seasonings. Broil the asparagus for about 4 minutes, until browned and just tender; check often to prevent the spears from burning. Remove the asparagus from the oven and let them cool slightly. Cut the spears crosswise into bite-size pieces. Transfer to a bowl.

Heat the remaining 1 tbsp oil and the butter in a large, heavy-bottomed pot over medium-low heat. When the butter is melted and begins to sizzle, add the onion and cook, stirring frequently, for 7 minutes, or until softened and translucent. Stir in the rice and 1 tsp salt and cook, stirring, for 2 to 3 minutes, until the rice grains are shiny and glassy-looking. Raise the heat to medium-high and pour in the wine. Let it bubble for a minute or so, until it is almost absorbed.

CONTINUED

Reduce the heat to medium-low and begin to add the broth, a ladleful at a time, stirring frequently, until the liquid is almost absorbed. You do not need to stir the risotto constantly, but be sure that you do stir it often, and take care that the grains do not stick to the bottom of the pot. Continue to cook the risotto and add broth, one or two ladlefuls at a time, for 18 to 20 minutes, until the rice is almost but not completely cooked. It should be al dente—still rather firm and chalky at the center. Check by tasting a few grains.

Gently stir in the asparagus and a little more broth. When the broth has been absorbed, stir in the cheeses and the parsley. Stir in a final ladleful of broth to achieve a creamy texture. The risotto should not be stiff or runny; it should mound softly on a spoon. Taste and season with salt and pepper if you like.

Spoon the risotto into shallow rimmed bowls and serve immediately.

SUMMER RISOTTO WITH ZUCCHINI BLOSSOMS

makes 6 servings

If you really want to make me happy, don't give me roses; give me zucchini flowers. Instead of putting them in water, I'll batter and fry them (see page 38), or toss them with linguine, or stir them into this gentle risotto. We'll open a bottle of Prosecco and toast *Madre Natura* for one of her most ingenious creations, the edible flower.

2 TBSP UNSALTED BUTTER

1 TBSP EXTRA-VIRGIN OLIVE OIL

1 SMALL RED ONION, DICED

3 CUPS/645 G ARBORIO, CARNAROLI, OR OTHER SHORT-GRAIN RICE

FINE SEA SALT

1/2 CUP/120 ML DRY WHITE WINE

7 TO 8 CUPS/1.7 TO 2 L VEGETABLE BROTH (PAGE 62), TOMATO-VEGETABLE BROTH (PAGE 63), OR BEST-QUALITY COMMERCIAL VEGETABLE BROTH, HEATED TO A SIMMER

GENEROUS PINCH OF SAFFRON THREADS

12 TO 15 ZUCCHINI BLOSSOMS, CUT CROSSWISE INTO THICK SHREDS

3/4 CUP/85 G FRESHLY GRATED PARMIGIANO-REGGIANO CHEESE

FRESHLY GROUND BLACK PEPPER

Melt 1 tbsp of the butter and the oil in a large, heavy-bottomed pot over medium-low heat. When the butter is melted and begins to sizzle, add the onion and cook, stirring frequently, for 7 minutes, or until softened and translucent. Stir in the rice and 1 tsp salt and cook, stirring, for 2 to 3 minutes, until the rice grains are shiny and glassy-looking. Raise the heat to medium-high and pour in the wine. Let it bubble for a minute or so, until it is almost absorbed. Reduce the heat to medium-low and begin to add the broth, a ladleful at a time, stirring frequently, until the liquid is almost absorbed. You do not need to stir the risotto constantly, but be sure that you do stir it often, and take care that the grains do not stick to the bottom of the pot. Continue to cook the risotto and add broth, 1 or 2 ladlefuls at a time, for 10 minutes.

In a small bowl, combine the saffron threads and 2 spoonfuls of hot broth and stir until the threads are partially dissolved. Pour the saffron mixture into the risotto. Continue to cook the risotto, adding broth as necessary, for another 8 to 10 minutes, until the rice is almost but not completely cooked. It should be al dente—still rather firm and chalky at the center. Check by tasting a few grains.

Gently stir in the zucchini blossoms and a little more broth. When the broth has been absorbed, stir in the remaining 1 tbsp of butter, the Parmigiano, and few grindings of pepper. Stir in a final ladleful of broth to achieve a creamy texture. The risotto should not be stiff or runny; it should mound softly on a spoon. Taste and season with salt or pepper if you like.

Spoon the risotto into shallow rimmed bowls and serve immediately.

AUTUMN RISOTTO WITH CHANTERELLE MUSHROOMS

makes 4 servings

Diane Morgan is a prolific cookbook author whose topics have ranged from holiday enter-taining to root vegetables. She is also a dear friend who has been the angel on my shoulder from the time I began working on my first cookbook, back in 2004. The only problem is that she lives on the other side of the universe, in Portland, Oregon. Happily, we have social media. One evening I happened to read an update that Diane posted on her Facebook page in which she mentioned she was making risotto with chanterelle mushrooms. I pounced and asked if she wouldn't mind sharing the recipe for this book, and she generously agreed. Fresh chanterelles are elegant and pretty, with a fleshy, ruffled, fan-shaped body and a toasted gold hue. They can be quite expensive, so be sure to save this risotto for someone who really deserves it, like a dear friend!

4 TBSP/55 G UNSALTED BUTTER

8 OZ/225 G CHANTERELLE MUSHROOMS, TRIMMED AND COARSELY CHOPPED (SEE COOK'S NOTE)

FINE SEA SALT

FRESHLY GROUND BLACK PEPPER

1 TBSP EXTRA-VIRGIN OLIVE OIL

2/3 CUP/80 G DICED WHITE ONION

1 1/2 CUPS/315 G ARBORIO, CARNAROLI, OR OTHER SHORT-GRAIN RICE

1 CUP/240 ML DRY WHITE WINE

6 CUPS/1.4 L MUSHROOM BROTH (PAGE 63), VEGETABLE BROTH (PAGE 62), OR BEST-QUALITY COMMERCIAL VEGETABLE OR CHICKEN BROTH, HEATED TO A SIMMER

1/4 CUP/60 ML HEAVY CREAM

1/4 CUP/30 G FRESHLY GRATED PARMIGIANO-REGGIANO CHEESE

2 TBSP FRESH FLAT-LEAF PARSLEY, COARSELY CHOPPED

In a large sauté pan over medium heat, melt 2 tbsp of the butter. Add the mush-rooms and cook, stirring frequently, for 15 minutes, or until the mushrooms are tender and the liquid they release has mostly evaporated. Season lightly with salt and pepper. Set aside.

Heat the remaining 2 tbsp butter and the oil in a large, heavy-bottomed pot over medium-low heat. When the butter is melted and begins to sizzle, add the onion and cook, stirring frequently, for 7 minutes, or until softened and translu-cent. Stir in the rice and 1 tsp salt and cook, stirring, for 2 to 3 minutes, until the grains are shiny and glassy-looking. Raise the heat to medium-high and pour in the wine. Let it bubble a minute or so, until it is almost absorbed.

Reduce the heat to medium-low and begin to add the broth, a ladleful at a time, stirring frequently, until the liquid is almost absorbed. You do not need to stir the risotto constantly, but be sure that you do stir it often, and take care that the rice grains do not stick to the bottom of the pot. Continue to cook the risotto and add broth, 1 or 2 ladlefuls at a time, for 18 minutes, until the rice is almost but not completely cooked. It should be al dente—still rather firm and chalky at the center. Check by tasting a few grains.

Stir in the mushrooms and the cream. Then stir in a final ladleful of broth to achieve a creamy texture. The risotto should not be stiff or runny; it should mound softly on a spoon. Stir in the Parmigiano and parsley. Taste and season with salt and pepper if you like.

Spoon the risotto into shallow rimmed bowls and serve immediately.

COOK'S NOTE: Fresh chanterelles are typically available from late summer and into fall. They can be prohibitively expensive. If you are unable to find them, or would rather not pay the price, you can substitute 8 oz/225 g mixed fresh mushrooms and ¾ oz/20 g dried chanterelles reconstituted in ¾ cup/180 ml water. Save the mushroom liquid and use it for cooking the risotto.

WINTER RISOTTO WITH BUTTERNUT SQUASH AND TUSCAN KALE

makes 4 servings

Whoever coined the phrase "opposites attract" must have had winter squash and Tuscan (or lacinato) kale in mind. One is sweet and smooth and the other is pungent and hearty. And yet, here they are, happily hand in hand in this colorful cold-weather risotto.

3 TBSP EXTRA-VIRGIN OLIVE OIL

1/2 CUP/60 G DICED YELLOW ONION

1 LB/455 G BUTTERNUT SQUASH, PEELED, SEEDED, AND CUT INTO 1/2-IN/12-MM CUBES

8 OZ/225 G TUSCAN KALE, COARSELY SHREDDED

1/2 TSP FINE SEA SALT

2 CUPS/430 G ARBORIO, CARNAROLI, OR OTHER SHORT-GRAIN RICE

1 CUP/240 ML DRY WHITE WINE

5 TO 6 CUPS/1.2 TO 1.4 L VEGETABLE BROTH (PAGE 62) OR BEST-QUALITY COMMERCIAL VEGETABLE OR CHICKEN BROTH

1 TBSP UNSALTED BUTTER

1/2 CUP/60 G FRESHLY GRATED PARMIGIANO-REGGIANO CHEESE, PLUS MORE FOR SERVING

FRESHLY GROUND BLACK PEPPER

Warm the olive oil and the onion in a large Dutch oven or other heavy-bottomed pot over medium-low heat. Cook, stirring often, for 7 to 8 minutes, or until the onion is softened and translucent. Add the squash and kale and toss to coat them with the oil. Sprinkle in the salt. Cover the pot and cook, stirring occasionally, for 15 to 20 minutes, or until the kale is completely wilted and the cubes of squash are just tender.

Stir in the rice and cook, stirring, for 2 to 3 minutes, until the grains are shiny and glassy-looking. Raise the heat to medium-high and pour in the wine. Let it bubble for a minute or so, until it is almost absorbed. Reduce the heat to medium-low and begin to add the broth, a ladleful at a time, stirring frequently, until the liquid is almost absorbed. You do not need to stir the risotto constantly, but be sure that you do stir it often, and take care that the rice grains do not stick to the bottom of the pot. Continue to cook the risotto and add broth, 1 or 2 ladlefuls at a time, for 20 to 25 minutes, until the rice is almost but not completely cooked. It should be al dente—still rather firm and chalky at the center. Check by tasting a few grains. Stir in the butter and cheese. Then stir in a final ladleful of broth to achieve a creamy texture. The risotto should not be stiff or runny; it should mound softly on a spoon. Taste and season with salt and pepper if you like.

Spoon the risotto into shallow rimmed bowls and serve immediately, with additional Parmigiano on the side.

POTATO GNOCCHI WITH FRESH BASIL PESTO

makes 8 servings

The first time my mom made gnocchi was for my dad, many years ago when they were a young couple in New York. More than five decades later, they still talk about those gnocchi and what an epic failure they were—so tough and gluey that my parents ended up going out to dinner that night. Failure in the kitchen does not sit well with my mom, and it wasn't long before she mastered the technique for making gnocchi. Hers are the best—light and tender but with just enough substance so that you don't feel like you're just chewing air. The most important advice my mom offers is to use a light hand, both when you are making the dough and when you are forming the gnocchi. She has another secret, too; she adds a splash of grappa to the dough. The alcohol adds a touch of moisture without promoting the formation of gluten. This, in turn, keeps the dough from developing that dreaded gluey texture. If you don't have grappa on hand, use vodka instead.

In winter, I dress gnocchi with a simple tomato or meat sauce, but in summer I like the bright perfume of fresh basil pesto.

2 LB/910 G RED BLISS AND YUKON GOLD POTATOES, ABOUT 2 LARGE POTATOES OF EACH TYPE

1¾ CUPS/205 G UNBLEACHED ALL-PURPOSE FLOUR, PLUS MORE FOR DUSTING THE WORK SURFACE

1 LARGE EGG, LIGHTLY BEATEN

¾ TSP FINE SEA SALT

1 TBSP GRAPPA OR VODKA (OPTIONAL)

SEMOLINA FLOUR FOR DUSTING THE WORK SURFACE

1 RECIPE FRESH BASIL PESTO (PAGE 64)

½ TBSP UNSALTED BUTTER (OPTIONAL)

FRESHLY GRATED PECORINO ROMANO OR PARMIGIANO-REGGIANO CHEESE FOR SERVING

Put the potatoes in a large pot with cold water to cover by 1 to 2 in/2.5 to 5 cm. Set the pot over medium-high heat and bring to a boil. Cook the potatoes for 25 to 30 minutes, or until they are tender. Drain the potatoes in a colander and let sit until cool enough to handle but still warm.

Peel them, cut them into big pieces, and force them through a ricer onto a clean work surface, forming an airy mound. Sprinkle the flour in a ring around the base of the mound. Make a small well in the center of the mound and carefully pour in the beaten egg. Sprinkle the salt over the egg and pour in the grappa, if using.

Using a fork or your fingers, begin incorporating the egg mixture into the potatoes, working outward and eventually incorporating the flour around the base as well. Knead the mixture lightly until it forms a soft, shaggy ball of dough—it should feel pliant and slightly tacky, and a bit rough rather than smooth. Cover the dough with a clean kitchen towel, and use a dough scraper to clean the work surface, discarding any bits of dough.

CONTINUED

Cover a large work surface, such as a kitchen table, with a clean tablecloth and sprinkle the cloth with a light coating of semolina flour. Or sprinkle semolina on two large, rimmed baking sheets. This is where you will put the gnocchi once you have formed them.

Sprinkle a little all-purpose flour onto the work surface. Slice off a piece of dough about the size of a tangerine and cover the remaining dough. With your palms, lightly roll the dough piece into a rope about 3/4 in/2 cm in diameter. Use the dough scraper or a knife to cut the rope into 1-in/2.5-cm pieces.

Holding a fork in one hand and a small nugget of dough in the other, roll the piece of dough down the curved tines of the fork. Use your index or middle finger to propel it downward and create a small indentation as you press. When you are done, the gnocco should have the ridges from the fork tines on one side and the groove from your finger on the other. These markings are important, as they play a role in helping the gnocchi to cook evenly and trap sauce. Continue to shape the remaining pieces and transfer them to the semolina-dusted tablecloth or baking sheets. Slice, roll, cut, and shape the rest of the dough in the same way.

Bring a very large pot of water to a boil over high heat and salt generously. While the water is heating, put the pesto in a saucepan and set it over very low heat. If the pesto is thick, loosen it with 1 to 2 tbsp of the hot gnocchi cooking water. It should have a thick but pourable consistency. If you want to enrich it a bit, add the butter as well and stir until it is melted.

Gently drop the gnocchi, in batches if necessary to avoid crowding them, into the boiling water. In about 2 minutes, before the water returns to a boil, the gnocchi will begin to float to the surface. Taste one to see if it is done; it should be soft and fluffy but cooked through and not raw-tasting.

Spoon some of the pesto into the bottom of a warmed serving bowl. Use a large skimmer to transfer the gnocchi to the serving bowl. Spoon the remaining pesto over the gnocchi and gently toss to coat them. Sprinkle with a few table-spoons of Pecorino Romano and serve immediately.

COOK'S NOTE: If you are not cooking the gnocchi soon after shaping them, arrange them in one layer on the semolina-dusted baking sheets and freeze for 1 hour or until firm. Transfer them to large ziplock freezer bags or tightly lidded containers and freeze for up to 1 month. Cook them directly from the freezer.

patate, semolina, farina,
pecorino, basilico

POLENTA AL FORNO WITH
SWISS CHARD–TOMATO SAUCE

makes 6 servings

Think of this as a happy mash-up of north and south. Polenta—the hearty cornmeal porridge that is a staple of northern Italy—is baked and then dressed with a Sicilian-inspired sauce of tomatoes simmered with silky chard and golden raisins. What you get is perfect harmony—at least when it comes to dinner.

SWISS CHARD–TOMATO SAUCE:

2 GARLIC CLOVES, SLICED PAPER-THIN

3 TBSP EXTRA-VIRGIN OLIVE OIL

1 LB/455 G SWISS CHARD, ENDS TRIMMED, STEMS CHOPPED, LEAVES CUT CROSSWISE INTO RIBBONS

1/2 TSP FINE SEA SALT

1 PEPPER, CHILE PEPPERS IN OLIVE OIL (PAGE 259), MINCED, OR A GENEROUS PINCH OF RED PEPPER FLAKES

1/4 CUP/40 G SULTANAS (GOLDEN RAISINS)

ONE 28-OZ/800-G CAN DICED TOMATOES

ONE 14-OZ/400-G CAN STEWED TOMATOES

POLENTA:

6 CUPS/1.4 L VEGETABLE BROTH (PAGE 62) OR BEST-QUALITY COMMERCIAL VEGETABLE OR CHICKEN BROTH

1 1/2 CUPS/280 G POLENTA

3 TBSP UNSALTED BUTTER

3/4 CUP/85 G PLUS 2 TBSP FRESHLY GRATED PARMIGIANO-REGGIANO CHEESE

1/2 TO 1 TSP FINE SEA SALT

EXTRA-VIRGIN OLIVE OIL FOR THE BAKING DISH

4 OZ/115 G SHREDDED ASIAGO FRESCO, PECORINO FRESCO, OR OTHER GOOD SHREDDING AND MELTING CHEESE

TO MAKE THE SAUCE: Warm the garlic in the olive oil in a large frying pan set over medium-low heat. Cook until the garlic softens and begins to release its fragrance, about 3 minutes. Stir in the chard stems, raise the heat to medium, and cook until softened, about 5 minutes. Add the chard leaves, cover, and cook until they are wilted, about 5 minutes more. Add the salt and chile pepper and cook, uncovered, until the chard is tender, about 15 minutes. Stir in the sultanas and the diced and stewed tomatoes. Cook, uncovered, at a gentle simmer until thickened, 30 to 40 minutes. Turn off the heat and cover to keep warm.

Heat the oven to 400°F/200°C/gas 6.

TO MAKE THE POLENTA: In a heavy-bottomed saucepan, bring the broth to a boil over medium-high heat. Sprinkle in the polenta in a continuous stream, stirring all the while with a wire whisk to prevent lumps from forming. Reduce the heat to medium and continue to cook the polenta, stirring frequently with a wooden spoon, for 30 to 40 minutes, or until it is thick and pulls away from the sides and bottom of the pan. Add in the butter, 3/4 cup/85 g Parmigiano, and 1/2 tsp salt and stir vigorously until they are well incorporated into the polenta. Taste and adjust the seasoning if you like.

Lightly oil a round or rectangular ovenproof baking dish large enough to hold the polenta. Spread half of the polenta into the baking dish and sprinkle the Asiago fresco over it. Spread the remaining polenta on top and use a silicone spatula to smooth it out. Sprinkle the remaining 2 tbsp of Parmigiano on top. Bake, uncovered, for 20 to 30 minutes, until firm and bubbly. (If you would like to brown the top more, briefly place the baking dish under the broiler.)

Bring the Swiss chard–tomato sauce to a simmer over medium heat and cook just until heated through.

To serve, cut the polenta into wedges or squares and place them in shallow rimmed bowls. Spoon some sauce over each portion and serve.

VARIATION: If you have a batch of Slow-Roasted Tomatoes (page 67) on hand, you can use them in place of the Swiss chard–tomato sauce. Just heat the slow-roasted tomatoes until warmed through and spoon over the baked polenta.

chapter 5

PIZZA, CALZONI, AND PANINI

pizze, calzoni, e panini

PIZZA, CALZONI, AND PANINI
pizze, calzoni, e panini

I do not have a wood-fired oven in my suburban Virginia home, but that doesn't mean I can't make great pizza. My mom made pizza from time to time when I was growing up, and whenever she did the kitchen was perfumed with the warm aroma of the rising dough. Pizza night always seemed a little special to me; it still does.

Dough is an important factor in making good pizza. The basic pizza dough recipe in this chapter yields a crust that is pleasantly yeasty in flavor and light in texture. It is versatile, too, and I use it not only to make pizza in the oven but also calzoni (stuffed pizzas) and pizza on the grill.

The best part about pizza is choosing what to put on it—or, in the case of calzoni (page 174), in it. You can go classic, with tomato and mozzarella (page 166), or elegant, with a savory white topping of roasted fennel and ricotta (page 168). The Roasted Mushrooms (page 69) and Grilled Peppers (page 74) in chapter 1 both make excellent pizza toppings.

In Rome, *pizza al taglio* ("pizza by the slice") is a popular street food. The pizza is baked in large rectangular pans and sold by weight. As a child my all-time favorite *pizza al taglio* was topped with paper-thin slices of potato and rosemary, and on page 167 you'll find my homemade version.

Where there is pizza there is bread, and where there is bread there is the panino, Italy's famed version of the sandwich. In this chapter, you'll find recipes for three hearty panini, piled high with good cheese and your choice of vegetables such as grilled peppers, mushrooms, fresh tomatoes, and fried zucchini blossoms. Ready to take a bite?

PIZZA DOUGH

makes 1½ lb / 680 g

If you have never made homemade pizza dough before, you will be pleasantly surprised at how easy and satisfying it is. The dough is pliable and fun to work with, and it perfumes the kitchen with its yeasty aroma. This recipe is versatile and I use it to make pizza in the oven, stuffed pizza (calzoni), and pizza on the grill.

2¾ CUPS/345 G BREAD FLOUR, PLUS MORE FOR DUSTING THE WORK SURFACE

¼ CUP/35 G SEMOLINA FLOUR

2 TSP RAPID-RISE YEAST

1½ TSP FINE SEA SALT

1 CUP/240 ML WARM WATER (100 TO 110°F/38 TO 43°C)

1 TO 2 TBSP EXTRA-VIRGIN OLIVE OIL, PLUS MORE FOR THE BOWL

Combine the bread flour and semolina flour, yeast, and salt in the work bowl of a food processor. Pulse to combine. With the motor running, drizzle the water and then 1 tbsp of the olive oil through the feed tube and process just until a ball of dough forms. If the mixture seems dry, add an additional 1 tbsp olive oil.

Turn the dough out onto a lightly floured work surface and knead until it is smooth and elastic, 3 to 5 minutes. Form the dough into a smooth ball. Coat the inside of a large ceramic or glass bowl with olive oil. Put the ball of dough in the bowl and turn to coat it completely with the oil. Cover the bowl with plastic wrap.

If you have the time, put the dough in the refrigerator and let it rise slowly for 6 to 8 hours. Otherwise, set it in a warm spot and let it rise until doubled in bulk, about 1½ hours. I find the slow rise in the fridge gives the dough more time to develop flavor and a somewhat chewier texture. But I have made dough both ways and either is fine. If the dough has risen in the refrigerator, remove it and let it come to room temperature before shaping it.

When the dough has doubled in size, turn it out onto a flour-dusted work surface and roll it into a ball. Cover it with a clean kitchen towel and let it sit for 20 to 30 minutes, until lightly puffed. Shape according to the individual recipe.

COOK'S NOTE: If you don't plan to use the dough immediately, wrap it tightly in plastic wrap after it has risen. Put the wrapped dough in a ziplock bag and store it in the refrigerator for 1 day or in the freezer for up to 1 month.

CLASSIC PIZZA
makes 4 to 6 servings

This is the homemade pizza I grew up with. It's not "authentic" Neapolitan pizza, or gooey New York pizza—just my mom's simple baked-in-a-pan pizza topped with tomato sauce and mozzarella. There are infinite ways to customize it with different toppings—Roasted Mushrooms (page 69), Sweet-and-Sour Eggplant Salad (page 92), or caramelized onions (see page 85) are but a few choices. You can vary the cheeses, too, substituting smoked mozzarella for fresh, or sprinkling shredded Fontina or Asiago fresco on top. This pizza is best fresh, though my husband has been known to polish off leftovers for breakfast.

1½ CUPS/360 G CANNED DICED TOMATOES

3 TBSP EXTRA-VIRGIN OLIVE OIL, PLUS MORE FOR THE BAKING SHEET

1 GARLIC CLOVE, LIGHTLY CRUSHED

5 FRESH BASIL LEAVES, SHREDDED

FINE SEA SALT

1 BATCH PIZZA DOUGH (PAGE 165), RISEN AND READY TO SHAPE

SEMOLINA FLOUR FOR DUSTING THE WORK SURFACE

12 TO 16 OZ/340 TO 455 G FRESH MOZZARELLA CHEESE, THINLY SLICED

Combine the tomatoes, 3 tbsp olive oil, garlic, basil, and ¼ tsp salt in a medium bowl. Let sit for 30 minutes or longer to allow the flavors to mingle.

Heat the oven to 500°F/260°C/gas 10.

Generously coat a 12-by-17-in/30.5-by-43-cm rimmed baking sheet with olive oil. With oiled fingers, gently stretch and press the dough out toward the rim. This will take a little while, since the dough will want to spring back toward the center. Let it rest for a few minutes and then continue to stretch and press the dough until it reaches the rim.

Spoon the tomato sauce evenly over the dough, leaving a 1-in/2.5-cm border. Arrange the mozzarella slices on top of the sauce. Bake the pizza for about 17 minutes, or until the cheese is melted and brown in spots and the crust is lightly crisp and puffed up around the edges.

Remove from the oven and let it rest for 5 minutes before cutting into rectangles and serving.

POTATO PIZZA

makes 4 to 6 servings

My three aunts—my mother's sisters—lived in a beautiful apartment in Rome not far from the city's largest park, Villa Ada. In summers, when we stayed with them, my sister and I would spend the morning playing at the park—I have a fuzzy memory of bumper cars and a giant slide. Sometimes, on the way home, we stopped at a place that sold *pizza al taglio*—pizza by the slice. There were all sorts of toppings—artichokes, eggplant, mushrooms, peppers—but our favorite was the crispy potato pizza. The flat baked dough was covered with a thin layer of sliced potatoes and seasoned simply with salt and rosemary. Here is my home version of one of my all-time favorite pizzas.

1 TBSP FINE SEA SALT

3 MEDIUM RED POTATOES, ABOUT 1½ LB/680 G

EXTRA-VIRGIN OLIVE OIL FOR THE BAKING SHEET AND FOR DRIBBLING

1 BATCH PIZZA DOUGH (PAGE 165), RISEN AND READY TO SHAPE

1 ROUNDED TBSP FRESH ROSEMARY LEAVES

COARSE SEA SALT

FRESHLY GROUND BLACK PEPPER

3 TO 4 OZ/85 TO 115 G SMOKED GOUDA CHEESE, SHREDDED

Dissolve the fine sea salt in a bowl of tepid water. Remove any eyes or blemishes from the potatoes but leave the skins on. Slice them very thinly—less than ⅛ in/ 3 mm thick. I use a mandoline for this task, but a sharp chef's knife will also do the job. Immerse the potato slices in the water as you go, which will keep them from turning brown. Soak the potatoes for about 1 hour, until they lose their crispness. Drain them in a colander, and then spread them out on a clean kitchen towel. Cover with another clean towel and pat dry.

Heat the oven to 500°F/260°C/gas 10.

Generously coat a 12-by-17-in/30.5-by-43-cm rimmed baking sheet with olive oil. With oiled fingers, gently stretch and press the dough toward the rim. This will take a little while, since the dough will want to spring back toward the center. Let it rest for a few minutes and then continue to stretch and press the dough until it reaches the rim.

Arrange the potato slices in rows on top of the dough, overlapping them slightly; leave a 1-in/2.5-cm border of dough. Dribble a little olive oil over the potatoes and use your fingers to coat them lightly with the oil. Sprinkle the rosemary leaves on top of the potatoes. Season the pizza with coarse sea salt and pepper. Scatter the cheese on top.

Bake the pizza for about 20 minutes, or until the cheese is melted and the potatoes and crust are browned and crisp.

Remove from the oven and let it rest for 5 minutes before cutting into rectangles and serving.

PIZZA BIANCA WITH ROASTED FENNEL
makes 4 to 6 servings

This pizza may not bear the name of Italy's onetime queen Margherita; that distinction belongs to the classic Neapolitan wood-fired tomato, mozzarella, and basil pie. But in my opinion it is no less worthy. The crispy-chewy crust is topped with sweet caramelized fennel, creamy cheese, and salty bits of pancetta. A royal combination if ever there was one, and I did sort of feel like I deserved a tiara after I came up with it.

4 TBSP/60 ML EXTRA-VIRGIN OLIVE OIL PLUS MORE FOR THE PIZZA PAN

FINE SEA SALT

FRESHLY GROUND BLACK PEPPER

1 BATCH PIZZA DOUGH (PAGE 165), RISEN AND READY TO SHAPE

4 OZ/115 G WELL-DRAINED FRESH COW'S MILK RICOTTA CHEESE

4 OZ/115 G FRESH MOZZARELLA CHEESE, THINLY SLICED

1 BATCH ROASTED FENNEL (PAGE 68) MADE WITH 2 FENNEL BULBS

2 OZ/55 G PANCETTA, DICED (OPTIONAL)

COARSE SEA SALT

Heat the oven to 500°F/260°C/gas 10.

Generously coat a 13- or 14-in/33- or 35.5-cm round pizza pan or a 12-by-17-in/30.5-by-43-cm rimmed baking sheet with olive oil. With oiled fingers, gently stretch and press the dough out toward the rim. This will take a little while, since the dough will want to spring back toward the center. Let it rest for a few minutes and then continue to stretch and press the dough until it reaches the rim.

In a small bowl, combine the ricotta with 1 tbsp olive oil and stir until smooth. Spoon little dollops of ricotta evenly over the dough, leaving a 1-in/2.5-cm border. Arrange the mozzarella slices over the top. Spread the roasted fennel over the cheeses and scatter the pancetta, if using, on top. Season the pizza with coarse sea salt and pepper.

Bake the pizza for about 20 minutes, or until the cheese is melted and beginning to bubble, the fennel is browned at the edges, and the crust is browned and crisp. Remove from the oven and let it rest for 5 minutes before slicing and serving.

finocchio, olio, sale, ricotta,
mozzarella, pancetta

GRILLED PIZZAS
makes 4 individual pizzas

Yes, a certain agility is required to successfully grill pizza. But the technique is not difficult to master, and it's worth the effort. For nothing beats a deliciously crisp-charred, hot-off-the-grill pizza on a summer night. Following are instructions for how to make pizzas on the grill, plus a selection of toppings from which you and your fellow *pizzaioli* (pizza makers) can choose. Although you may want to shower your pizza with all sorts of toppings, it would be best to limit yourself to three, or at most four—one cheese, plus two or three other toppings. Otherwise you will end up with a soggy, droopy affair instead of an artful balance of bread and toppings.

VEGETABLE OIL FOR THE GRILL GRATE

SEMOLINA OR ALL-PURPOSE FLOUR FOR DUSTING

1 BATCH PIZZA DOUGH (PAGE 165), RISEN AND READY TO SHAPE

CHEESE, 1/2 CUP/115 G SHREDDED CHEESE PER PIZZA (SEE LIST, FACING PAGE)

VEGETABLES, SMALL AMOUNT OF TWO OR THREE SELECTIONS PER PIZZA (SEE LIST, FACING PAGE)

HERBS AND VEGETABLES, SMALL AMOUNTS TO SPRINKLE, FOR SERVING (SEE LIST, FACING PAGE)

EXTRA-VIRGIN OLIVE OIL FOR BRUSHING THE DOUGH

FINE SEA SALT (OPTIONAL)

Prepare a hot charcoal grill or preheat a gas grill to high. If you are using charcoal, spread the hot coals across half of the bottom of the grill and leave the other half clear to create a cool zone. If you are using gas, turn one of the burners to low. Lightly oil the grill grate with vegetable oil.

Have ready a large baking sheet lightly dusted with flour. Place the ball of pizza dough on a flour-dusted work surface. Cut it into quarters and reshape so that you have four balls of dough. Cover three of the balls with a clean kitchen towel. Using your hands or a rolling pin, roll and stretch the remaining piece of dough into a circle about 10 in/25 cm in diameter and 1/4 in/6 mm thick.

Carefully transfer the rolled-out dough to the baking sheet and lay a sheet of parchment paper over it. Roll out the remaining pieces of dough in the same way, and stack them on the baking sheet between sheets of parchment.

Have all of your topping selections ready. Brush one side of a dough disk with olive oil and place it, oiled-side down, on the hot part of the grill. Grill for about 2 minutes—just until it has puffed and begun to turn crispy and is slightly charred on the underside. Use tongs and a wide spatula (or a pizza peel if you have one) to flip the dough to the cool side of the grill.

Top the pizza with a selected cheese and a judicious amount of other ingredients (for example, tomato slices and a scattering of olives, or grilled peppers and red onions). Return the topped pizza to the hot side of the grill for 30 to 60 seconds, until the bottom is browned. Slide the pizza back to the cool side, close the grill, and grill for 3 minutes, or until the cheese has melted.

Using wide spatulas, carefully lift the pizza off the grill and transfer it to a large plate. Keep the pizza warm in an oven set to 225°F/110°C, if you like, while you grill the remaining pizzas. Just before serving, scatter a few leaves of basil, arugula, or spinach on top of the pizza and finish with a drizzle of olive oil and a sprinkle of salt.

TOPPING OPTIONS:

CHEESE TOPPINGS:

FRESH MOZZARELLA, THINLY SLICED

CAPRINO (FRESH GOAT CHEESE)

SCAMORZA OR SMOKED SCAMORZA, THINLY SLICED OR SHREDDED

VEGETABLE TOPPINGS:

RIPE TOMATOES, THINLY SLICED

RED ONION, THINLY SLICED

GRILLED EGGPLANT IN OLIVE OIL (PAGE 261)

SWEET-AND-SOUR EGGPLANT SALAD (PAGE 92)

ROASTED MUSHROOMS (PAGE 69)

GRILLED PEPPERS (PAGE 74)

GAETA OR KALAMATA OLIVES

VEGETABLE TOPPINGS FOR GARNISHING THE GRILLED, HOT PIZZA:

HANDFUL OF FRESH BASIL LEAVES, WHOLE OR SHREDDED

ARUGULA LEAVES

FRESH BABY SPINACH LEAVES

rucola, cipolle, peperoni, semolina, scamorza, caprino, fou

CALZONI WITH THREE FILLINGS

makes 4 calzoni

Leave it to the ingenious Neapolitans to give the world not only pizza, but also stuffed pizza. For that is what a calzone is—pizza dough folded around a rich, cheesy filling. Calzoni are easy to make and a great way to get children into the kitchen—what kid doesn't love to handle pizza dough? The hard part is choosing a filling. Here I've included options for three of my favorites—sautéed rapini and scamorza; roasted mushroom and Fontina; and grilled peppers, prosciutto, and ricotta. Choose one of these or make up your own.

EXTRA-VIRGIN OLIVE OIL FOR THE BAKING SHEETS AND BRUSHING THE DOUGH

1 BATCH PIZZA DOUGH (PAGE 165), RISEN AND READY TO SHAPE

BREAD FLOUR OR UNBLEACHED ALL-PURPOSE FLOUR FOR DUSTING THE WORK SURFACE

ONE OF THE THREE FILLING OPTIONS (SEE FACING PAGE)

1 LARGE EGG, LIGHTLY BEATEN

Heat the oven to 400°F/200°C/gas 6. Lightly oil two large rimmed baking sheets.

Place the ball of pizza dough on a flour-dusted work surface. Cut it into quarters and reshape so that you have four balls of dough. Cover three of the balls with a clean kitchen towel. With lightly oiled fingers, stretch and press the remaining ball into a 9-in/23-cm circle.

Layer one-fourth of the filling ingredients on one-half of the dough circle. Brush a little beaten egg around the edges of the circle and fold the dough over the filling to form a half-moon shape. Press the edges to seal, and then roll them to create a rolled seam. Brush a little olive oil on top of the calzone. With a sharp knife, make 2 or 3 slashes on top of the calzone to let steam escape during baking. Use a pizza peel, if you have one, or two large spatulas to carefully transfer the calzone to one of the oiled baking sheets. Leave enough room for a second calzone.

Form the remaining three calzoni in the same way, and transfer them to the oiled baking sheets (two calzoni per baking sheet). Bake the calzoni for 25 to 30 minutes, until they are golden-brown on top and along the edges. Remove from the oven and let rest for 5 to 10 minutes before serving.

FILLING OPTIONS:

RAPINI AND SCAMORZA FILLING:

1 BATCH SAUTÉED RAPINI (PAGE 75)

8 OZ/225 G SCAMORZA, SMOKED SCAMORZA, OR SMOKED MOZZARELLA CHEESE, THINLY SLICED

4 OZ/115 G FRESH MOZZARELLA CHEESE, THINLY SLICED

MUSHROOM AND FONTINA FILLING:

1 BATCH ROASTED MUSHROOMS (PAGE 69)

8 OZ/225 G FONTINA VAL D'AOSTA, THINLY SLICED

4 OZ/115 G FRESH MOZZARELLA CHEESE, THINLY SLICED

PEPPERS, RICOTTA, AND PROSCIUTTO FILLING:

1 BATCH GRILLED PEPPERS (PAGE 74)

8 THIN SLICES (8 OZ/225 G) PROSCIUTTO DI PARMA

8 OZ/225 G WELL-DRAINED FRESH COW'S MILK RICOTTA CHEESE

4 OZ/115 G FRESH MOZZARELLA CHEESE, THINLY SLICED

ZUCCHINI BLOSSOM, TOMATO, AND MOZZARELLA PANINO

makes 1 panino

It isn't often that we have leftover fried zucchini blossoms at our house. They are usually the first things to disappear when I make them. But one day it happened, a few stragglers remained on the platter (I must have fried *a lot*). I wrapped them in plastic and put them in the fridge. The following day, I made myself this spectacular sandwich, colorfully layered with slices of ripe summer tomato, creamy mozzarella, and fried squash blossoms. Now I fry zucchini blossoms expressly for this purpose and serve the sandwiches for dinner in late summer, when the flowers are abundant and when tomatoes are at their best.

1 FRESH CIABATTA ROLL OR OTHER ITALIAN COUNTRY ROLL

1 TBSP BEST-QUALITY EXTRA-VIRGIN OLIVE OIL

2 TSP AGED BALSAMIC VINEGAR

1 SMALL TO MEDIUM RIPE SUMMER TOMATO, THINLY SLICED

COARSE SEA SALT

2 OZ/55 G FRESH MOZZARELLA CHEESE, SLICED

4 OR 5 FRIED ZUCCHINI BLOSSOMS (PAGE 38)

1 OR 2 BASIL LEAVES, TORN (OPTIONAL)

Slice the ciabatta roll in half horizontally and set cut-side up on the work surface. In a small bowl, whisk together the olive oil and vinegar and drizzle it over both slices. Arrange the tomato slices on the bottom half of the roll and season with a pinch of salt. Top with the mozzarella slices and then the zucchini blossoms. Sprinkle the basil leaves on top, if using. Place the upper half of the roll on top and press down gently for just a few seconds to lightly compress the sandwich. Cut the panino in half, and eat with pleasure.

fiore de zucca, mozzarella, pomodori, basilico

ROASTED PEPPER, CAPRINO, AND COPPA PANINO

makes 1 panino

This is the panino to take on a picnic, whether you're headed for the countryside, the seashore, or your local city park. It's a hearty sandwich, practically a meal in itself—with tangy goat cheese, silky sweet grilled peppers, and, as if that weren't enough, hot, spicy coppa. You need only to uncork a bottle of chilled Prosecco and let the al fresco dining begin.

1 TBSP EXTRA-VIRGIN OLIVE OIL

1 TO 2 TSP AGED BALSAMIC VINEGAR

1 SMALL GARLIC CLOVE, LIGHTLY CRUSHED

1 GRILLED PEPPER (SEE PAGE 74), CLEANED, SEEDED, AND CUT INTO STRIPS; OR 1 TO 2 BOTTLED ROASTED PEPPERS, CUT INTO STRIPS

2 TBSP CAPRINO (FRESH GOAT CHEESE) (SEE PAGE 44)

1 FRESH CIABATTA ROLL OR OTHER ITALIAN COUNTRY ROLL, OR 2 THICK SLICES ITALIAN COUNTRY BREAD

1 OZ/30 G HOT COPPA (SEE PAGE 46), THINLY SLICED

In a small bowl, mix together the oil and vinegar. Drop in the garlic clove and stir in the pepper strips. Let them steep for a while—up to 1 hour.

Spread the caprino cheese on the inside of the bottom half of the roll or one slice of bread. Top with the sliced coppa. Mound the peppers on top of the coppa and spoon the dressing over them. Cover with the top half of the roll or second slice of bread, and press down gently to compress the sandwich. Cut the panino in half. Now comes the best part: take a bite.

GRILLED PORTOBELLO PANINI

makes 4 panini

Portobello mushrooms may lack the rich, woodsy flavor of Italian porcini, but they have an appealing, firm texture and are really good grilled. Topped with a slice of sharp cheese and dressed with a little balsamic mayonnaise, they make a satisfying sandwich.

1/2 CUP/120 ML MAYONNAISE	FINE SEA SALT
1 TSP FRESHLY SQUEEZED LEMON JUICE	FRESHLY GROUND BLACK PEPPER
2 TSP PLUS 2 TBSP AGED BALSAMIC VINEGAR	4 FRESH CIABATTA ROLLS OR OTHER ITALIAN COUNTRY ROLLS, SPLIT HORIZONTALLY
1/3 CUP/75 ML EXTRA-VIRGIN OLIVE OIL	
1 GARLIC CLOVE, LIGHTLY CRUSHED	FOUR 1-OZ/30-G SLICES PROVOLONE OR SMOKED PROVOLONE CHEESE
4 LARGE PORTOBELLO MUSHROOM CAPS, ABOUT 4 IN/10 CM IN DIAMETER	HANDFUL OF ARUGULA LEAVES

In a small bowl, whisk together the mayonnaise, lemon juice, and 2 tsp of the vinegar. Cover and refrigerate until ready to use.

In another small bowl, whisk together the oil and the 2 tbsp vinegar. Drop in the garlic clove and let the mixture steep for 30 minutes.

Prepare a medium-hot charcoal grill or heat a gas grill to medium-high. Alternatively, position an oven rack 4 in/10 cm from the broiler and turn the broiler on.

Using a small paring knife, scrape away the brown gills on the underside of the portobello caps. Brush the oil and vinegar mixture on both sides of the caps, coating them well. Lightly season them with salt and pepper. Grill the caps for 2 to 3 minutes, until browned and lightly charred on the bottom; turn and grill for another 2 to 3 minutes, until browned. If broiling, put the caps in a broiler pan. Broil the caps for 2 to 3 minutes, until browned on top; turn and broil the other side for another 2 to 3 minutes.

Spread the balsamic mayonnaise on the cut sides of the rolls. Place a warm portobello on each bottom half of the rolls and top with a slice of Provolone cheese. Place a small mound of the arugula leaves on top of the cheese. Cover with the top halves of the rolls and press down gently. Enjoy while still warm.

chapter 6

MAIN COURSES

secondi

MAIN COURSES
secondi

My brother-in-law John stopped eating meat for a few years. He gave it up for Lent one year and kept on going. I enjoyed having him over to dinner because it gave me an opportunity to cook creatively rather than fall back on the usual dinner party roast. Grilled Summer Vegetables alla Parmigiana (page 194) and Crêpe Cannelloni with Mushrooms and Zucchini (page 189) are just two of my favorite vegetarian entrées that came into being thanks to John.

A couple of years ago John went back to eating meat—he was done in by a beef burrito. But I still cook a lot of vegetarian dinners for my family. Frittatas and vegetable tarts, such as the pretty Asparagus and Ricotta Tart on page 185, make frequent appearances on weeknights. And no one complains about the absence of meat when a beautiful dish of baked jumbo shells, bubbly and brown on top and filled with Swiss chard and three kinds of cheese, arrives at the table.

On the other hand, we do eat meat and seafood at our house. I make an effort to support the farmers in my area by buying locally raised and processed meat, and when buying seafood I look for varieties that have not been overfished and that are sustainably farmed. Over the years, these practices have become increasingly important to me as a consumer.

I am especially fond of dishes that bring meat—or seafood, for that matter—and vegetables together harmoniously, one complementing the other. So at the end of the chapter, I have included a sampling of those types of dishes: Clam Stew with Greens and Tomatoes (page 205); Chicken Thighs Braised with Escarole (page 208); and Grilled Lamb Spiedini on a Bed of Caponata (page 209).

TUSCAN KALE FRITTATA

makes 4 servings

A vegetable frittata of one kind or another has saved dinner at my house more times than I can count. It's especially true of this version, featuring Tuscan kale, a nutritious member of the cabbage family with dark, slender, crinkled leaves and a rich, sweet flavor that contrasts nicely with the sharp Pecorino Romano cheese. In winter, I like to serve this dish with a side of sautéed or Roasted Mushrooms (page 69)—though sometimes the mushrooms end up in the frittata instead.

¼ CUP/60 ML EXTRA-VIRGIN OLIVE OIL	1 TSP FINE SEA SALT
3 GARLIC CLOVES, SLICED PAPER-THIN	8 LARGE EGGS
8 OZ/225 G TUSCAN KALE, CUT CROSSWISE INTO WIDE STRIPS	½ CUP/60 G FRESHLY GRATED PECORINO ROMANO CHEESE

Heat the olive oil and garlic in a 10-in/25-cm broiler-proof nonstick skillet placed over low to medium-low heat (I use a well-seasoned cast-iron skillet). Cook, stirring once or twice, for 3 minutes, or until the garlic is softened and fragrant but not browned. Add the kale to the skillet by the handful, using tongs to toss and coat the leaves with the oil. Cover and cook, stirring occasionally, for about 20 minutes or until the kale is completely wilted, tender, and deep green-black in color. Season with ½ tsp of the salt.

Position an oven rack 4 to 6 in/10 to 15 cm from the broiler and turn the broiler on.

In a medium bowl, whisk together the eggs, Pecorino Romano, and the remaining ½ tsp of salt. Slowly pour the egg mixture over the greens. Cook the eggs without stirring for 8 minutes, or until the top is almost set. You may need to adjust the heat if the bottom is browning too quickly.

Transfer the skillet to the broiler and broil for 3 minutes, or until the top of the frittata is browned. Check often to make sure it does not burn. Remove the frittata from the oven and let it sit for 1 or 2 minutes.

Using a spatula that won't scratch the pan, coax the frittata out of the skillet and transfer it to a serving platter. Serve hot, warm, or at room temperature.

ZUCCHINI BLOSSOM AND RICOTTA FRITTATA

makes 4 servings

I used to have to search high and low for zucchini blossoms. Nowadays, farmers' markets across the country carry them, packed in little baskets in tidy ruffled rows. One day, while playing around with this recipe, I arranged the lightly sautéed blossoms into the shape of a flower in the skillet and poured the eggs over them. The finished frittata was *almost* too pretty to eat. Serve this warm or at room temperature, with a juicy, high-summer tomato salad on the side.

¼ CUP/60 ML EXTRA-VIRGIN OLIVE OIL

2 GARLIC CLOVES, MINCED

12 ZUCCHINI BLOSSOMS OR OTHER SUMMER SQUASH BLOSSOMS, GENTLY RINSED AND PATTED DRY

6 LARGE EGGS, LIGHTLY BEATEN

8 OZ/225 G FRESH SHEEP'S MILK OR WELL-DRAINED COW'S MILK RICOTTA CHEESE

½ TSP FINE SEA SALT

FRESHLY GROUND BLACK PEPPER

1 TBSP MINCED FRESH BASIL

Position an oven rack 4 to 6 in/10 to 15 cm from the broiler and turn the broiler on.

Heat the olive oil and garlic in a 10-in/25-cm broiler-proof nonstick skillet placed over low to medium-low heat (I use a well-seasoned cast-iron skillet). Cook, stirring often, for 3 minutes, or until the garlic is softened and fragrant but not browned. Add the zucchini blossoms and toss gently to coat them with oil. Cook gently until the blossoms are just wilted, no more than 5 minutes. Using a fork or tongs, gently arrange the blossoms in a flower shape with the stem ends toward the center of the skillet and their petals flared out.

In a medium bowl, whisk together the eggs, ricotta, the salt, a grinding of pepper, and the basil. Slowly pour the egg mixture over the blossoms. Cook the eggs without stirring for 8 minutes, or until the top is almost set.

Transfer the skillet to the broiler and broil for 3 minutes, or until the top of the frittata is browned. Check often to make sure it does not burn. Remove the frittata from the oven and let it sit for 1 or 2 minutes.

Using a spatula that won't scratch the pan, coax the frittata out of the skillet and transfer it to a serving platter. Serve hot, warm, or at room temperature.

ASPARAGUS AND RICOTTA TART

makes 4 to 6 servings

Torte salate, or savory vegetable tarts, abound in Italian home cooking, and like so much of the country's cuisine, they tend to follow the seasons. In spring, I make this simple asparagus tart, sometimes for dinner, sometimes for Sunday brunch, and serve it with good bread and a salad of lightly dressed baby greens.

1 LB/455 G ASPARAGUS

1 TBSP UNSALTED BUTTER

1 TO 2 TBSP EXTRA-VIRGIN OLIVE OIL

1/2 CUP/60 G DICED WHITE ONION

FINE SEA SALT

FRESHLY GROUND BLACK PEPPER

4 OZ/115 G FRESH SHEEP'S MILK OR WELL-DRAINED COW'S MILK RICOTTA CHEESE

1/2 CUP/120 ML HEAVY CREAM

3 LARGE EGGS, LIGHTLY BEATEN

2 OZ/60 G PECORINO FRESCO OR OTHER TANGY SEMISOFT SHEEP'S MILK CHEESE, SHREDDED

FLOUR FOR DUSTING THE WORK SURFACE

1 BATCH FLAKY PASTRY DOUGH (PAGE 60)

Remove the tough stem ends from the asparagus. Set aside 4 whole trimmed asparagus spears. Cut the remaining spears crosswise into 1/2-in/12-mm pieces.

Melt the butter in the oil in a large skillet over medium heat. When the butter is melted and begins to sizzle, stir in the onion and reduce the heat to medium-low. Cook, stirring frequently, for 7 to 8 minutes, or until the onion is softened and translucent. Add the asparagus pieces and sprinkle with 1/2 tsp salt and a grinding of pepper. Cook, stirring occasionally, for 5 minutes, or until the pieces of asparagus are bright green and just tender. Transfer the asparagus pieces to a bowl and set aside. If the skillet is dry, pour in 1 tbsp of olive oil. Add the whole spears to the skillet and cook, turning them a few times, for 5 minutes, or until they are just tender. Transfer them to a plate and set aside.

Heat the oven to 375°F/190°C/gas 5.

Put the ricotta in a large bowl and stir with a fork until it is creamy. Add the cream and stir until well combined. Gently whisk in the eggs and pecorino fresco and season with 1/4 tsp salt and a grinding of pepper.

CONTINUED

On a lightly floured work surface, roll the dough out into an 11-in/28-cm circle. Carefully wrap the dough around the rolling pin and drape it over a 9-in/23-cm round fluted tart pan with a removable bottom. Gently press the dough into the bottom of the pan and up the sides. Trim the overhang to about 1/2 in/12 mm and fold it in, pressing it against the inside rim to reinforce the sides of the tart shell. Use the rolling pin or the palm of your hand to press around the perimeter of the pan to cut off any excess dough. Place the tart pan on a rimmed baking sheet.

Spread the asparagus pieces on the bottom of the tart shell. Pour the ricotta mixture over the asparagus. Arrange the 4 whole asparagus spears in a decorative pattern on top of the tart—I arrange them in a diamond pattern with the spears slightly overlapping.

Bake the tart for 45 minutes, or until it is puffed and golden brown on top and just set in the center. Remove from the oven and let cool 5 to 10 minutes.

Serve hot or warm.

BAKED SMOKED SCAMORZA
WITH SAUTÉED PEPPERS
makes 4 servings

Smoked scamorza—slightly aged mozzarella that has been smoked—is one of the best cheeses for melting, turning supple and stretchy when put to the flame. Scamorza, both smoked and unsmoked, is typically found in parts of southern Italy, including Abruzzo, Campania, and Puglia. If the cheese is dry enough, you can plop fat slices of it right on the grill and grill them like you would a hamburger. Or, in chilly weather, you can bake the slices, as in this recipe. Add sautéed peppers to the mix, and you've got dinner covered.

3 TBSP EXTRA-VIRGIN OLIVE OIL, PLUS MORE FOR THE BAKING DISH

2 GARLIC CLOVES, LIGHTLY CRUSHED

1 ROUNDED CUP/140 G THINLY SLICED RED ONION

1½ LB/680 G SWEET BELL PEPPERS (ABOUT 3 LARGE), TRIMMED AND CUT LENGTHWISE INTO THIN SLICES

1 TSP FINE SEA SALT

1 TBSP MINCED FRESH HERBS (I USE A MIX OF FLAT-LEAF PARSLEY AND OREGANO)

8 OZ/225 G SMOKED SCAMORZA CHEESE, CUT INTO ½-IN/12-MM SLICES

Heat the oven to 400°F/200°C/gas 6.

Warm the olive oil and garlic in a large skillet placed over medium-low heat. When the garlic is fragrant and begins to sizzle, add the onion to the pan and toss to coat with the oil. Cook, stirring often, for 5 minutes, or until the onion just begins to soften. Add the peppers, salt, and herbs. Cook, stirring occasionally, for 30 minutes, or until the onion and peppers are tender and the peppers are browned in spots.

Lightly coat a 9-by-6-in/23-by-15-cm oval or rectangular baking dish with olive oil. Spoon the onions and peppers into the baking dish and spread them evenly over the bottom. Arrange the scamorza slices slightly overlapped on top of the peppers in one layer.

Bake for 20 minutes, or until the cheese is melted. Remove from the oven. Position an oven rack 4 in/10 cm below the broiler and turn the broiler on. Broil the scamorza for 1 to 2 minutes, just enough to give the cheese a bubbly browned surface.

Serve immediately (I suggest serving with good, crusty bread on the side).

porcini, funghi, prezzemolo
mozzarella, noce moscato, zucch
ricotta, parmigiano

CRÊPE CANNELLONI WITH MUSHROOMS AND ZUCCHINI

makes 8 to 12 servings

Crespelle is the Italian word for crêpes, and although they are mostly associated with French cuisine, they also figure prominently in the traditional cooking of my mother's native region of Abruzzo. In this recipe, they are stuffed with a savory filling of mushroom and zucchini, bathed in porcini-flavored *balsamella* sauce (the Italian version of béchamel sauce), and baked until beautifully browned and bubbly. This is definitely a dish fit for company.

CRÊPES:

8 LARGE EGGS

2 CUPS/480 ML WHOLE MILK

3 TBSP MINCED FRESH FLAT-LEAF PARSLEY

1½ CUPS/175 G UNBLEACHED ALL-PURPOSE FLOUR

1 TSP SEA SALT

FRESHLY GROUND BLACK PEPPER

SMALL PINCH OF FRESHLY GRATED NUTMEG

2 TBSP UNSALTED BUTTER, OR MORE AS NEEDED FOR THE CRÊPE PAN

FILLING:

½ OZ/15 G DRIED PORCINI MUSHROOMS

1 CUP/240 ML BOILING WATER

2 TBSP EXTRA-VIRGIN OLIVE OIL

1 TBSP UNSALTED BUTTER

1 LARGE SHALLOT (2 OZ/55 G), MINCED

1 LB/455 G MIXED FRESH MUSHROOMS, SUCH AS CREMINI, PORTOBELLO, AND SHIITAKE, COARSELY CHOPPED

1 TBSP MINCED FRESH FLAT-LEAF PARSLEY

1 TSP FINE SEA SALT

1 LB/455 G ZUCCHINI, CUT INTO THIN HALF-COINS OR DICED

FRESHLY GROUND BLACK PEPPER

½ CUP/120 ML DRY WHITE WINE

1 TBSP MINCED FRESH BASIL

1½ CUPS/340 G WELL-DRAINED WHOLE COW'S MILK RICOTTA CHEESE

4 OZ/115 G FRESH MOZZARELLA CHEESE, DICED

½ CUP/60 G FRESHLY GRATED PARMIGIANO-REGGIANO CHEESE

BALSAMELLA SAUCE:

2½ CUPS/600 ML WHOLE OR 2-PERCENT MILK

RESERVED LIQUID FROM RECONSTITUTED PORCINI

4 TBSP/55 G UNSALTED BUTTER

¼ CUP/30 G UNBLEACHED ALL-PURPOSE FLOUR

1 TSP FINE SEA SALT

FRESHLY GROUND BLACK PEPPER

PINCH OF FRESHLY GRATED NUTMEG

UNSALTED BUTTER FOR THE BAKING DISHES, SOFTENED

1 CUP/115 G FRESHLY GRATED PARMIGIANO-REGGIANO CHEESE

CONTINUED

TO MAKE THE CRÊPES: In a large bowl, whisk together the eggs, milk, and parsley. In a separate large bowl, combine the flour, salt, a few grindings of pepper, and nutmeg. Slowly pour the egg mixture into the flour mixture, whisking all the while to avoid lumps. Cover the crêpe batter with plastic wrap and let stand for 30 minutes.

Melt a little butter in a 9-in/23-cm nonstick skillet placed over medium heat (I use a well-seasoned cast-iron skillet). When the pan is hot, pour in 1/4 cup/60 ml of the crêpe batter and quickly swirl it around to completely coat the bottom of the pan, forming a thin pancake. Cook for 30 to 45 seconds, until just set. Use a small angled spatula to lift up one edge of the crêpe. Flip the crêpe and cook on the other side for 20 to 30 seconds. Transfer the crêpe to a plate. Continue to make crêpes until you have used all the batter, making sure to grease the pan from time to time with a thin film of butter. You should end up with 24 crêpes. Cover the crêpes with plastic wrap until you are ready to assemble the cannelloni.

TO MAKE THE FILLING: Put the dried porcini in a small heatproof bowl and pour the boiling water over them. Let stand for 20 to 30 minutes, or until softened. Drain the porcini in a fine-mesh sieve lined with a damp paper towel, reserving the liquid. Chop the mushrooms coarsely and set the mushrooms and liquid aside separately.

Warm the oil and butter in a large skillet placed over medium-low heat. When the butter is melted, add the shallot and cook, stirring often, for 5 to 7 minutes, or until they are softened but not browned. Add the porcini mushrooms and the mixed fresh mushrooms and stir to coat them with the oil. Sprinkle the parsley and salt over the mushrooms and toss gently. Raise the heat to medium and cook, stirring from time to time, for 10 minutes, or until the liquid released by the mushrooms has mostly evaporated. Add the zucchini to the pan and season with pepper. Cook, stirring from time to time, for 10 to 15 minutes, or until the mushrooms and zucchini are tender and there is little liquid left in the pan. Raise the heat to medium-high and pour in the wine. Let it bubble for 1 or 2 minutes, until most of the wine is evaporated. Remove from the heat and stir in the basil. Transfer the mushroom-zucchini mixture to a medium bowl and let it cool for 10 minutes.

In a separate medium bowl, stir the ricotta with a fork until it is creamy. Fold in the mozzarella and Parmigiano. Then fold the cheeses into the mushroom-zucchini mixture. Cover with plastic wrap and set aside.

TO MAKE THE SAUCE: Pour the milk into a medium saucepan. Pour the reserved porcini liquid into a glass measuring cup, and add enough water so that the liquid equals 1 cup/240 ml. Pour the liquid into the pan with the milk. Bring just to a boil over medium heat and then turn off the heat.

Melt the butter in a large heavy-bottomed saucepan over medium heat. Whisk in the flour and cook, stirring constantly, for 2 minutes. Add the hot milk mixture in driblets, whisking constantly and taking care to eliminate lumps and avoid scorching. The mixture will look like it's breaking but it will come together again and become smooth. When all of the milk mixture has been added, cook the sauce, stirring it frequently, for 10 to 15 minutes, or until it is thick enough to coat the back of a wooden spoon. Season with the salt, pepper, and nutmeg, and remove from the heat.

TO ASSEMBLE AND BAKE THE CANNELLONI: Heat the oven to 375°F/190°C/gas 5. Have the crêpes, filling, and *balsamella* sauce at the ready. Lightly coat three 8-by-12-in/20-by-30.5-cm baking dishes with butter. Spread a thin layer of *balsamella* sauce in the bottom of each dish.

Place a crêpe on a clean work surface. Spoon about 2 tbsp of the mushroom-zucchini filling across the bottom third of the crêpe. Roll it up, jelly-roll style, and place it seam-side down in the baking dish. Continue filling and rolling the crêpes, arranging them side by side in a single layer in each baking dish. You should be able to fit 8 crêpes in each baking dish.

Divide the remaining *balsamella* sauce among the three baking dishes, spreading it over the filled cannelloni. Sprinkle one-third of the Parmigiano cheese over each assembled dish. Cover the dishes with aluminum foil. Bake for 15 minutes. Uncover and bake for an additional 20 to 25 minutes, or until the cheese and *balsamella* sauce are bubbly and the top is golden brown.

Serve the cannelloni piping hot from the oven.

COOK'S NOTE: This dish is not difficult to make, but it is a bit labor intensive. The good news is that it is worth every bit of effort, and most of the work can be done in advance. The crêpes may be made in advance and refrigerated, tightly wrapped, for up to 3 days or frozen for up to 1 month. The filling may be made in advance and refrigerated for up to 3 days. The dish may be assembled in advance and refrigerated for up to 3 days. Bring it to room temperature before baking.

VEGETABLE-STUFFED PASTA SHELLS
makes 8 to 9 servings

My affection for stuffed shells is a fairly recent development. My Italian mother did not make them when I was growing up, preferring the more "authentic" cannelloni. And I did not start making them until I created a meat-stuffed version for *The Glorious Pasta of Italy*. The shells were such a hit with my kids that I put them on our regular dinner rotation. Their enthusiasm prompted me to start playing around with a meatless version. Here it is, and it's every bit as good as the original (and as my mom's cannelloni, for that matter—but don't tell her I said that).

1 LB/455 G RAINBOW OR SWISS CHARD, STEMS REMOVED AND RESERVED FOR ANOTHER USE, LEAVES COARSELY CHOPPED

2 TBSP EXTRA-VIRGIN OLIVE OIL, PLUS MORE FOR DRIZZLING AND FOR THE PAN

1 TBSP UNSALTED BUTTER

1 GARLIC CLOVE, MINCED

2 RED OR GREEN SCALLIONS, SLICED CROSSWISE

2 MEDIUM ZUCCHINI (ABOUT 12 OZ/ 340 G), SHREDDED AND SQUEEZED TO REMOVE EXCESS LIQUID

1 TSP FINE SEA SALT

FRESHLY GROUND BLACK PEPPER

3 OZ/85 G SHREDDED SEMISOFT CHEESE, SUCH AS AN ITALIAN *TOMA*, FRENCH *TOMME,* OR FONTINA

4 OZ/115 G FRESH MOZZARELLA CHEESE, DICED

1 CUP/115 G FRESHLY GRATED PARMIGIANO-REGGIANO CHEESE

2 LARGE EGGS, LIGHTLY BEATEN

ONE 12-OZ/340-G BOX JUMBO DRIED PASTA SHELLS (36 SHELLS)

1 RECIPE SIMPLE TOMATO SAUCE (PAGE 66), HEATED TO A SIMMER

Rinse the chopped chard leaves in cold water. Place the leaves, with the water still clinging to them, into a large skillet or shallow sauté pan, cover, and set over medium heat. If the leaves are dry, add 2 tbsp water to the pan. Cook the chard, tossing from time to time, for 15 to 20 minutes or until tender and most of the water has evaporated. Turn off the heat, transfer the chard to a colander, and let it cool. Then squeeze as much excess water from it as you can. Transfer the chard to a cutting board and chop finely. Set aside.

Wipe the skillet clean and add the oil and butter. Place over medium-low heat. When the butter is melted add the garlic and scallions. Cook, stirring frequently, for 7 minutes, or until the scallions are softened but not browned. Stir in the zucchini and season with the salt and a grinding of pepper. Raise the heat to medium and cook, stirring from time to time, for 5 minutes, or until the zucchini is bright green. Add the cooked, chopped chard and stir to combine. Cook for 5 more minutes, or until the chard is heated through. Transfer the mixture to a large bowl and let cool for at least 10 minutes.

When the greens are cool, gently fold in the *toma*, the mozzarella, and ½ cup/ 60 g of the Parmigiano. Gently mix in the beaten eggs. Cover and refrigerate until ready to use.

Heat the oven to 350°F/180°C/gas 4.

Bring a large pot of water to a boil over high heat and salt generously. Add the pasta shells, stir to separate, and cook according to the package instructions until not quite al dente. (They should be slightly underdone, because they will finish cooking in the oven.) Drain the shells in a colander and transfer them to a large bowl. Drizzle 1 or 2 tbsp olive oil over the shells—just enough to coat them so they do not stick to one another—and toss gently with a wooden spoon or silicone spatula.

Lightly coat a 10-by-15-in/25-by-38-cm baking dish or two smaller dishes with olive oil. Spoon 1½ to 2 cups/360 to 480 ml of the tomato sauce into the bottom of the dish to make a soft bed for the shells. Fill each shell with a scant 2 tbsp of the stuffing and arrange them, filling-side up, in the dish. Spread more sauce over the shells—enough to cover them well but not drown them (there may be some sauce left over). Sprinkle the remaining ½ cup/55 g of Parmigiano cheese on top.

Bake the shells, uncovered, for 35 to 45 minutes, or until the sauce is bubbling and the cheese is browned. Serve the shells from the baking dish or spoon them into warmed shallow individual bowls.

GRILLED SUMMER VEGETABLES
ALLA PARMIGIANA
makes 8 servings

I did not think it was possible to improve on classic eggplant alla Parmigiana (eggplant Parmesan), the comfort food of choice for legions of Italian Americans. But then it struck me one day, as I returned from the farmers' market laden with bags of summer vegetables, that a mix of eggplant, zucchini, and peppers could be a wonderful riff on tradition. And it is. Grilling the vegetables first gives them that rich, smoky summer flavor that is enhanced by smoked scamorza cheese. This is party fare, Italian style!

1 LB/455 G EGGPLANT, ENDS TRIMMED, CUT LENGTHWISE INTO 1/3-IN/8-MM SLICES

KOSHER OR SEA SALT

1 LB/455 G ZUCCHINI, ENDS TRIMMED, CUT LENGTHWISE INTO 1/3-IN/8-MM SLICES

EXTRA-VIRGIN OLIVE OIL FOR BRUSHING THE VEGETABLES AND FOR THE BAKING DISH

1 BATCH GRILLED PEPPERS (PAGE 74)

FRESHLY GROUND BLACK PEPPER

6 TBSP/45 G DRIED BREAD CRUMBS

1 RECIPE SIMPLE TOMATO SAUCE (PAGE 66), HEATED TO A SIMMER

8 OZ/225 G LOW-MOISTURE MOZZARELLA CHEESE, THINLY SLICED

8 OZ/225 G SMOKED SCAMORZA OR SMOKED MOZZARELLA CHEESE, THINLY SLICED

1/2 CUP/115 G PECORINO FRESCO, SHREDDED

1/2 CUP/60 G FRESHLY GRATED PARMIGIANO-REGGIANO CHEESE

Sprinkle both sides of the eggplant slices with salt and place them in a colander set on a plate. Put another plate on top of the eggplant and weight it down with a heavy object. Let the eggplant slices sit for 30 to 60 minutes to leach out their bitter juices. Pat the slices dry with a paper towel and set them aside on a clean plate.

Prepare a medium-hot charcoal grill or heat a gas grill to medium-high.

Brush the eggplant and zucchini slices with olive oil and season lightly with salt and pepper. Grill the eggplant and zucchini for 2 to 4 minutes per side, depending on how hot your flame is. You are aiming for grill marks and a few blackened spots, but you do not want to burn them and you want to give them enough time to soften a bit. If the flame is too hot, move the slices to the outer part of the grill grate. Using tongs, carefully transfer the slices to a plate.

Slice the grilled peppers lengthwise into quarters. Set them on a plate.

Heat the oven to 375°F/190°C/gas 5.

Lightly coat a 9-by-13-in/23-by-33-cm ovenproof ceramic baking dish with olive oil. Coat the bottom and sides of the dish with 2 tbsp of the bread crumbs. Spread ½ cup/120 ml of tomato sauce into the bottom of the dish. Arrange the eggplant slices in the dish in one layer, overlapping the slices if necessary. Sprinkle a little salt and pepper over the eggplant and arrange one-third of the mozzarella, scamorza, and pecorino fresco on top.

Spoon a second layer of sauce—about ½ cup/120 ml—over the cheeses, then sprinkle with 2 tbsp of the bread crumbs. Arrange the peppers in one layer, overlapping if necessary. Sprinkle with a little salt and pepper, and then top with another one-third of the mozzarella, scamorza, and pecorino fresco.

Spoon a third layer of sauce—about ½ cup/120 ml—over the cheeses, then sprinkle with the remaining 2 tbsp of the bread crumbs. Arrange the zucchini slices in one layer, overlapping if necessary. Sprinkle with a little salt and pepper, and then top with the remaining mozzarella, scamorza, and pecorino fresco.

Spoon a final layer of sauce over the cheeses (you may not use all of the sauce; reserve any leftovers for another use). Sprinkle the Parmigiano cheese on top.

Bake uncovered for 30 to 40 minutes, until it is bubbling and the top is nicely browned. Remove it from the oven and let it sit for 10 minutes before serving.

Serve warm or at room temperature.

STUFFED SUMMER VEGETABLE PLATTER

makes 4 servings

Once or twice during our summer months in Italy, my mother would prepare stuffed vegetables for dinner. She would use whichever suitable vegetables she found at the market, mix together a variety of fillings, and by the time her two lazybones daughters returned from the beach, a gorgeous platter of colorful vegetables spilling with stuffing was already waiting at the table. I hope my mom knows how much I appreciated those lunches (I know she does because I told her so again just the other day!).

This recipe is a bit simpler, in that it calls for just one stuffing of seasoned bread crumbs. You can use the vegetables listed here, or try others—squat scallop-edged summer squashes, onions, and mushrooms are all great vessels for stuffing. I like to serve this dish together with cheese and thinly sliced prosciutto to round out the meal.

4 SMALL RIPE TOMATOES

4 SMALL OR 2 MEDIUM ZUCCHINI (ABOUT 12 OZ/340 G)

1 LARGE RED BELL PEPPER

1 LARGE YELLOW BELL PEPPER

4 CUPS/460 G FRESH BREAD CRUMBS

2 GARLIC CLOVES, MINCED

3 TBSP MINCED FRESH FLAT-LEAF PARSLEY

8 TO 9 TBSP/120 TO 135 ML EXTRA-VIRGIN OLIVE OIL

1/2 CUP/120 G FINELY CHOPPED GABRIELLA'S GIARDINIERA (PAGE 256) OR BOTTLED *GIARDINIERA*

2 TBSP CAPERS, RINSED, DRAINED, AND FINELY CHOPPED

1/2 CUP/60 G FRESHLY GRATED PARMIGIANO-REGGIANO CHEESE

1/2 CUP/60 G FRESHLY GRATED PECORINO ROMANO CHEESE

1/2 CUP/60 G SHREDDED SCAMORZA OR PART-SKIM MOZZARELLA CHEESE

1 TSP FINE SEA SALT

FRESHLY GROUND BLACK PEPPER

2 CUPS/480 ML FRESH TOMATO SAUCE (PAGE 65) OR ONE 14 1/2-OZ/415-G CAN DICED TOMATOES, WITH THEIR JUICE

Slice off the tops of the tomatoes and use a melon baller to hollow out the insides. Discard the insides (or save for another use) and set the tomato shells upside-down on a paper towel–lined plate to drain.

If the zucchini are small, trim the ends off. Use a corer or the tip of a vegetable peeler to hollow out the interior of the zucchini, leaving the shell intact. If the zucchini are medium, trim off the ends and cut the zucchini in half crosswise before hollowing out the interiors. Set aside.

Cut the red and yellow peppers in half lengthwise, cutting through the stems so that each pepper half has a decorative stem end. Remove the seeds and white pith from the inside of the peppers. Set aside.

Heat the oven to 375°F/190°C/gas 5.

Combine the bread crumbs, garlic, and parsley in a large bowl. In a large skillet, heat 4 tbsp of the olive oil over medium heat. Add the bread crumb mixture to the skillet and cook, stirring frequently, for 7 to 8 minutes, or until the bread crumbs are pale golden and starting to crisp. Spoon the bread crumbs back into the bowl and add the *giardiniera*, capers, cheeses, salt, and a generous grinding of pepper.

Put the prepared vegetables on a large cutting board. Spoon the bread crumbs-and-cheese filling into the tomatoes and peppers, and with your fingers, stuff the zucchini, taking care not to overpack them.

Lightly coat a 12-in/30.5-cm round or 9-by-13-in/23-by-33-cm rectangular baking dish with 2 tbsp olive oil. Spread two-thirds of the tomato sauce in the bottom of the baking dish. Arrange the stuffed vegetables snugly in the baking dish and spoon the remaining tomato sauce over them. Drizzle with 2 to 3 tbsp olive oil.

Bake the vegetables for 1 hour, or until they are nicely browned and tender. Turn off the oven and let the vegetables sit in the oven 15 minutes, to settle.

Serve the stuffed vegetables from the baking dish warm or at room temperature.

pomodori, zucc...
aglio, giardi...

ne, peperoni,
era, scamorza, parmigiano-reggian

patate, funghi, panna, sale
scamora, uova,
parmiziano-rezziano

POTATO AND MUSHROOM GATTŌ

makes 8 servings

Gattō is the French word *gâteau* turned into Neapolitan dialect. It means "cake" and that is essentially what this rich dish is—a savory cake of seasoned mashed potatoes and cheese. The classic version of *gattō* also calls for cubed salami. But here I've used meaty roasted mushrooms. You can serve this dish as a main course—it's certainly substantial enough—or serve it (in judicious portions) alongside roast chicken or grilled salmon.

3 LB/1.4 KG YELLOW POTATOES, SUCH AS YUKON GOLD

KOSHER SALT

1 CUP/115 G FRESHLY GRATED PARMIGIANO-REGGIANO CHEESE

½ CUP/120 ML HEAVY CREAM

2 TBSP MINCED FRESH FLAT-LEAF PARSLEY

1 EGG, LIGHTLY BEATEN

½ TSP FINE SEA SALT

FRESHLY GROUND BLACK PEPPER

BUTTER FOR THE CAKE PAN AND TO DOT THE SURFACE OF THE *GATTŌ*

3 TBSP DRIED BREAD CRUMBS

4 OZ/115 G SMOKED SCAMORZA OR SMOKED MOZZARELLA, DICED

1 LB/455 G ROASTED MUSHROOMS (PAGE 69)

4 OZ/115 G FRESH MOZZARELLA, DICED

Put the potatoes in a large pot with cold water to cover by 1 to 2 in/2.5 to 5 cm. Salt generously. Set the pot over medium-high heat and bring to a boil. Cook the potatoes for 25 to 30 minutes, or until they are tender. Drain the potatoes in a colander and let sit until the potatoes are cool enough to handle but still warm.

Heat the oven to 400°F/200°C/gas 6.

Peel the potatoes and cut them into large chunks. Press them through a ricer into a large bowl. Let them cool slightly if they are still steaming hot. Add the Parmigiano cheese, cream, parsley, egg, salt, and a generous grinding of pepper. Fold everything together gently but thoroughly.

Lightly coat a 10-in/25-cm round cake pan or baking dish with butter. Coat the bottom and sides of the pan with 2 tbsp of the bread crumbs. Spread two-thirds of the potato mixture into the pan. Scatter the scamorza over the potatoes. Spread the roasted mushrooms on top of the scamorza. Scatter the mozzarella over the mushrooms. Spread the remaining potato mixture over the mozzarella. Use the tines of a fork to score a swirling pattern on top of the *gattō* if you like. Sprinkle the remaining 1 tbsp bread crumbs on top and dot the surface with a little butter.

Bake the *gattō* uncovered for 30 to 40 minutes, or until beautifully browned on top and hot throughout. Remove from the oven and let rest for 5 to 10 minutes before serving.

EGGPLANT "MEATBALLS" IN TOMATO SAUCE
makes 4 to 5 servings

This recipe sounds contrived, doesn't it? An effort to create a meat-like dish out of a vegetable. But resourceful Italian cooks have been participating in such trickery for centuries. After all, meat was a scarcity in most Italian homes until fairly recently. Eggplant, with its meaty yet silky texture and its ability to absorb flavor, makes an excellent stand-in in this southern Italian classic. My kids like these patties as much as they like real meatballs.

1 LARGE (1 LB/455 G) SHINY PURPLE OR LAVENDER EGGPLANT

3 ROUNDED CUPS/170 G FRESH BREAD CRUMBS

2 LARGE EGGS, LIGHTLY BEATEN

2 GARLIC CLOVES, PRESSED

1/2 TSP FINE SEA SALT

2 OZ/60 G PECORINO ROMANO CHEESE, FRESHLY GRATED

1 TBSP MINCED FRESH BASIL

1 TBSP MINCED FRESH FLAT-LEAF PARSLEY

UNBLEACHED ALL-PURPOSE FLOUR FOR DREDGING

VEGETABLE OIL FOR FRYING

3 CUPS/720 ML FRESH TOMATO SAUCE (PAGE 65) OR SIMPLE TOMATO SAUCE (PAGE 66), HEATED TO A SIMMER IN A SAUCEPAN BIG ENOUGH TO HOLD ALL THE EGGPLANT "MEATBALLS"

FRESHLY GRATED PARMIGIANO-REGGIANO OR PECORINO ROMANO CHEESE FOR SERVING

Heat the oven to 350°F/180°C/gas 4.

Using the tines of a fork, prick the eggplant here and there a few times. Set on a small rimmed baking sheet and bake for about 1 hour, or until the skin is crinkled and collapsed and the interior is completely tender. Remove from the oven and let sit briefly to cool. Slice the eggplant open lengthwise and scoop the flesh onto a cutting board. Discard the skin.

Mash the eggplant with a potato masher, or chop it coarsely with a chef's knife. Scoop the flesh into a large bowl and add the bread crumbs, eggs, garlic, salt, Pecorino Romano, basil, and parsley. Fold everything together gently but thoroughly with a wooden spoon or silicone spatula.

Spoon about 1 cup/115 g of flour into a shallow bowl. Have ready a platter lined with waxed paper. Using your hands, form the eggplant mixture into golf ball-size balls. Dredge the balls in the flour and place them on the prepared platter. Press down on them gently to flatten them just a bit. You should end up with about fifteen 2-in/5-cm eggplant meatballs.

CONTINUED

melanzana, aglio, basilico, uova

salsa fresca

Pour enough vegetable oil into a deep frying pan or cast-iron skillet to reach a depth of at least 1 in/2.5 cm. Place over medium-high heat and heat the oil to about 375°F/190°C on a deep-frying thermometer. If you do not have a thermometer, drop a tiny ball of the eggplant mixture into the oil; if it sizzles immediately, the oil is hot enough.

Working in two batches, add the eggplant meatballs to the hot oil and fry until golden-brown on the bottom, 2 to 3 minutes. Turn with a spatula and fry the other side until golden-brown, 2 minutes more.

Transfer the eggplant meatballs from the frying pan directly to the pan of sauce that is simmering on the stove over medium-low heat. Cook, turning the eggplant meatballs once or twice, until heated through, about 10 minutes. If the sauce seems too thick—the eggplant meatballs will absorb some of it—add 1 or 2 tbsp of water and gently stir it into the sauce.

Serve the eggplant meatballs hot, with a little tomato sauce spooned over them and a sprinkle of Parmigiano cheese on top.

CLAM STEW WITH GREENS AND TOMATOES
makes 4 to 6 servings

I can't remember a time when I didn't love clams. When I was a kid, I used to dig for *telline*—tiny, oval-shaped clams—beside the shallow waters of the Adriatic Sea. This required little effort on my part. I merely had to stick my hand down into the wet sand and pull up the clams, which I would pry open and pop in my mouth. As much as I enjoy clams on their own, they are even better when mixed with braised hearty greens and tomatoes. All of the robust flavors come together to form a rich stew, perfect for a chilly evening in late fall.

GREENS:

3 TBSP EXTRA-VIRGIN OLIVE OIL

3 LARGE GARLIC CLOVES, SLICED PAPER-THIN

8 OZ/225 G TUSCAN KALE, COARSELY SHREDDED

8 OZ/225 G SAVOY CABBAGE (USE THE DARK OUTER LEAVES), HALVED LENGTHWISE AND SHREDDED

FINE SEA SALT

GENEROUS PINCH OF RED PEPPER FLAKES

2 CUPS/480 G CHOPPED CANNED TOMATOES, WITH THEIR JUICE

CLAMS:

¼ CUP/60 ML EXTRA-VIRGIN OLIVE OIL

1 TBSP MINCED GARLIC

GENEROUS PINCH OF RED PEPPER FLAKES

1 CUP/240 ML DRY WHITE WINE

4 DOZEN FRESH LITTLENECK OR OTHER SMALL CLAMS, SCRUBBED CLEAN

4 TO 6 THICK SLICES BRUSCHETTA (PAGE 86)

TO MAKE THE GREENS: Warm the olive oil and garlic in a large saucepan or deep-sided skillet over medium-low heat. Cook until the garlic is soft and translucent, 7 to 8 minutes. Add the greens by the handful—as much as will fit in the pan. Cover and cook for about 5 minutes, or until the greens begin to wilt. Continue to add more greens to the pan and cook until they are all wilted. Season with salt and the red pepper flakes and cover. Raise the heat to medium and cook, stirring occasionally, until the greens are tender, 20 to 25 minutes. Pour in the chopped tomatoes and bring to a simmer. Cover partially, reduce the heat to medium-low, and cook at a gentle simmer for 15 to 20 minutes, or until the tomatoes have thickened slightly to a sauce consistency.

CONTINUED

TO COOK THE CLAMS: While the greens are cooking, warm the olive oil, garlic, and red pepper flakes in a large frying pan over medium heat. Cook until the garlic is fragrant, about 3 minutes. Raise the heat to medium-high and pour in the wine. Add the clams and cover the pan. Cook the clams at a lively simmer for 5 to 8 minutes, or until they just open. Using tongs, remove the clams to a large bowl as they open; discard any that are not open. Once all the clams have been removed, strain the liquid through a fine-mesh sieve lined with damp cheesecloth into a small bowl. Pour the strained liquid into the saucepan with the greens, and then add the clams. Using a large serving spoon, gently incorporate the clams into the greens. Heat briefly until the greens and clams are warmed through.

Place a slice of bruschetta in the bottom of four or six shallow rimmed bowls. Spoon the clams and greens, as well as some of the liquid, into each bowl and serve.

CLAM STEW WITH PANCETTA VARIATION: To say that pancetta goes well with clams and greens would be an understatement. The three make a perfect, if unconventional, marriage. To add pancetta, put 1 to 2 oz/30 to 55 g diced pancetta in the large saucepan where you will cook the greens. Do this *before* you add the sliced garlic. Cook until the pancetta is just crisp and has rendered some fat. Add the garlic, and 1 tbsp of oil if you like, and proceed with the recipe as directed.

cavolo, pomodori, vongole, aglio, vino, bruschetta

CHICKEN THIGHS BRAISED WITH ESCAROLE

makes 4 servings

Escarole is one of those vegetables that when cooked is completely different from when it is raw. In this recipe, simmered with chicken thighs and wine, it turns from a sturdy, crunchy green into a savory, pulpy sauce, absorbing the rich flavors in the pan. Serve this dish with good bread or plain rice for sopping up the juices.

2 TBSP EXTRA-VIRGIN OLIVE OIL

8 SKIN-ON, BONE-IN CHICKEN THIGHS

FINE SEA SALT

FRESHLY GROUND BLACK PEPPER

3 SPRING BULB ONIONS, RED OR GREEN, BULB AND LIGHT GREEN PARTS ONLY, THINLY SLICED CROSSWISE

2 TBSP MINCED FRESH FLAT-LEAF PARSLEY

½ CUP/120 ML DRY WHITE WINE

1 HEAD ESCAROLE (ABOUT 1 LB/455 G), COARSELY CHOPPED OR SHREDDED

½ CUP/120 ML BEST-QUALITY COMMERCIAL CHICKEN BROTH

Heat the olive oil in a large deep skillet over medium heat. When the oil is shimmering, lay 4 of the thighs, skin-side down, in the pan and season them with salt and pepper. Cook, without turning, for 5 to 6 minutes or until crispy and golden brown on the bottom. Turn the thighs over, season with salt and pepper, and cook for 3 to 4 minutes more, or until browned on the second side. Using tongs, transfer the browned thighs to a plate. Brown the remaining 4 thighs in the same way and transfer them to the plate. Pour off and discard all but about 2 tbsp of the fat in the skillet.

Reduce the heat to medium-low and add the onions and parsley to the skillet, turning them to coat with oil. Cook, stirring frequently, for 7 to 8 minutes, or just until the onions are softened and translucent. Return all of the chicken thighs, skin-side up, to the skillet, raise the heat to medium-high. Pour in the wine and let it bubble for 1 to 2 minutes. Add the escarole to the skillet, and then add the chicken broth. Reduce the heat to medium-low, cover the pan, and simmer, stirring occasionally, for about 30 minutes, or until the juices run clear and the chicken is tender. Taste and season with additional salt or pepper if you like. Serve immediately.

GRILLED LAMB SPIEDINI ON A BED OF CAPONATA
makes 6 servings

Lamb and eggplant love each other, and I love them both, so why choose? Here, simply seasoned lamb skewers are served on a bed of caponata, the traditional sweet-and-sour eggplant salad from Sicily. There are many ways to enjoy caponata beyond this dish: serve it warm—or cold—on bruschetta, with a fried egg or a frittata, or with a good, sharp sheep's milk cheese.

CAPONATA:

1 MEDIUM EGGPLANT, CUT INTO
3/4-IN/2-CM DICE

FINE SEA SALT

4 TBSP/60 ML EXTRA-VIRGIN OLIVE OIL

1 LARGE RED ONION, CUT INTO
1/2-IN/12-MM DICE

2 RIBS CELERY, CUT CROSSWISE INTO
1/4-IN/6-MM SLICES

1 CUP/155 G COARSELY CHOPPED PITTED
GREEN OLIVES

1 CUP/240 G CANNED DICED TOMATOES,
WITH THEIR LIQUID

1 TBSP MINCED FRESH FLAT-LEAF
PARSLEY, PLUS A SPRIG FOR GARNISH

1 TBSP CAPERS, RINSED, DRAINED, AND
COARSELY CHOPPED

1 TBSP SUGAR

4 TO 5 TBSP RED WINE VINEGAR

LAMB SKEWERS:

3 LB/1.4 KG BONELESS LEG OF LAMB
WITH SOME MARBLING OF FAT, CUT INTO
3/4-IN/2-CM CUBES

1/4 CUP/60 ML EXTRA-VIRGIN OLIVE OIL

2 GARLIC CLOVES, SLICED PAPER-THIN

TWELVE 12-IN/30.5-CM WOODEN
SKEWERS, SOAKED IN COLD WATER FOR
30 MINUTES AND DRAINED

FINE SEA SALT

FRESHLY GROUND BLACK PEPPER

TO MAKE THE CAPONATA: Sprinkle the diced eggplant with salt and place them in a colander set on a plate. Put another plate over the eggplant and weight it down with a heavy object. Let the eggplant pieces sit for 30 to 60 minutes, to leach out their bitter juices. Pat the pieces dry with a paper towel.

CONTINUED

Heat 3 tbsp of the olive oil in a large skillet over medium-high heat. When the oil is shimmering, add the eggplant cubes and toss to coat with the oil. Cook, turning them occasionally, for 5 minutes, or until they are golden brown on several sides. Reduce the heat to medium if the eggplant seems to be browning too quickly. Transfer the eggplant to a paper towel–lined plate.

Reduce the heat to medium and add the remaining 1 tbsp of olive oil to the skillet. When it is shimmering, add the onion and celery. Cook, stirring frequently, for 8 minutes, or until the onion is translucent. Add the olives and diced tomatoes and season with 1/2 tsp salt. Bring to a simmer and cook for 5 minutes. Stir in the parsley, capers, sugar, and 4 tbsp vinegar, and let the mixture bubble for a minute or so. Then return the eggplant to the pan, stir to combine, and cook at a gentle simmer for 10 minutes, or until the sauce has thickened. Taste and adjust the seasoning with salt and the additional 1 tbsp of vinegar if you like. Remove from the heat and let cool while you grill the lamb.

TO PREPARE THE LAMB: In a large bowl, toss the lamb cubes with the olive oil and garlic. Let the lamb sit for 30 minutes to give the flavors time to mingle. Place the lamb cubes on the skewers, threading them tightly so they are touching and leaving a length of skewer empty at one end to use as a handle. Season with a little salt and a generous grinding of pepper.

Prepare a hot charcoal grill or preheat a gas grill to high. Arrange the skewers on the grill and sear for about 3 minutes, or until browned on the first side. Turn and sear until browned on the second side, about 2 minutes. The interior of the meat should still be rosy pink. Using tongs, transfer the skewers to a plate.

To serve, spoon the caponata into a deep serving dish and arrange the skewers of grilled lamb on top. Garnish with a sprig of fresh parsley, if you like, and serve.

melanzane, cipolle, pomodor

io d'oliva, agnello

chapter 7
SIDE DISHES
contorni

SIDE DISHES
contorni

I mention this sentiment elsewhere in this book, but it bears repeating here: Even as side dishes, vegetables enjoy a place of honor at the Italian table. They demand it, really, with their glorious colors and sheer variety. In fact, I had a difficult time whittling down which recipes to include in this chapter. Most of them, you'll find, require little preparation because the vegetables themselves are the stars and stars should be left to shine.

I am hugely fond of snap beans—green beans, wax beans, flat Romano beans, and so I've included a couple of recipes for preparing them simply—roasted with herbs (see page 226), and lightly sautéed and dressed with olive oil, lemon, and *peperoncino* (see page 221). But did you know that green beans are also delicious cooked until very tender and then . . . mashed? The recipe for Smashed Green Beans and Potatoes with Pancetta (page 230) comes from a country restaurant in the hills of Abruzzo, and like so many dishes from my family's beloved region, its appeal lies in its rustic simplicity.

And I would be remiss if I didn't also point out two of my childhood favorites—my mother's Braised Sweet-and-Sour Savoy Cabbage (page 222) and her Cauliflower with Oil-Cured Olives and Anchovies (page 217). Both of these dishes were served every year on Thanksgiving and we looked forward to them as much as we did the turkey or the pumpkin pie. I'm happy to share them with you here.

GRILLED ASPARAGUS WITH SPECK

makes 4 to 6 servings

Grilling season starts early in Virginia, where I live, and happily it coincides with the arrival of local asparagus. Nothing could be simpler than tossing fat, fresh spears in a little olive oil and giving them a quick char on the grill. The crisped speck garnish is an optional step, but I like the crunch that the sautéed smoked prosciutto provides and the way it underlines the smoky flavor of the grilled asparagus spears.

1 LB/455 G ASPARAGUS, PREFERABLY THICK SPEARS, TOUGH ENDS TRIMMED

3 TBSP EXTRA-VIRGIN OLIVE OIL

FINE SEA SALT

FRESHLY GROUND BLACK PEPPER

1 TBSP FRESHLY SQUEEZED LEMON JUICE

2 OZ/55 G IMPORTED SPECK (SEE PAGE 46), DICED OR CUT INTO THIN STRIPS

Prepare a medium-hot charcoal grill or preheat a gas grill to medium-high. Or position an oven rack 4 in/10 cm from the broiler and turn the broiler on.

In a baking dish, toss the asparagus with 2 tbsp of the olive oil, taking care to coat them thoroughly. Grill or broil the asparagus, turning them two or three times as they cook, for 5 minutes, or until just tender and browned in spots. Return the asparagus spears to the baking dish. Season lightly with salt and pepper, and dribble a little lemon juice over them. Use tongs to gently toss the asparagus.

In a small skillet, heat the remaining 1 tbsp olive oil over medium-high heat and add the speck. Cook, stirring often, 5 to 7 minutes, or until the speck is browned and crisped.

Sprinkle the speck and any pan drippings over the asparagus and serve.

BROCCOLINI WITH LEMON-MUSTARD DRESSING

makes 4 servings

Broccolini *seems* Italian, with its crunchy green florets and tender stalks. But in fact, it's a clever cross between standard broccoli and gai lan, Chinese broccoli. This is a good marriage, and, not surprisingly, broccolini is as comfortable in a stir-fry as it is tossed with this Italian-style dressing.

½ TSP MINCED GARLIC

1 TBSP FRESHLY SQUEEZED LEMON JUICE

1 TSP COARSE DIJON MUSTARD

3 TBSP EXTRA-VIRGIN OLIVE OIL

FINE SEA SALT

FRESHLY GROUND BLACK PEPPER

1 LB/455 G BROCCOLINI, STEM ENDS TRIMMED

KOSHER OR SEA SALT

In a small bowl, whisk together the garlic, lemon juice, and mustard. Whisk in the oil, and season with salt and pepper.

Bring a large saucepan of water to a boil and salt generously. Cook the broccolini for 3 minutes, until bright green and just tender—they should still have some crunch. Drain the broccolini.

Put the broccolini in a shallow serving bowl. Drizzle the dressing over them and toss to coat thoroughly. Serve immediately.

CAULIFLOWER WITH OIL-CURED OLIVES
AND ANCHOVIES

makes 8 servings

This dish is so much more than a recipe to me. Together with Braised Sweet-and-Sour Savoy Cabbage (page 222), it has been present at almost every Christmas Eve dinner that I have sat down to, and almost as many Thanksgiving dinners. It is my mother's creation, and it may very well be the dish most responsible for my lifelong love affair with vegetables. And olives. And anchovies.

KOSHER OR SEA SALT

2 MEDIUM HEADS CAULIFLOWER (ABOUT 2 LB/910 G), CUT INTO BITE-SIZE FLORETS

2 TBSP EXTRA-VIRGIN OLIVE OIL

2 GARLIC CLOVES, LIGHTLY CRUSHED

1 CUP/170 G PITTED OIL-CURED OLIVES

12 RIZZOLI-BRAND *ALICI IN SALSA PICCANTE* (SEE PAGE 43) OR BEST-QUALITY IMPORTED ITALIAN OR SPANISH ANCHOVY FILLETS IN OLIVE OIL

1½ TBSP CAPERS, RINSED, DRAINED, AND COARSELY CHOPPED

2 TBSP RED WINE VINEGAR

Bring a large pot of water to a boil over high heat and salt generously. Add the cauliflower florets, cover, and cook for 2 to 3 minutes, until they are barely tender and still quite firm. Drain them in a colander.

In a large skillet, heat the olive oil and garlic over medium heat. Cook, pressing down on the garlic cloves to release their fragrance, until the garlic is sizzling but not browned. Add the olives, anchovies, and capers, and mix everything together, pressing down lightly with a wooden spoon or silicone spatula to mash up the anchovies.

Add the cauliflower to the pan, and gently toss to combine the florets with the olives, capers, and anchovies. Reduce the heat to low, cover, and cook, stirring from time to time, for 20 minutes, or until the cauliflower is tender but not mushy.

Raise the heat to medium-high and sprinkle in the vinegar. Stir gently to combine, and cook for another 2 to 3 minutes, until the vinegar has been absorbed. Taste and add additional salt if you like—though between the olives, capers, and anchovies you probably won't need to. Serve immediately.

COOK'S NOTE: This recipe is easily halved to serve 4.

peperoni, *va*

SWEET-AND-SOUR PEPPERS
WITH OIL-CURED OLIVES
makes 4 to 6 servings

In summertime in Italy, you can hardly walk down the street—whether you're in a city or a small hill town—without catching the aroma of peppers roasting or frying. This scent fills me with wonderful memories of casual trattoria lunches and leisurely family dinners at our beach house on the Adriatic coast. Whenever I feel nostalgic for those days, which is often, I slice a couple of peppers and start them sizzling in a frying pan. Here's my latest variation, a sweet-and-sour version, with some salty cured olives tossed in for good measure.

3 TBSP EXTRA-VIRGIN OLIVE OIL

2 LARGE RIPE RED BELL PEPPERS, TRIMMED, SEEDED, AND CUT LENGTHWISE INTO 3/4-IN/2-CM SLICES

2 LARGE RIPE YELLOW BELL PEPPERS, TRIMMED, SEEDED, AND CUT LENGTHWISE INTO 3/4-IN/2-CM SLICES

1 CUP/115 G THINLY SLICED RED ONION (ABOUT 1/2 LARGE ONION)

1 TSP FINE SEA SALT

1 TBSP SUGAR

3 TBSP WHITE WINE VINEGAR

1/4 LIGHTLY PACKED CUP/45 G PITTED OIL-CURED OLIVES, HALVED LENGTHWISE

In a large skillet, warm the oil over medium heat. When it begins to shimmer, add the peppers and onion and cook, tossing and stirring often, for 15 minutes, or until the vegetables have begun to soften. Sprinkle in the salt and cook for another 15 minutes, until the peppers and onions are soft and browned in spots.

Sprinkle the sugar over the peppers and onions, and drizzle in the vinegar. Raise the heat to medium-high and cook for 1 or 2 minutes, until most of the vinegar has been absorbed. Stir in the olives and cook about 2 minutes more, just until the olives are warmed through.

Transfer the peppers to a serving platter and serve hot, warm, or at room temperature.

COOK'S NOTE: There are many ways to enjoy these peppers. Serve them as a side dish with roast chicken, pork, or a frittata. Or stir them into the frittata. You can also turn them into a topping for pizza or toss them with hot cooked pasta such as penne or cavatappi for a one-dish meal.

ESCAROLE ALL' ANTICA

makes 4 servings

Like radicchio, escarole is transformed by heat. It turns soft and pulpy, and its bitter flavor becomes mellow. For years, my mom was the only one in our house who liked escarole, so every now and again she would cook a small head of it and keep it in the refrigerator, to be enjoyed, presumably, when the kids were at school and my dad at work. I actually remember the time, during my teen years, when, in a moment of curiosity, I opened the container she stored it in, picked up a few shreds with my fingers, and tasted it. I can't say for sure, but I might have polished off the entire container right there in front of the fridge.

This recipe is as plain as they come, but it is so good. If you want to add a little more zest, you can stir in some chopped capers, a couple of minced anchovy fillets, or garnish it with shaved Parmigiano-Reggiano cheese.

1 HEAD ESCAROLE (ABOUT 1 LB/455 G), CORED, SEPARATED INTO LEAVES, AND THOROUGHLY WASHED

1/4 CUP/60 ML EXTRA-VIRGIN OLIVE OIL, PLUS MORE FOR DRIZZLING

4 GARLIC CLOVES, SLICED PAPER-THIN

1/2 TSP FINE SEA SALT

GENEROUS PINCH OF RED PEPPER FLAKES

1 LEMON, CUT INTO WEDGES

Bring a large pot of water to a boil. Drop in the escarole leaves and use tongs or a wooden spoon to submerge them. Cook, uncovered, for 3 to 4 minutes, until the escarole is wilted. Drain in a colander.

In a large frying pan, heat the oil and garlic over medium-low heat until the garlic begins to soften, about 3 minutes. Do not let it brown. Add the escarole to the pan and toss to coat it with the olive oil. Sprinkle in the salt and red pepper flakes and cook for 3 to 5 minutes, until heated through.

Transfer the warmed greens to a serving platter and garnish with a drizzle of olive oil. Arrange the lemon wedges around the platter and serve.

SAUTÉED DRAGON TONGUE BEANS WITH LEMON ZEST AND PEPERONCINO

makes 4 to 6 servings

Dragon Tongue beans are somewhat flat beans similar to Romano beans, but instead of being green they are a pale, creamy yellow with streaks of purple. They are versatile: they can be harvested as snap beans when young, as shell beans once their purple streaks have turned red, and as beans for drying when fully matured. The young snap beans called for in this recipe have a pleasantly firm texture and an appealing fresh bean flavor that shines in this simple sauté. If you are unable to find Dragon Tongue beans, substitute Romano beans or even young green beans or wax beans.

1 LB/455 G YOUNG DRAGON TONGUE OR ROMANO BEANS, STEM ENDS TRIMMED, SLICED ON THE DIAGONAL INTO 2-IN/5-CM PIECES

¼ CUP/60 ML EXTRA-VIRGIN OLIVE OIL

6 GARLIC CLOVES, MINCED

2 FRESH OREGANO SPRIGS

1 SMALL FRESH *PEPERONCINO* OR OTHER HOT CHILE PEPPER, MINCED; OR A GENEROUS PINCH OF RED PEPPER FLAKES

1 TBSP FINELY GRATED LEMON ZEST

FINE SEA SALT

Place a steamer basket in a large saucepan and fill the pan with water up to but not touching the bottom. Bring the water to a boil over high heat. Arrange the beans in the steamer basket, cover, and steam until just tender, 3 to 4 minutes, and the beans have lost their purple streaks. Remove from the heat and transfer the beans to a bowl.

Warm the oil, garlic, and oregano sprigs in a large skillet over low heat. Cook, stirring from time to time, for about 10 minutes, or until the garlic is softened but not browned. Stir in the *peperoncino* and lemon zest and cook for about 2 minutes, until the zest begins to release its fragrance. Add the reserved beans to the pan and toss to coat with the oil. Raise the heat to medium-low and cook, stirring occasionally, for 10 minutes, or until the beans are tender but not mushy. You should be able to easily pierce them with a fork. Season lightly with salt. Remove from the heat and remove and discard the oregano sprigs.

Transfer the beans to a serving bowl and spoon the warm oil over them (including the garlic and bits of *peperoncino* and lemon zest). Serve warm or at room temperature.

BRAISED SWEET-AND-SOUR SAVOY CABBAGE

makes 6 to 8 servings

My mom has been making this recipe—succulent Savoy cabbage braised in a rich, sweet and savory broth—since before I can remember, and it has always held a place of honor at our holiday feasts, especially on Thanksgiving and Christmas Eve. It goes beautifully with roast turkey, pork, or sautéed fish.

1 HEAD SAVOY CABBAGE (ABOUT 1½ LB/680 G), QUARTERED, CORED, AND COARSELY SHREDDED

⅓ CUP/75 ML EXTRA-VIRGIN OLIVE OIL

4 GARLIC CLOVES, LIGHTLY CRUSHED

1 TSP FINE SEA SALT

FRESHLY GROUND BLACK PEPPER

½ CUP/120 ML VEGETABLE BROTH (PAGE 62) OR BEST-QUALITY COMMERCIAL VEGETABLE OR CHICKEN BROTH

¼ TO ⅓ CUP/60 TO 75 ML DRY WHITE WINE

3 TBSP SUGAR

3 TBSP WHITE WINE VINEGAR

Place the cabbage in a large pot and cover with cold water. Bring the water to a boil over high heat and boil the cabbage for 3 to 5 minutes, until it is wilted but still a bit firm. Drain in a colander and set aside.

In a large heavy-bottomed sauté pan, heat the olive oil and garlic over medium heat. Cook, pressing down on the garlic cloves, for 3 to 4 minutes, or until the garlic is fragrant but not browned. Add the cabbage and toss to combine with the olive oil. Season with the salt and a generous grinding of pepper, and pour in the broth. Raise the heat to medium-high, bring to a simmer, then cover the pan and reduce the heat to medium-low. Cook, stirring occasionally, for 20 to 25 minutes, until the cabbage is tender.

Raise the heat to medium-high and add the wine. Let it bubble for about 2 minutes, and then add the sugar and vinegar. Cook at a lively simmer for about 5 minutes, or until some, but not all, of the liquid is absorbed. Taste and add additional salt or pepper if you like. Serve immediately.

BRAISED RADICCHIO WITH PANCETTA AND CREAM

makes 4 servings

Remember this dish when it's the middle of winter and you're feeling like the vegetable world has left you high and dry. It makes a great accompaniment to a simple roast beef or roast chicken dinner, and would be perfectly at home sharing the plate with a frittata. I've also turned this braise into a fine sauce for pasta.

1 TBSP EXTRA-VIRGIN OLIVE OIL	$1/2$ TSP FINE SEA SALT
6 OZ/170 G PANCETTA, DICED	FRESHLY GROUND BLACK PEPPER
2 SMALL SHALLOTS, THINLY SLICED	$1/4$ CUP/60 ML DRY WHITE WINE
1 LB/455 G RADICCHIO DI CHIOGGIA, QUARTERED, CORED, AND COARSELY SHREDDED	$1/2$ TO $3/4$ CUP/120 TO 180 ML HEAVY CREAM

Heat the oil and pancetta in a large skillet placed over medium heat. Cook, stirring frequently, until the pancetta is browned and crisped, about 8 minutes. With a slotted spoon, transfer the pancetta to a paper towel–lined plate and set aside.

Reduce the heat to medium-low and stir in the shallots. Cook, stirring frequently, until softened but not browned, about 7 minutes. Add the radicchio, in batches if necessary, along with the salt. Cover the pan, raise the heat to medium-high, and cook the radicchio for about 8 minutes, or until it is all wilted. Uncover the pan and season with several grindings of pepper. Pour in the wine and let it bubble for about 2 minutes. Stir in the cream and cook for about 2 minutes more, until the sauce is thickened. Return the pancetta to the pan and stir to combine with the radicchio. Serve immediately.

RAPINI BRAISED IN TOMATO SAUCE

makes 4 servings

Amy Brandwein is a chef in Washington, DC, and an Italophile. We share a love of rapini (broccoli rabe), the pungent green popular in Southern Italian cooking. One day, when Amy and I were having lunch together, she introduced me to her favorite way to enjoy rapini — braised in tomato sauce. Until then I had always made rapini with plenty of garlic and oil and, usually, a splash of dry white wine—but no tomato. One bite of Amy's version and I was hooked. I asked Amy if I could adapt her recipe and she generously agreed.

1 LB/455 G RAPINI, WELL RINSED, TOUGH STEM TRIMMED

3 TBSP EXTRA-VIRGIN OLIVE OIL, PLUS MORE FOR DRIZZLING

2 GARLIC CLOVES, MINCED

1 TO 2 SMALL CHILE PEPPERS IN OLIVE OIL (PAGE 259), MINCED, OR A GENEROUS PINCH OF RED PEPPER FLAKES

1 TSP FINE SEA SALT

ONE 14½-OZ/415-G CAN DICED TOMATOES, WITH THEIR JUICE

Put the rapini, with the rinse water still clinging to it, in a large pot and place over medium-high heat. Cover and cook, using tongs to turn the greens occasionally, for 15 minutes, or until completely wilted.

Meanwhile, in a large skillet, heat the olive oil with the garlic over medium-low heat. Cook, stirring often, for 3 to 4 minutes, or until the garlic is softened and fragrant but not browned. Stir in the chile peppers. Using tongs, transfer the rapini from the pot to the skillet and gently toss to coat with the olive oil. Add the salt. Cover partially and cook for 5 minutes. Raise the heat to medium-high, stir in the diced tomatoes, and bring to a simmer. Reduce the heat to medium-low, cover partially, and simmer for 30 to 40 minutes, turning occasionally, until the greens are tender and the tomatoes have thickened to a sauce consistency.

Transfer the greens to a serving bowl and drizzle a few drops of olive oil over them. Serve hot.

ROASTED FENNEL WITH
SULTANAS AND CHILE PEPPER
makes 6 to 8 servings

This recipe was originally given to me by John Coletta, chef and partner at Quartino, an Italian restaurant in Chicago. It's one of my favorite ways to enjoy fennel and I make it often. Over the years I have played around with the flavors. Here is my latest riff, bright with freshly squeezed orange juice and fresh rosemary.

1/2 CUP/80 G SULTANAS (GOLDEN RAISINS)

2 STRIPS ORANGE ZEST AND 2/3 CUP/165 ML FRESHLY SQUEEZED ORANGE JUICE

1/3 CUP/75 ML DRY WHITE WINE

2 SMALL FRESH ROSEMARY SPRIGS

1 BATCH ROASTED FENNEL (PAGE 68), USING 3 BULBS

1 TO 2 TBSP AGED BALSAMIC VINEGAR

1 TBSP EXTRA-VIRGIN OLIVE OIL

1 SMALL FRESH CHILE PEPPER, MINCED

FINE SEA SALT

Put the sultanas, orange zest and juice, white wine, and 1 rosemary sprig in a small saucepan and bring to a simmer over medium-high heat. Reduce the heat to medium-low and simmer for 10 to 15 minutes, until the raisins are plumped and tender. Drain the sultanas in a small strainer and discard the liquid and rosemary sprig.

In a large bowl, combine the roasted fennel with the poached sultanas. Add 1 tbsp balsamic vinegar and 1 tbsp olive oil. Add the minced chile pepper and toss everything together gently. Taste and season with salt or more vinegar if you like.

Transfer the salad to a decorative bowl or platter and garnish with the remaining rosemary sprig. Serve warm or at room temperature.

ROASTED WAX BEANS WITH CHOPPED HERBS AND FETA

makes 4 to 6 servings

I wish I had tried wax beans years ago. I thought their pale hue meant they had a pale flavor to match. I couldn't have been more wrong. They are lovely, crisp-tender, and sweet, and taste slightly grassy and buttery. And they are pretty, too, especially when they are picked young and their luminous pods are still tinged with green. Most of the time, I do nothing more than steam them and toss them with good olive oil, but this slightly more elaborate preparation is a nice change.

1 LB/455 G FRESH YELLOW WAX BEANS, STEM ENDS SNAPPED OFF

4 TBSP/60 ML EXTRA-VIRGIN OLIVE OIL

1/2 TSP FINE SEA SALT

FINELY GRATED ZEST AND JUICE OF 1 SMALL LEMON

1 GARLIC CLOVE, LIGHTLY CRUSHED

2 TBSP COARSELY CHOPPED FRESH HERBS (I USE A MIX OF BASIL, MINT, AND OREGANO)

2 OZ/60 G GREEK FETA CHEESE, CRUMBLED

Heat the oven to 425°F/220°C/gas 7.

Place the beans on a small, rimmed baking sheet and drizzle 2 tbsp of the oil over them. Toss to coat, and then arrange them in a single layer. Sprinkle the salt over them. Roast, uncovered, for 10 minutes, until the beans are just tender.

Using tongs, transfer the beans to a shallow serving bowl. Add the lemon zest, lemon juice, garlic, herbs, and the remaining 2 tbsp olive oil. Toss to combine thoroughly. Sprinkle the feta over the beans and toss again. Some of the feta will break up more and become part of the dressing.

Cover the beans and let sit for about 10 minutes to allow the flavors to mingle before serving.

ROASTED ROMANESCO WITH ANCHOVY SAUCE

makes 4 servings

I met Amy Albert when she was an editor at *Fine Cooking* and I was writing my first piece for the magazine. She came to my home in Virginia to take pictures of me making sauce in my kitchen. I was all nerves and excitement, and she was the perfect counterbalance—warm, friendly, calm, and professional. We hit it off and stayed in touch. When I was looking for a recipe to honor this unique vegetable, Romanesco cauliflower, with its Fibonacci spirals, soft green hue, and mild, sweet flavor, Amy came through with this simple, classic preparation, in which the roasted florets are tossed with a savory anchovy sauce. Amy's method calls for using a mortar and pestle (see page 51) to make the sauce. If you don't have one, you can use a sharp chef's knife to mash the ingredients together, or zap them in a small food processor.

1 GARLIC CLOVE

GENEROUS PINCH OF COARSE SEA SALT OR KOSHER SALT

2 RIZZOLI-BRAND *ALICI IN SALSA PICCANTE* (SEE PAGE 43) OR BEST-QUALITY IMPORTED ITALIAN OR SPANISH ANCHOVY FILLETS IN OLIVE OIL

1 PEPPER, CHILE PEPPER IN OLIVE OIL (PAGE 259), MINCED, OR A GENEROUS PINCH OF RED PEPPER FLAKES

4 TBSP/60 ML EXTRA-VIRGIN OLIVE OIL

1 HEAD (1½ LB/680 G) ROMANESCO CAULIFLOWER, OR COMMON CAULI-FLOWER OR BROCCOLINI, TRIMMED AND CUT INTO FLORETS, CORE CUT INTO BITE-SIZE PIECES

JUICE OF ½ LEMON

1 TBSP MINCED FRESH FLAT-LEAF PARSLEY

Heat the oven to 350°F/180°C/gas 4.

In a mortar, pound the garlic with the salt. Add the anchovies and pepper and pound everything together to a paste. Slowly work in 2 tbsp of the olive oil until incorporated.

Spread the Romanesco out on a heavy-duty rimmed baking sheet and drizzle the remaining 2 tbsp of the olive oil over them. Toss to coat the florets with the oil. Roast for 13 minutes. Remove the florets from the oven, pour the anchovy sauce over them, and toss to coat well. Roast for another 10 to 12 minutes, until the florets are just tender and lightly browned in spots.

Transfer the cauliflower florets to a serving bowl and sprinkle the lemon juice and chopped parsley over them. Toss well to combine and serve.

HONEY-BALSAMIC ROASTED CARROTS

makes 4 servings

You know why I love carrots? Because they are always there for me. Literally. I always have a bag of them in the vegetable bin in my fridge, and I'm guessing you do, too. Roasting them with a touch of honey and balsamic vinegar gives them the star treatment they deserve. Use everyday orange carrots, or mix in some colorful heirloom ones—red, purple, and golden—for a little variety.

1 LB/455 G CARROTS, CUT IN HALF CROSSWISE, EACH HALF CUT LENGTHWISE INTO QUARTERS

2 TBSP EXTRA-VIRGIN OLIVE OIL

1 TBSP GOOD-QUALITY FLAVORFUL HONEY

2 TSP AGED BALSAMIC VINEGAR, PLUS MORE FOR SPRINKLING

1/2 TSP COARSE SEA SALT, PLUS MORE FOR SPRINKLING

FRESHLY GROUND BLACK PEPPER

Heat the oven to 375°F/190°C/gas 5.

Put the carrots in a roasting pan. In a small bowl, whisk together the olive oil, honey, and 2 tsp vinegar. Pour over the carrots. Season with 1/2 tsp salt and a generous grinding of pepper. Toss gently to combine. Roast the carrots for 10 minutes; toss, and roast for 15 minutes more, or until the carrots are tender and browned in spots.

Transfer to a serving dish and sprinkle a few more drops of vinegar and some sea salt on top. Serve hot or warm.

BEET AND BEET GREEN GRATIN
WITH FONTINA AND GORGONZOLA

makes 4 servings

Honestly? Beets are not the first vegetable that comes to my mind when I think of Italian cooking. My mother, who is from Abruzzo, rarely made them. But in fact they do turn up in the cooking of Italy's northern regions, which is where I got the inspiration for this colorful gratin. Sweet, earthy beets pair beautifully with the creamy, assertive cheeses of the north, and since I couldn't choose between Fontina and Gorgonzola, I used both.

2^1/2 LB/1.2 KG BEETS WITH THEIR GREEN TOPS, WASHED THOROUGHLY TO REMOVE ANY GRIT

3 TBSP EXTRA-VIRGIN OLIVE OIL, PLUS MORE FOR THE BAKING DISH

2 GARLIC CLOVES, SLICED PAPER-THIN

FINE SEA SALT

FRESHLY GROUND BLACK PEPPER

SHREDDED FONTINA VAL D'AOSTA CHEESE

^{3}/4 CUP/85 G CRUMBLED GORGONZOLA DOLCE OR GORGONZOLA PICCANTE CHEESE

1^1/4 CUP/60 ML HEAVY CREAM

3 TBSP COARSELY CHOPPED WALNUTS

Cut off the beet tops from the beets. Cut the red stems from the leafy part of the beet tops. Chop the stems into 1-in/2.5-cm pieces and coarsely chop the greens. Trim the tops and bottoms off the beets and slice them into thin rounds.

In a large skillet, heat the olive oil and the garlic over medium-low heat. Cook, stirring frequently, for about 5 minutes, or until the garlic is softened but not browned. Toss in the beet green stem pieces and cook, stirring often, for 6 minutes, or until they begin to soften. Begin to add the chopped leaves by the handful, using tongs to toss them in the oil. Continue to add more greens as those in the pan start to wilt, until you have added them all. Sprinkle in ^{1}/2 tsp salt, toss, and cover partially. Cook for 10 to 15 minutes, until the greens and stems are tender. Taste and add additional salt if you like. Transfer the cooked beet tops to a bowl.

Heat the oven to 375°F/190°C/gas 5. Lightly coat an 8-by-8-in/20-by-20-cm ovenproof baking dish with olive oil.

Arrange half of the sliced beets in the bottom of the baking dish. Season with a little salt and pepper. Scatter half the Fontina over the beet slices. Spread all of the cooked beet tops over the cheese, and dot with half of the Gorgonzola. Arrange the remaining beet slices on top and season with salt and pepper. Top with the remaining Fontina and Gorgonzola, and add a final few grindings of pepper. Drizzle the cream over the gratin and sprinkle the walnuts on top.

Bake the gratin for 45 to 50 minutes, or until the beets are tender and the cheese and walnut topping is nicely browned. Serve hot.

SMASHED GREEN BEANS AND POTATOES
WITH PANCETTA
makes 6 servings

La Loggia Antica is an agritourism restaurant situated high in the hills above Bisenti, in Abruzzo's Teramo province. The small, informal restaurant is known for the creative ways in which it features local vegetables. My friend Marcello de Antoniis, a local expert on the area's cuisine, recommended the restaurant to my family and me when we were visiting in 2009, and it turned out to be one of the (many) highlights of our trip. I remember making a point to write down, in the food journal I carried everywhere with me, the many dishes we enjoyed that day, including this rustic mash of potatoes and green beans seasoned simply—but deliciously—with good olive oil and crispy pancetta.

1 LB/455 G MEDIUM-SIZE YELLOW POTATOES, SUCH AS YUKON GOLD, PEELED AND CUT IN HALF CROSSWISE

1 LB/455 G FRESH YOUNG GREEN BEANS, ENDS TRIMMED

4 OZ/115 G PANCETTA, DICED

1/3 CUP/75 ML GOOD-QUALITY EXTRA-VIRGIN OLIVE OIL, PLUS MORE FOR DRIZZLING

FINE SEA SALT

FRESHLY GROUND BLACK PEPPER

Put the potatoes and green beans in a large pot and fill with cold water to cover. Set the pot over high heat and salt generously. Bring the water to a boil and reduce the heat to medium-high to maintain a lively (but not violent) simmer. Boil the vegetables until they are very tender, about 25 minutes.

While the potatoes and green beans are cooking, place the pancetta in a medium skillet (I use a well-seasoned cast-iron skillet) and set over medium heat. Sauté the pancetta, turning it frequently, for about 10 minutes, until it has rendered some of its fat and has just begun to crisp and turn brown. Remove from the heat and cover to keep warm.

When the vegetables are tender, drain them in a colander. Return them to the pot and slowly drizzle in the olive oil. Use a potato masher to mash the potatoes and green beans together as you drizzle. What you're aiming for is a somewhat lumpy, textured mash—no need to purée completely.

With a spatula or wooden spoon, scrape the pancetta and drippings into the pot and stir to combine with the potato-bean mash. Season with salt and pepper.

Spoon the mixture into a serving bowl and drizzle with a little more olive oil if you like. Serve warm or at room temperature.

patate, olio d'oliva, sale, fazioli, peperoni, pancetta

SWEET-AND-SOUR WINTER SQUASH

makes 4 servings

I am not exaggerating when I tell you that winter squash prepared in this way is as good as candy. The vegetable's natural sugar caramelizes as the slices cook in the skillet. The syrupy sweet-and-sour sauce gives the squash a beautiful lacquered finish.

⅓ CUP/75 ML EXTRA-VIRGIN OLIVE OIL

2 TO 3 GARLIC CLOVES, LIGHTLY CRUSHED

1 LB/455 G DELICATA OR BUTTERNUT SQUASH, TRIMMED, PEELED, HALVED LENGTHWISE, SEEDED, AND CUT INTO ¼-IN-/6-MM HALF-MOON SLICES (IF USING DELICATA, PEELING IS OPTIONAL)

1 TBSP LIGHT BROWN SUGAR

3 TBSP WHITE WINE VINEGAR

¼ TSP FINE SEA SALT

FRESHLY GROUND BLACK PEPPER

1 TSP MINCED FRESH MINT

Heat the oil and garlic in a large skillet over medium-low heat. Cook until the garlic is softened and fragrant but not browned, 3 to 4 minutes. Press down on the cloves to release their flavor. Remove the garlic from the skillet and set aside.

Arrange a layer of squash slices in the skillet and fry, turning once or twice, until they are lightly browned on both sides and just tender. Using a slotted spoon, transfer the slices to a platter. Continue to fry the squash in batches until you have fried them all.

In a small bowl, dissolve the sugar in the vinegar. Carefully return all of the squash slices to the skillet. Sprinkle the sugar-vinegar mixture over the squash and season with the salt and pepper. Cook, gently moving the pieces of squash around, for 2 to 3 minutes, or until the sauce is reduced to a thick syrup. Sprinkle the mint on top.

Return the squash slices to the platter, cover loosely, and let sit for about 30 minutes to allow the flavors to mingle. If you want more prominent garlic flavor, tuck the reserved garlic cloves in among the squash pieces before covering. Serve at room temperature.

BAKED DELICATA SQUASH
WITH CREAM AND PARMIGIANO

makes 4 servings

I did not grow up with baked acorn squash, a classic American autumn side dish of scooped-out squash halves filled with butter, brown sugar, and raisins. Although I enjoy that version, I really love this pared down "Italianized" rendition that I created for dinner one cold night. I use delicata, a slim squash with a thin striped rind and sweet gold flesh. Most farmers' markets and supermarkets carry delicata in fall and winter, but you can substitute acorn squash.

2 DELICATA OR ACORN SQUASHES (2½ TO 3 LB/1.2 TO 1.4 KG), HALVED LENGTHWISE, SEEDED, EACH HALF CUT IN HALF CROSSWISE TO YIELD A TOTAL OF 4 PIECES

¼ CUP/60 ML HEAVY CREAM

FINE SEA SALT

FRESHLY GROUND BLACK PEPPER

PINCH OF FRESHLY GRATED NUTMEG

¼ CUP/30 G FRESHLY GRATED PARMIGIANO-REGGIANO CHEESE

Heat the oven to 400°F/200°C/gas 6.

Arrange the pieces of squash, cut-side up, on a rimmed baking sheet or in a large baking dish. Drizzle the heavy cream on the squash pieces and use a pastry brush to spread it around. Season with a little salt and a few grindings of pepper. Sprinkle a little nutmeg over each piece (I grate the nutmeg directly over the pieces), and then sprinkle on the Parmigiano.

Bake the squash for 30 to 40 minutes if using delicata squash, or 45 minutes if using acorn squash. Baste the squash once or twice during baking. The squash is done when the cream is thickened and lightly browned and the flesh is tender and easily pierced with the tip of a knife.

Transfer the baked squash to a decorative platter and serve immediately.

, panna, sale, pepe, noce mosca
zziano

CARDOON SFORMATI

makes 6 servings

My friend Joe Gray is the food editor at the *Chicago Tribune*. We share an Italian heritage (both of us have family who came from Abruzzo) and a passion for Italian cooking. A couple of years ago, Joe went on a quest to master the art of the *sformato*, a savory baked custard made with vegetable purée—the word *sformato* means "unformed" or "unmolded" and refers to the way the custard is served, turned out from the mold in which it is baked. Through trial and error and with the help of a recipe from Marcella Hazan, Joe came up with what is, to me, the perfect master *sformato* recipe, rich and refined yet simple to execute. After his recipe ran in the *Trib*, I asked Joe if he wouldn't mind sharing it, and he and the paper kindly agreed. I chose cardoons, which are popular in Italian cooking but not so well known over here, for this version; see Variations below for many other choices.

BALSAMELLA SAUCE:	2 TBSP EXTRA-VIRGIN OLIVE OIL
1 CUP/240 ML WHOLE MILK	1/2 CUP/60 G DICED YELLOW ONION
1 TBSP UNSALTED BUTTER	1 GARLIC CLOVE, MINCED
1 1/2 TBSP UNBLEACHED ALL-PURPOSE FLOUR	1/4 TSP FINE SEA SALT
1/4 TSP FINE SEA SALT	2 LARGE EGGS
PINCH OF FRESHLY GRATED NUTMEG	1 CUP/115 G FRESHLY GRATED PARMIGIANO-REGGIANO CHEESE
CARDOON PURÉE:	UNSALTED BUTTER FOR THE RAMEKINS
FRESHLY SQUEEZED JUICE OF 1 LEMON	3 TO 4 TBSP DRIED BREAD CRUMBS
2 LB/910 G TENDER CARDOON STALKS, TOUGH OUTER STALKS AND ANY STRINGS REMOVED, CUT INTO 2-IN/5-CM PIECES	6 SMALL FRESH FLAT-LEAF PARSLEY SPRIGS FOR GARNISH

TO MAKE THE SAUCE: Pour the milk into a small saucepan. Bring just to a boil over medium heat and then turn off the heat.

Melt the butter in a small heavy-bottomed saucepan over medium heat. Whisk in the flour and cook, stirring constantly, for 2 minutes. Add the hot milk in driblets, whisking constantly and taking care to eliminate lumps and avoid scorching. The mixture will look like it's breaking but it will come together again and become smooth. When all of the milk has been added, cook the sauce, stirring it frequently, for 10 to 15 minutes, or until it is thick enough to coat the back of a wooden spoon. Reduce the heat to medium-low if necessary to prevent scorching. Season with the salt and the nutmeg, and remove from the heat. Cover until ready to use.

TO PREPARE THE PURÉE: Bring a large pot of water to a boil over high heat and add the lemon juice. Add the cardoons and bring to a boil. Reduce the heat to medium or medium-low and let the cardoons simmer for 45 minutes, or until completely tender. Drain in a colander.

In a large skillet, heat the olive oil, onion, and garlic over medium-low heat. Cook, stirring often, for 5 minutes, or until the onion is beginning to soften. Add the drained cardoons to the pan and season with the salt. Cook, stirring occasionally, for 5 minutes to blend the flavors. Let cool for 5 minutes. Transfer to a food processor fitted with the metal blade and purée until smooth.

Heat the oven to 400°F/200°C/gas 6.

Beat the eggs in a large bowl. Gently whisk in the *balsamella*. Gently stir in the cardoon purée and two-thirds of the Parmigiano cheese.

Lightly coat six 6-oz/180-ml ramekins with butter, then sprinkle in the bread crumbs, thoroughly coating the inside of each ramekin. Pour the cardoon custard into the six ramekins, dividing it among them, and sprinkle the remaining Parmigiano on top.

Bake the *sformati* for 30 minutes or until they are firm and a light golden crust forms on top. Remove the *sformati* from the oven and let sit for about 5 minutes.

To unmold, place a small plate upside down over a ramekin and invert. Holding the ramekin firmly to the plate, lift the plate up and then sharply down to break the suction and release the *sformato*. Unmold the remaining *sformati* in the same way. Garnish each *sformato* with a small parsley sprig if you like, and serve.

VARIATIONS: You can turn any number of vegetables into *sformati*—asparagus, broccoli, carrots, cauliflower, fennel, green beans, spinach, and winter squash are all good candidates. Just substitute an equal quantity of your vegetable of choice for the cardoons. You can either boil the vegetable or cook it in a steamer basket set over simmering water until tender. Or in the case of winter squash, use the basic recipe for Roasted Winter Squash Purée (page 70). Cooking times for boiling or steaming the vegetables before adding them to the custard will vary depending on the vegetable—asparagus and spinach will be done in a few minutes, but other vegetables will take longer.

chapter 8
DESSERTS
Dolci

DESSERTS
Dolci

You didn't think we were going to skip dessert, did you?

Here I'm offering a small but delicious selection of some of my favorite desserts that feature vegetables. These recipes, by the way, are not an attempt to manipulate vegetables into roles they are not designed to play. So you will not see, for example, a recipe for cardoon or eggplant gelato, though I am sure they exist somewhere. What you will find is a luscious Pumpkin Gelato (page 250), spiked with liqueur and fragrant with spice. Pumpkin and gelato were made for each other.

Pumpkin, or more accurately, winter squash, is also the star in a rich, beautifully burnished lattice-top Buttercup Squash and Ricotta Crostata (page 242), a rustic dessert that has been the finale at many a winter dinner party at my house.

Borrowing a page from my childhood, I created an Italian-ized version of the classic chocolate zucchini cake that was so popular in the 1970s. But this cake (page 244), is much different, dense and pudding-like, yet somehow light-textured. You'll have to make it to see what I mean.

My favorite recipe of the bunch might be the simplest one of all, a golden Carrot Polenta Cake with Marsala (page 246). It has a light, tender, orange-flecked crumb and a warm flavor infused with Marsala wine and citrus zest. Serve it, dusted with powdered sugar, for dessert, or enjoy it as an afternoon snack— with an espresso, of course.

SWEET POTATO FRITTELLE
makes 2 dozen fritters

There are many variations of Italian traditional Carnival fritters. In Venice, you will find them made with diced apples and raisins, and with puréed winter squash. I happened to have some mashed Japanese sweet potato in my fridge, so that is what I put into my batter. My kids ate them all as soon as they came out of the fryer.

Take note that making these fritters can be a little bit tricky—the oil for frying should be hot, but not so hot that they brown too quickly. Otherwise you will end up with fritters that aren't fully cooked inside. Be sure to turn them over in the oil a few times so that they cook evenly. You can either roll the fitters in granulated sugar or sprinkle with confectioners' sugar. I prefer the confectioners' sugar, because it makes the fritters look festive and as if they've been dusted with snow.

½ CUP/85 G MASHED COOKED JAPANESE SWEET POTATO, SWEET POTATO (SEE COOK'S NOTE), OR ROASTED WINTER SQUASH PURÉE (PAGE 70)

FINELY GRATED ZEST OF 1 ORANGE

1 LARGE EGG, LIGHTLY BEATEN

¼ CUP/50 G GRANULATED SUGAR

¾ CUP/90 G UNBLEACHED ALL-PURPOSE FLOUR

1 TSP BAKING POWDER

PINCH OF FRESHLY GRATED NUTMEG

VEGETABLE OIL FOR FRYING

CONFECTIONERS' SUGAR FOR DUSTING

Combine the mashed sweet potato with the orange zest in a mixing bowl. Add the egg and granulated sugar and combine them thoroughly with a wooden spoon or silicone spatula. Add the flour, baking powder, and nutmeg and stir well, until you have a thick, smooth batter. Let the batter rest for 15 to 20 minutes.

Pour enough oil into a deep sauté pan or pot to reach a depth of about 3 in/ 7.5 cm. Place the oil over medium high heat and heat to 350°F/190°C on a deep-frying thermometer. Test it by dropping in a tiny dollop of batter; it should sizzle gently and puff up quickly. Use two teaspoons to form rounded mounds of batter—no more than a scant tsp of batter for each fritter—and drop the mounds into the hot oil. Take care not to crowd the skillet. Fry the batter, turning the fritters occasionally, until they are a deep golden brown on the outside, about 3 minutes. With a mesh strainer or slotted spoon, transfer the fritters to a paper towel–lined plate. Let them cool slightly.

Dust the still-warm fritters with confectioners' sugar, and serve warm.

COOK'S NOTE: Japanese sweet potatoes are similar to the standard sweet potatoes available in grocery stores. However, their skin is purple-red and their flesh is creamy white. They have a sweet, almost floral taste that makes them great for using in desserts. They are also delicious roasted or baked in their skins. For this recipe, I baked a whole Japanese sweet potato in its skin, wrapped in foil, and then let it cool and scooped out the flesh.

BUTTERCUP SQUASH AND RICOTTA CROSTATA

makes one 9-in / 23-cm lattice-top crostata; 8 servings

Buttercup squash is not as well known as other varieties of winter squash such as butternut or acorn—but it should be. Buttercup is squat and round with a hard, dark green striped rind. Beneath that rind is bright orange flesh that is smooth, dense, and sweet when cooked. Look for buttercup squash (see page 41) at farmers' markets and well-stocked supermarkets through fall and into winter. Be sure to use good-quality ricotta cheese (see page 45)—it makes a difference.

1 BATCH SWEET PASTRY DOUGH (PAGE 61)

8 OZ/225 G WELL-DRAINED FRESH COW'S MILK RICOTTA CHEESE

8 OZ/225 G ROASTED WINTER SQUASH PURÉE (PAGE 70), MADE WITH BUTTERCUP SQUASH

3/4 CUP/85 G CONFECTIONERS' SUGAR, PLUS MORE FOR DUSTING

2 LARGE EGGS, SEPARATED

2 TBSP PUNCH ABRUZZO (PAGE 48), DARK RUM, OR BRANDY

1/2 TSP PURE VANILLA EXTRACT

1/4 TSP GROUND CINNAMON

1/8 TSP FINE SEA SALT

1/8 TSP CREAM OF TARTAR

WHIPPED CREAM FOR SERVING

Cut the dough disk into two portions, one slightly larger than the other. Rewrap the smaller portion and refrigerate. On a lightly floured surface, roll out the larger portion into an 11-in/28-cm round about 1/8 in/3 mm thick. Carefully wrap the dough around the rolling pin and drape it over a 9-in/23-cm fluted tart pan with a removable bottom. Gently press the dough into the bottom of the pan and up the sides. Use the rolling pin or the flat of your hand to press around the perimeter of the pan, cutting off any excess dough. Put the lined tart pan in the refrigerator to chill for 30 minutes.

Heat the oven to 350°F/180°C/gas 4.

In a large bowl, beat together the ricotta and the squash purée. Beat in the sugar, and then the egg yolks, liqueur, vanilla, and cinnamon. In a separate bowl, using clean beaters, beat the egg whites with the salt and cream of tartar until stiff peaks form. Gently fold the egg whites into the ricotta-squash mixture.

Remove the tart shell from the refrigerator. Gently spoon the ricotta-squash mixture into the shell and smooth it with a spatula. Roll out the remaining dough portion into a 10-in/25-cm round about 1/8 in/3 mm thick, and cut it into 3/4-in /2-cm strips with a fluted pastry wheel. Carefully place the strips over the filling in a lattice pattern, gently pressing the ends of the strips into the metal rim of the tart pan with the palm of your hand to cut off the excess. If you like, you can arrange more strips around the outer rim of the pan to form a border. Press these into the metal rim to cut off any excess dough.

Bake the crostata for 50 to 60 minutes, until the crust is golden and the filling is puffed and just set—the center should not wobble. Remove from the oven and place it on a wire rack to cool for 20 minutes.

Remove the fluted rim of the tart pan and transfer the crostata to a decorative serving platter. Serve warm with a dollop of whipped cream on top.

CHOCOLATE ZUCCHINI CAKE

makes one 8-in / 20-cm cake; 6 to 8 servings

I am old enough to remember when zucchini bread was all the rage in the 1970s. Sweet, spicy, moist, and tender, were it not for the little flecks of green we might not have known the cake-like quick bread contained any of the vegetable at all. Indeed, that is the appeal of using zucchini in baking; it does its job quietly, adding moistness without overwhelming a cake's flavor. Still, when I incorporated grated zucchini into the batter for this simple chocolate cake, I wasn't sure what to expect. What I got was a delightful surprise—a rich, deep chocolate flavor and a dense, pudding-like texture that retained a certain lightness about it. There's no need to frost this cake—a dusting of confectioners' sugar is perfect.

2 MEDIUM ZUCCHINI (ABOUT 1$\frac{2}{3}$ CUPS/ 170 G), SHREDDED ON THE LARGE HOLES OF A BOX GRATER

$\frac{1}{2}$ CUP/50 G COCOA POWDER

$\frac{1}{2}$ CUP/120 ML BOILING WATER

2 LARGE EGGS

1$\frac{1}{4}$ CUP/250 G GRANULATED SUGAR

$\frac{2}{3}$ CUP/165 ML EXTRA-VIRGIN OR LIGHT OLIVE OIL, PLUS MORE FOR THE PAN

$\frac{1}{2}$ TSP PURE VANILLA EXTRACT

$\frac{1}{4}$ TSP PURE ALMOND EXTRACT

2 TBSP PUNCH ABRUZZO (PAGE 48), GRAND MARNIER, OR DARK RUM (OPTIONAL)

$\frac{1}{2}$ CUP/60 G UNBLEACHED ALL-PURPOSE FLOUR, PLUS MORE FOR DUSTING THE PAN

$\frac{1}{2}$ CUP/70 G ALMOND FLOUR OR ALMOND MEAL

$\frac{1}{4}$ TSP BAKING SODA

$\frac{1}{4}$ TSP FINE SEA SALT

CONFECTIONERS' SUGAR FOR DUSTING

Heat the oven to 325°F/165°C/gas 3. Lightly coat an 8-in/20-cm round baking pan with olive oil. Sprinkle a little flour into the pan and coat the interior, tapping out any excess.

Place the shredded zucchini in a medium bowl lined with paper towels to absorb some of the liquid. Set aside.

In a small bowl, whisk together the cocoa powder and boiling water until smooth. Set aside to cool.

In a large bowl, whisk together the eggs and granulated sugar until pale, thick, and frothy. Slowly whisk in the olive oil until well blended. Stir in the cocoa mixture, vanilla extract, almond extract, and the liqueur, if using.

In a separate medium bowl, whisk together the flour, almond flour, baking soda, and salt. Pour the flour mixture into the egg mixture, whisking all the while to avoid lumps. Using a silicone spatula or wooden spoon, stir in the shredded zucchini. Scrape the batter into the prepared baking pan.

Bake for 55 to 65 minutes, or until a cake tester inserted into the center of the cake comes out clean. Transfer the pan to a rack to cool for 20 to 30 minutes. Remove the cake from the pan and set it on the rack to cool to room temperature.

Transfer the cooled cake to a decorative platter. Dust the cake lightly with confectioners' sugar right before serving.

CARROT POLENTA CAKE WITH MARSALA

makes one 8-in / 20-cm cake; 6 to 8 servings

Have you ever experimented with a recipe that turned out so well that you can't quite believe you made it? This is that recipe. I made this simple cake on a brisk, cold day in January. As the cake baked, it filled the kitchen with the warm scent of Marsala and citrus, so that even before I tasted it, I had a feeling it would be more than the sum of its parts. This cake has a lovely, tender crumb thanks to the olive oil and grated carrots. It is a typical Italian home dessert, not at all fancy, and a good companion to an afternoon espresso—or hot tea, if that is your preference.

½ CUP/120 ML EXTRA-VIRGIN OR LIGHT OLIVE OIL, PLUS MORE FOR THE PAN

1 CUP/200 G GRANULATED SUGAR

2 LARGE EGGS

½ CUP/120 ML DRY MARSALA WINE

FINELY GRATED ZEST OF 1 LEMON

FINELY GRATED ZEST OF 1 ORANGE

1¼ CUPS/145 G UNBLEACHED ALL-PURPOSE FLOUR

½ CUP/70 G FINELY GROUND POLENTA

2 TSP BAKING POWDER

¾ TSP FINE SEA SALT

PINCH OF FRESHLY GRATED NUTMEG

2 CUPS/175 G SHREDDED CARROTS (ABOUT 3 LARGE)

CONFECTIONERS' SUGAR FOR DUSTING

Heat the oven to 375°F/190°C/gas 5. Lightly coat an 8-in/20-cm square or round baking pan with olive oil and set aside.

In a large bowl, whisk together the olive oil, granulated sugar, eggs, Marsala, and the lemon and orange zests until well blended (the sugar will not completely dissolve).

In a separate medium bowl, whisk together the flour, polenta, baking powder, salt, and nutmeg. Pour the flour mixture into the egg mixture, whisking all the while to avoid lumps. Using a silicone spatula or wooden spoon, stir in the shredded carrots. Scrape the batter into the prepared baking pan.

Bake for 35 minutes, or until a cake tester inserted into the middle of the cake comes out clean. Transfer the pan to a rack to cool for 20 to 30 minutes. Remove the cake from the pan and set it on the rack to cool to room temperature.

Transfer the cake to a decorative platter. Dust the cake lightly with confectioners' sugar right before serving.

carote, limone, marsala, farina
noce moscato, uova, aranc

WINTER SQUASH PANNA COTTA

makes 8 servings

I still remember the first time I had panna cotta. My mom and I had been wandering around Rome's historic *centro*, shopping and sightseeing, when we found a small restaurant tucked somewhere behind the Spanish Steps. The panna cotta was served in a balloon glass, and the custard was thick and silky and tasted like fresh cream spiked with vanilla. Now this dessert is world famous and comes in countless exotic flavors. My feeling, though, is that simple is best, so I've added just a touch of spice and a little roasted winter squash, both for color and for the sweet earthy flavor it adds. It makes a delicious fall or winter dessert.

3 CUPS/720 ML HEAVY CREAM

²/₃ CUP/130 G SUGAR

½ VANILLA BEAN

¼ TSP GROUND CINNAMON

PINCH OF FRESHLY GRATED NUTMEG

ONE ¼-OZ/7-G ENVELOPE UNFLAVORED GELATIN

1 CUP/225 G ROASTED WINTER SQUASH PURÉE (PAGE 70)

4 OZ/115 G MASCARPONE CHEESE, AT ROOM TEMPERATURE

Combine the cream and sugar in a large heavy-bottomed saucepan. Scrape in the seeds from the vanilla bean and toss in the pod. Whisk in the cinnamon and nutmeg. Cook over medium heat, stirring often, for 7 minutes, or until the mixture is almost at a simmer. Remove from the heat, cover, and let steep for 20 minutes.

Pour 3 tbsp cold water into a small bowl. Sprinkle the gelatin over the water and let stand for 5 minutes.

In a large bowl, fold together the squash purée and mascarpone.

Uncover the cream mixture and bring it just to a simmer over medium heat. Gently whisk in the gelatin mixture, stirring until it is completely dissolved. Remove from the heat and let cool 5 minutes. Then slowly pour the cream mixture into the squash purée and mascarpone, gently whisking constantly. Pour the panna cotta into eight dessert cups or goblets or into a decorative bowl. Cover with plastic wrap and refrigerate until completely set, at least 3 hours and up to overnight.

To serve, unmold the panna cotta onto small dessert plates or onto a dessert platter, and serve. Or, rather than unmold it, serve the panna cotta in the dessert cups or goblets, or spoon it from the decorative bowl into dessert cups.

panna,
mascarpone, car

PUMPKIN GELATO
makes about 1 qt; 6 servings

There was a time when most *gelaterie* featured pretty much the same parade of flavors—fresh fruit varieties such as strawberry or pineapple, plus the usual lineup of *crema, cioccolata, gianduja, nocciola, stracciatella,* and *torroncino*. Then came the '80s and everything changed—mostly for the better, I say. Yes, there were oddities such as olive oil gelato (not such an oddity anymore) and garlic gelato (which was and still is a bad idea). But we also started to see more whimsy, with popular desserts such as tiramisú and crème caramel reinterpreted as ice cream; and more seasonal flavors, such as fig in late summer and chestnut or pumpkin in fall. This is my own version of pumpkin gelato. I use roasted winter squash purée in place of pumpkin purée to give it a more robust flavor. A gelato this good needs no embellishment, but feel free to crush some amaretto cookies on top if you are feeling extravagant.

1½ CUPS/360 ML WHOLE MILK

1½ CUPS/360 ML HEAVY CREAM

½ VANILLA BEAN

3 STRIPS LEMON ZEST

2 CUPS/455 G ROASTED WINTER SQUASH PURÉE (PAGE 70) OR PUMPKIN PURÉE

1 CUP/200 G SUGAR

4 LARGE EGG YOLKS

½ CUP/120 ML SUNFLOWER OR CHESTNUT HONEY, OR ANOTHER FLAVORFUL HONEY

PINCH OF FINE SEA SALT

¼ TSP GROUND CINNAMON

PINCH OF FRESHLY GRATED NUTMEG

1 TBSP PUNCH ABRUZZO (PAGE 48), AMARETTO, MARSALA, OR DARK RUM

AMARETTO COOKIES FOR SERVING (OPTIONAL)

Pour the milk and cream into a large saucepan. Split the vanilla bean open lengthwise and scrape the seeds into the saucepan. Toss in the pod and the lemon zest. Bring the milk-cream mixture to a simmer over medium heat. Then turn off the heat and cover the pot. Let steep for about 20 minutes.

Combine the squash purée and ½ cup/100 g of the sugar in a separate medium saucepan and place over medium-low heat. Cook, stirring often, until the sugar is dissolved and the purée is a shade darker and glossy, about 10 minutes. Remove from the heat and let cool.

In a medium bowl, whisk together the egg yolks, the remaining ½ cup/100 g sugar, the honey, and the salt until thick and creamy. Slowly drizzle in a ladleful of the hot milk mixture, whisking constantly to prevent the eggs from curdling. Whisk in another ladleful of the hot milk mixture. Then slowly whisk the egg mixture into the saucepan with the rest of the milk mixture. Place over medium-low heat and cook, stirring constantly with a wooden spoon or silicone spatula for about 15 minutes, or until a thin custard forms that lightly coats the back of the spoon. Remove from the heat and gently whisk in the sweetened squash purée. Strain the hot custard through a fine-mesh sieve into a heatproof bowl. Whisk in the cinnamon, nutmeg, and liqueur.

Place a sheet of plastic wrap directly on the surface of the custard to prevent a skin from forming. Refrigerate for at least 4 hours and up to overnight. Freeze the custard in an ice cream machine according to the manufacturer's instructions. Scoop the thickened custard into a container with a tight-fitting lid. Cover and freeze until firm.

To serve, scoop the gelato into dessert bowls. Serve as is, or with amaretto cookies on the side or crumbled on top if you like.

chapter 9
PRESERVES AND CONDIMENTS
conserve di casa

PRESERVES AND CONDIMENTS
conserve di casa

It is wonderful to see the art of preserving making a comeback in the United States. Movements such as Canning Across America have turned a new generation of cooks on to making their own jams and pickles with fruits and vegetables from their own gardens or local farmers' markets.

Home-canned goods have always been an essential part of the Italian pantry. Wherever you go in Italy, in restaurants or in someone's home, you can be sure you will to be treated to house-made preserves of some sort, whether bottled tomato sauce (see page 263), silky eggplants submerged in olive oil (see page 261), or sweet, vinegary peppers (see page 258). In Abruzzo, where my family is from, it is likely to be *peperoncini*— hot chile peppers preserved in oil or vinegar. Most Abruzzesi wouldn't think of sitting down to a meal without a jar of those peppers on the table.

My mom, who came to the States as a young woman in the 1950s, always seemed to be canning something when I was growing up. Every year she made jars of her vinegar-steeped *giardiniera* and green tomato marmalade. I think it made her feel closer to the homeland she missed. But I also think she did it out of love, and for the sheer pleasure of it.

I share her passion, and in this chapter you'll find my adaptations of those treasured recipes. To me, there is nothing more satisfying than dipping into the pantry and opening a jar of something I made the previous summer. In some small but important way, those jars make me feel connected—to the land, to the seasons, and to a people who have been practicing this art for centuries.

SWEET-AND-SOUR CIPOLLINE
makes 2 pt / 960 ml

You have probably come across cipolline in the grocery store or at farmers' markets and in restaurants. They are those small, saucer-shaped onions that might be described as cute if such a word could ever apply to onions. Their size makes them ideal for pickling—they readily absorb the spiced vinegar brine but keep their appealing crunch. In this book, these onions are folded into Insalata di Riso (page 126). But you can put them out as part of an antipasto platter; slice them into a salad or a panino; or mince them and mix them into your favorite hard-boiled egg filling.

1½ LB/680 G RED OR YELLOW CIPOLLINE ONIONS

1 CUP/240 ML AGED BALSAMIC VINEGAR

½ CUP/120 ML WHITE WINE VINEGAR

½ CUP/120 ML WATER

⅓ CUP/65 G SUGAR

1 TSP FINE SEA SALT

1 BAY LEAF

1 TSP BLACK PEPPERCORNS

1 FRESH ROSEMARY SPRIG

Wash and then sterilize one 2-pt/960-ml glass jar or two 1-pt/480-ml glass jars and their lids by immersing them in boiling water for 10 minutes.

Peel the onions and immerse them in a bowl of cold water for 30 minutes.

While the onions are soaking, combine the vinegars, water, sugar, salt, bay leaf, peppercorns, and rosemary sprig in a medium saucepan and bring to a simmer over medium heat. Stir to dissolve the sugar.

Drain the onions and add them to the saucepan. Raise the heat to medium-high and bring to a boil. Boil the onions for 10 minutes, or until you can pierce a fork through them with a bit of resistance—you want them to be tender but not too soft.

With a slotted spoon, remove the onions from the liquid and pack them snugly into the jar. Pour the pickling liquid through a fine-mesh strainer over the onions. There should be enough liquid to cover them completely. Use a bubble remover or a clean fork handle to get rid of any bubbles that may be trapped. Screw the lid on tightly and process for 10 minutes in a boiling water bath.

Store in a cool dark place for up to 1 year. Or store them in the refrigerator for at least 2 months. They will get more flavorful as time goes by.

GABRIELLA'S GIARDINIERA

makes 5 pt / 2.4 L

My mother made *giardiniera*—the classic Italian mixed pickled vegetables—often when I was growing up. There always seemed to be a jar in our fridge, and at least one waiting on a pantry shelf. Oddly, I did not start making it myself until recently; it was too easy to grab a jar off the shelf at my local Italian deli. But, of course, the homemade version is better, and this is doubly true if you use fresh farmers' market vegetables. I like my *giardiniera* tart and tangy, but you can mellow the brine a bit by cutting the vinegar with a little more water. Serve the *giardiniera* as part of an antipasto platter or as a side to boiled beef. I also mince it finely and use it in my filling for stuffed peppers and for Italian-style deviled eggs.

1 MEDIUM HEAD CAULIFLOWER (ABOUT 1 LB/455 G), TRIMMED AND CUT INTO BITE-SIZE FLORETS	2 TBSP KOSHER SALT
	1 TBSP SUGAR
4 MEDIUM CARROTS, SLICED ON THE BIAS	2 TSP BLACK PEPPERCORNS, LIGHTLY CRUSHED
2 RIBS CELERY, SLICED ON THE BIAS	1 TSP RED PEPPER FLAKES
1 LARGE HEAVY RIPE RED BELL PEPPER, CUT INTO THIN STRIPS	1/2 TSP WHOLE CLOVES
15 CIPOLLINE OR 20 PEARL ONIONS, PEELED	1 BAY LEAF
	1 TBSP FRESH OREGANO LEAVES
4 CUPS/960 ML CIDER VINEGAR	2 GARLIC CLOVES, SLICED PAPER-THIN
4 CUPS/960 ML WATER	

Have the cauliflower, carrots, celery, red bell pepper, and cipolline onions peeled, trimmed, sliced, and ready.

Wash and then sterilize five 1-pt/480-ml glass jars and their lids by immersing them in boiling water for 10 minutes.

In a pot or saucepan large enough to hold the vegetables, combine the vinegar, water, salt, sugar, peppercorns, red pepper flakes, cloves, and bay leaf and bring to a boil over high heat. Add the vegetables, oregano leaves, and garlic and stir. Turn off the heat and cover the pot. Let the vegetables steep in the brine for 1 minute.

Pack the vegetables into the sterilized jars, taking care to get a mix of vegetables and some spices in each one. Pour the hot brine over the vegetables, filling the jars to 1/2 in/12 mm below the top. Use a bubble remover or a clean fork handle to get rid of any bubbles that may be trapped. Screw the lids on tightly, and process for 10 minutes in a boiling water bath.

Let the *giardiniera* cure for at least 1 week before serving. Store the sealed jars in a cool dark place, where they will last up to 1 year.

PICKLED SNACKING PEPPERS
makes about 1 pt / 480 ml

Snacking peppers are dainty little bell peppers, about 2 in/5 cm long. They turn from green to yellow to bright orange and red as they ripen, and are sweet, with few seeds. It was my friend Cathy Barrow's idea to pickle them. Cathy is a master in the art of preserving and author of the blog Mrs. Wheelbarrow's Kitchen. She preserves everything from homemade Concord grape juice to fresh tuna in oil, and pretty much everything in between. Prunes in Armagnac? Yep, she's done it. Ginger confit? Of course! Cathy and I got together in her kitchen one day to play around with peppers, and this recipe was born. Look for snacking peppers at farmers' markets and at well-stocked supermarkets. Otherwise, use regular bell peppers: grill them and clean them according to the instructions on page 74, cut them into strips, and then proceed with the recipe.

1 LB/455 G SNACKING PEPPERS, STEMS REMOVED

2 RED CIPOLLINE ONIONS, THINLY SLICED (ABOUT ½ CUP/60 G), OR ½ MEDIUM RED ONION, THINLY SLICED

½ CUP/120 ML WHITE WINE VINEGAR

¼ CUP/60 ML BOTTLED LEMON JUICE

¼ CUP/60 ML EXTRA-VIRGIN OLIVE OIL

¼ TSP KOSHER OR SEA SALT

Wash and then sterilize two ½-pt/240-ml glass jars and their lids by immersing them in boiling water for 10 minutes.

Make sure the peppers are clean and free of blemishes. Pierce each one and make a small slit, which will allow the brine to penetrate.

Prepare a medium-hot charcoal grill or preheat a gas grill to medium-high. Alternatively, position an oven rack 7 in/17 cm from the broiler and turn the broiler on. If grilling, put the peppers on a perforated grill pan. Grill, turning them with tongs from time to time, until they are softened and lightly charred. The time will depend on how hot your grill is. If broiling, arrange the peppers on a rimmed baking sheet. Broil, turning them with tongs a few times, for 15 to 20 minutes, or until they are softened and lightly charred. (If you are using snacking peppers there is no need to peel them.)

In a medium saucepan, bring the onions, vinegar, lemon juice, olive oil, and salt to a boil over medium-high heat. Reduce the heat to low, so the brine is just simmering.

Pack the peppers tightly in the sterilized jars. Pour the hot brine over the peppers, filling the jars to ½ in/12 mm below the top. Use a bubble remover or a clean fork handle to get rid of any bubbles that may be trapped. Screw the lids on tightly, and process for 10 minutes in a boiling water bath.

Let the peppers cure for at least 1 week before serving. Store the sealed jars in a cool dark place, where they will last up to 1 year.

CHILE PEPPERS IN OLIVE OIL

makes about ½ pt / 240 ml

The best hot peppers I ever had were given to me by my friend Titti Pacchione—tiny, marble-size *really hot* cherry peppers that she grew in her garden and packed in oil. Titti lives in Abruzzo, where hot peppers are set out at every meal except breakfast. I have been unable to find that variety of peppers here—the cherry peppers are much larger and not nearly as hot. However, I did find something called a super chile plant at my farmers' market that is a great substitute: it is a compact bush, but a prolific producer, with small, very spicy, horn-shaped peppers. If you are unable to find super chiles, you can substitute cayenne or Thai chile peppers—or whatever variety suits your own heat index.

When it came time to test this recipe, I enlisted the help of my friend Cathy Barrow (see Pickled Snacking Peppers, facing page). Working from my friend Titti's admittedly vague instructions and our own trials, we came up with the following method.

Timing and care are the keys to the success of this recipe. First, before being packed in oil, the peppers must sit out to dry for at least 1 week, usually longer, until they are wrinkled but still flexible and not completely dry. Once partially dried, they must be fried—for the briefest moment—in hot oil, just enough time for them to puff up in the pan but not long enough for them to discolor and turn black. Here you must pay careful attention, not only to the color of the peppers but also because the oil may pop and spatter when you add the peppers to the pan.

Are they worth the effort? To me, yes, without a doubt. I use these peppers in all sorts of pasta dishes and soups, in sauces, and in stews. Not only do the peppers keep for several months in the refrigerator, but the longer they sit, the spicier the oil in which they are suspended becomes. You can use this oil to add heat to sauces, soups, and more.

4 OZ/113 G SUPER CHILE PEPPERS
OR OTHER SMALL CHILE PEPPERS
(2 LOOSELY PACKED CUPS)

2 CUPS/480 ML EXTRA-VIRGIN OLIVE OIL,
PLUS MORE AS NEEDED

½ TSP FINE SEA SALT

With a small paring knife, remove the stems from the peppers but keep the peppers intact. Set them out on a cooling rack and let them dry for about 1 week, until the peppers are wrinkled but still soft and flexible. (If you live in a dry, sunny area, you can let them dry outside in a protected area, though the amount of drying time may be less.) The peppers should give when you pinch them with your fingers, but they should not break or crumble. Your aim is to rid the peppers of moisture to prevent mold from forming later on. But don't let them dry out too much; otherwise they will not fry properly and they will not soften in the oil.

Check the peppers and discard any that are blemished or on which mold has formed.

CONTINUED

Wash and then sterilize one ½-pint/240-ml glass jar and the lid by immersing them in boiling water for 10 minutes.

Pour enough olive oil into a medium skillet to reach a depth of ½ in/12 mm. Place over medium heat and heat the oil to about 300°F/150°C on a deep-frying thermometer. Fry the peppers in batches, for a few seconds only—just until they puff up—moving them around in the pan. Work quickly and watch out for spattering oil. Remove the pan from the heat if necessary to prevent the peppers from burning. With a slotted spoon, transfer the peppers to the sterilized jar, taking care to pack them tightly, and sprinkle in a little salt. Continue to fry and pack the peppers in the jar until you have packed them all. Let the olive oil cool for 5 to 10 minutes, and then pour it over the peppers. If the peppers are not completely submerged in oil, add more until they are covered. This will keep bacteria from growing.

Screw the lid on the jar and let it come to room temperature. Refrigerate for at least 1 week before using. As you use the peppers and their spicy oil, make sure you top off with more oil so that the peppers are always completely submerged.

GRILLED EGGPLANT IN OLIVE OIL

makes 2 pt / 960 ml

Italians have a long tradition of preserving vegetables in oil. Artichokes, mushrooms, sun-dried tomatoes, and peppers—all the traditional antipasto vegetables—take well to a leisurely soak. Eggplant, with its silky texture and tendency to absorb liquid, is my favorite vegetable preserved this way. I grill the eggplant slices first, since this preparation imparts a lovely smoky flavor that tastes of summer and lunches at side-street trattorias. Serve these eggplant slices as part of an antipasto platter, in a panino, or as a topping for pizza.

2 LB/910 G DARK PURPLE EGGPLANT, SUCH AS VIOLETTA LUNGA (ABOUT 3 1/2 IN/9 CM WIDE AT ITS WIDEST POINT), CUT CROSSWISE INTO SLICES ABOUT 1/4 IN/6 MM THICK

FINE SEA SALT

EXTRA-VIRGIN OLIVE OIL

1/2 CUP/120 ML WHITE WINE VINEGAR

1 TSP CRUSHED DRIED OREGANO LEAVES

2 GARLIC CLOVES, LIGHTLY CRUSHED

Sprinkle both sides of the eggplant with salt and place them in a colander set on a plate. Put another plate on top of the eggplant and weight it down with a heavy object. Let the eggplant slices sit for 4 hours or, better yet, overnight. This will leach out the bitter juices and allow the slices to soften and dry a little.

In a small bowl, vigorously whisk together 1/2 cup/120 ml olive oil, the vinegar, 1 tsp salt, and the oregano until the mixture is emulsified. Add the garlic cloves and set aside for at least 30 minutes to give the flavors a chance to mingle. Be sure to whisk the dressing again right before using.

Prepare a medium-hot charcoal grill or heat a gas grill to medium-high and lightly brush the grate with olive oil. Or heat a grill pan over medium-high heat and coat it lightly with olive oil. Grill the eggplant slices, in batches if necessary, until they are slightly blackened in spots on the bottom—this will take only about 2 minutes, depending on how hot your grill is, so watch carefully. Use tongs to turn the slices and slightly blacken the other side. Transfer the grilled slices to a plate.

Wash and then sterilize two 1-pt/480-ml glass jars and their lids by immersing them in boiling water for 10 minutes. Set one of the jars on the counter and pour in 1 tbsp of the emulsified dressing. Carefully stack about 4 eggplant slices in the jar. Pour another spoonful of dressing over the eggplant, then stack 4 more slices on top. Continue until the stack is slightly below the top of the jar. Pack the second jar in the same way.

CONTINUED

CONTINUED

Pour enough dressing into the jars so that the eggplant is completely submerged. Use a bubble remover or clean fork handle to get rid of any air bubbles that may be trapped. Screw the lids onto the jars and refrigerate for at least 3 days before serving. The eggplant will keep for at least 2 months in the refrigerator.

COOK'S NOTE: The olive oil in the dressing will congeal in the refrigerator. To serve, you can either remove the jar from the fridge and let the oil warm to room temperature and liquefy before removing any eggplant slices, or you can remove the quantity of eggplant that you need and wipe off any excess oil. These eggplant slices are especially good in panini, as the bread will soak up the flavor-infused oil.

SMALL-BATCH TOMATO SAUCE

makes 2 pt / 960 ml

For the longest time, I avoided canning my own tomato sauce. The thought of peeling, seeding, cooking, and processing 20 to 30 lbs/9 to 14 kg of tomatoes did not appeal to me at all. What's more, my standard winter tomato sauce, made from good commercial canned tomatoes was—and is—plenty good (see page 66). But a couple of summers ago, I dipped my toe in and made a small batch of home-canned sauce—just a couple of jars. I stored them in a cupboard and promptly forgot about them. The following January, when a hand injury prevented me from being able cook for several weeks, I remembered those jars. Not only did my sauce save us from yet another night of takeout, it was a most welcome taste of summer in the middle of winter.

1/4 CUP/60 ML EXTRA-VIRGIN OLIVE OIL

2 GARLIC CLOVES, LIGHTLY CRUSHED

4 LB/1.75 KG RIPE PLUM TOMATOES, GRATED (SEE PAGE 65), TO YIELD ABOUT 3 LB/1.4 KG (6 CUPS/1.4 L) PULP AND JUICE

1 TSP FINE SEA SALT

6 FRESH BASIL LEAVES

2 TBSP FRESHLY SQUEEZED LEMON JUICE

Wash and then sterilize two 1-pt/480-ml glass jars and their lids by immersing them in boiling water for 10 minutes.

In a large heavy-bottomed saucepan, warm the olive oil and garlic over medium heat. Cook, stirring frequently, for 1 to 2 minutes, until the garlic is fragrant. Do not let it brown. Carefully pour in the tomatoes—the oil will spatter—and stir to incorporate with the oil. Raise the heat to medium-high and bring the tomatoes to a boil. Reduce the heat to medium-low and simmer for about 30 minutes, until the tomatoes have broken down but still have a fresh tomato flavor. Season with the salt and cook for 10 to 15 more minutes, until the tomatoes have thickened to a sauce consistency. Fish out the garlic cloves and discard. Stir in the basil leaves.

Pour 1 tbsp of the lemon juice into each of two 1-pt/480-ml sterilized jars. Ladle the sauce into the jars, leaving 1/2 in/12 mm of space at the top. Screw the lids on tightly and process for 35 minutes in a boiling water bath. Store in a cool, dark place for up to 1 year.

TOMATO MARMALADE
makes about 2½ pt / 1 L

This is the marmalade of my dreams—thick and shiny and gloriously red. It tastes of ripe late-summer tomatoes and bright lemon, and has a spicy kick from chile peppers, cloves, and fragrant bay leaves. I suppose it's not technically a marmalade since it's not citrus-based. But it does have lots of lemon peel and a consistency that resembles marmalade. Spread this on crostini and top with a sharp or pungent cheese. Or spread it on your favorite panino, on a smoked turkey and Cheddar cheese sandwich, or even a ham biscuit (that's the Virginian in me talking).

5 LB/2.3 KG RIPE PLUM TOMATOES, WASHED

2 CUPS/400 G SUGAR

ZEST AND FRESHLY SQUEEZED JUICE OF 2 LARGE LEMONS, ZEST CUT INTO STRIPS

1 TO 2 TBSP GOOD-QUALITY AGED BALSAMIC VINEGAR

1 TSP SEA SALT

8 WHOLE CLOVES

2 BAY LEAVES

2 FRESH CHILE PEPPERS, SUCH AS CAYENNE OR SUPER CHILES, MINCED

Wash and then sterilize five ½-pt/240-ml glass jars and their lids by immersing them in boiling water for 10 minutes.

Trim the stem end off the tomatoes. With a vegetable peeler, slice the skin off the tomatoes in strips and discard. Cut the tomatoes in half lengthwise and push out the seeds with your thumb (I do this over the sink). Cut the tomato halves in half again lengthwise, and then cut each quarter into 3 or 4 pieces. Toss the tomato pieces into a large heavy-bottomed nonreactive saucepan.

Put the sugar, lemon zest and juice, vinegar, salt, cloves, bay leaves, and chile peppers into the pot with the tomatoes. Set the pot over medium heat and bring to a simmer. Cook at a fairly lively simmer for about 1½ hours or until the marmalade is glossy and thick enough to spread. Be sure to stir often to prevent burning. When the marmalade is ready, remove the bay leaves and the cloves.

Spoon the marmalade into the sterilized jars, screw the lids on tightly, and process for 15 minutes in a boiling water bath. Store in a cool dark place for up to 1 year. Or store the marmalade in the refrigerator, where it will keep for at least 2 months.

pomodori, limone, balsamico
foglia di alloro,

SOURCES

For Italian heirloom vegetable seeds
Seeds from Italy
P.O. Box 3908
Lawrence, KS 66046
www.growitalian.com
(785) 748-0959

For a variety of vegetables, including baby artichokes, cardoons, summer and winter squash, greens, and more
Melissa's Produce
www.melissas.com

For Rogue Creamery Smokey Blue and other artisan cheeses
Rogue Creamery
311 N. Front Street
Central Point, OR 97502
www.roguecreamery.com
(866) 396-4704

For a variety of Italian and other cheeses
Murray's
254 Bleeker Street
New York, NY 10014
www.murrayscheese.com
(212) 243-3289; (888) MYCHEEZ

For Italian artisan pasta, cheese, olive oil and other products from Italy's Abruzzo region:
Abruzzo Pantry
www.abruzzopantry.com

For Punch Abruzzo liqueur
A Cork Above
www.acorkabove.com
info@acorkabove.com
(727) 259-5801

For almond flour or almond meal
Trader Joe's
Various locations
www.traderjoes.com

For a variety of Italian ingredients, including Rizzoli *alici in salsa piccante* and other types of anchovies; dried beans, chickpeas, and lentils; chestnut, sunflower and other types of honey; dried porcini mushrooms; saffron; '00' flour and semolina flour for pasta; and other specialty products:

A.G. Ferrari Foods
Various locations in California
agferrari@mail.agferrari.com
(877) 878-2783

Gustiamo, Inc.
1715 West Farms Road
Bronx, N.Y. 10460
www.gustiamo.com
(718) 860-2949

La Cuisine
323 Cameron Street
Alexandria, VA 22314
www.lacuisineus.com
(703) 836-8925; (800) 521-1176